SPORTS BUBBLE BLUES

SPORTS BUBBLE BLUES

A COLLECTION OF ESSAYS FROM THE MID-MAJORITY'S SEASON 5

KYLE WHELLISTON

Copyright © 2004, 2008, 2009 by Kyle Whelliston
All rights reserved.

Illustrations by Kyle Whelliston. Illustrations copyright © 2008, 2009 Kyle Whelliston
Photographs courtesy of the author. Used by permission.

Printed in the United States of America
First printing: August 2009
10 9 8 7 6 5 4 3 2 1

LIBRARY OF CONGRESS CATALOGUING-IN-PUBLICATION DATA
Whelliston, Kyle.
Sports Bubble Blues: A Collection of Essays From The Mid-Majority's Season 5 / Kyle Whelliston.
    p.   cm.
ISBN 978-0-578-03314-3
1. Basketball.   2. Whelliston, Kyle – Travel.   I. Title.

Book design by Roni Lagin

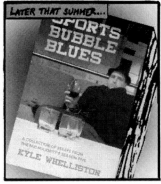

FOREWORD

JUL 1, 2009

As I sit here in mid-summer on the elevated back porch of my home in Pawtucket, I look out across a clear sky as blue as The Citadel's road uniforms, across a patchwork of swaying trees and the rooftops of a nearby Portuguese neighborhood. I reach for a 16-ounce glass, sweat beads glistening in the heat, full of 99-cent Sunpop from the Stop & Shop. It's all a moment's respite, a few seconds to catch breath and avert my gaze from my overpriced, underperforming laptop, an escape from the job of reviewing words and phrases I wrote many months ago, in a different time and in other places, about things like jump shots and arena rock.

This, here, is the first attempt to collect and print material from The Mid-Majority (midmajority.com), a small sports website I've maintained since November of 2004. For the past five winters, I've been travelling from coast to coast following and covering teams from the small-college end of Division I, the over 200 teams in 21 conferences that stand at a distinct competitive disadvantage against the household-name powerhouses of the NCAA's top tier, but still fight every season for the same National Championship that Kansas and North Carolina do. While this end of the pool doesn't interest many sports fans, I've been fortunate and blessed to turn a humble career from it.

But the site's format—five months on, and seven months dark—contributes towards an odd personality split. These words now, in the heat of summer, seem like the work of someone else entirely. These trips to places like Moraga and Carbondale and Martin seem the adventures of another: someone with a big-media gig, someone married, someone who hadn't divulged the strange health problems that plagued a 109-game, 26,000-mile trek across America in another attempt to find college basketball's true soul.

It's almost as if I'm reading this for the first time. I can only hope that loyal Mid-Majority readers will feel the same about so much recycling.

Culling tens of thousands of words out of the body of work presented on the site from last November to this March has not been all that difficult. Content on The Mid-Majority is generally divided into two types: the disposable kind—that is, hyperlink-ridden game recaps and weekly ratings and daily observations, outdated and discardable mere hours after initial posting—and that which is, on the other hand, slightly less disposable. The latter category includes essays and passages that could have been theoretically posted at any time, or at least in any year during a similar month. That's what is included in the pages following. We'll begin with one of the most-requested reprints from the site, the post that began the journey five years ago.

As an added bonus, if you can call it that, the 109 games I travelled to during the past season can be relived through their Twittercasts, except when insufficient connectivity at the time disallowed them. This may be the first-ever volume of any type for which "tweets" of 140 characters or less make up so much of the body text—we'll get that researched right away—but it's most assuredly the first time such a large volume of Twitter content has been printed and organized in reverse order, least recent first.

Thanks to my friend Robert Workman, who copy-edited these words so I didn't have to, and rooted out all the typos. Double-thanks to my colleague and associate Roni Lagin, who designed and typeset the book. But my most heartfelt appreciation is reserved for you, the reader, whether this is your first time with this material or your second. Without your generosity and thoughtfulness, none of these travels would even be possible.

— *Kyle Whelliston*

CONTENTS

THE BEAUTIFUL SEASON

NOV 13, 2004

It is designed to do a lot of things, but it certainly is not designed to break your heart. The game begins in the late autumn, when everything else has shriveled and fallen and died. Its blossoms come slowly in winter's course like crocus starts popping through icefields. And when it does stop, it leaves you to face the bursting glory of a fresh spring. What the hell's wrong with that?

Each November, college basketball fades in slowly, takes its dutiful place in the blurry background of the American sports landscape. Only in recent years have the the Men In Charge decided that the season's opening stages needed to be sexed up to compete with the dominant late-year sports stories—the national pastime that is the NFL, convoluted college gridiron bowl jostlings, the annual start of the increasingly ridiculous soap-opera/freak-show that used to be a pro basketball league. They've done this by staging made-for-television invitationals, power-conference challenges, and sham tournaments with worthless trophies.

But I say that while none of this has ruined anything, none of this is necessary in the least. The six weeks that end a calendar year and begin the school hoops season are crucial to the unfolding story.

When the first "Midnight Madness" events are staged in October, each and every one of the 342 Division I teams has a perfect 0-0 record and a theoretical chance of winning the national championship. The path is clear. Win your conference, or play well enough to please the gatekeepers on the selection committee, and you're on the March bracket. Go on a six-game winning streak, and you've achieved eternal glory.

November and December effectively crush many of these irrational and romantic hoop dreams. Early games serve to define and enforce the natural stratification that occurs when differing levels of strength, speed and skill enter into the arena. By the time the new year ticks over, it's usually apparent who the real contenders are, who the potential surprise teams are, and what the true worth of your season tickets are.

So guarantee games, 30-point blowouts and walkovers are not inherently "ugly," they are an example of the necessary elements of any Darwinist construct. We need to differentiate between the big fish, the little fish, and the sorta-kinda-middle-sized fish. To buck nature's way and to test your fish improperly can turn a 8-0 record at Christmas into a 10-18 disaster. And a few holiday upsets here and there signal that flaws are to be addressed, or act as urgent warnings that the conventional wisdom is in need of adjustments.

The early season also allows stratification on a local level, a chance for local teams in separate conferences to vie for regional supremacy and set brother-versus-brother bragging rights: the "unofficial" Big Five tournament in Philadelphia, SEC vs. ACC matchups, Kentucky vs. Western Kentucky, the little California schools of the Big West against their big brothers in the Pac-10.

And then comes the new year. Conference season. The games that are so important that they are recorded separately, in parentheses.

The league season brings a structure heretofore lacking. Cold Saturdays (Fridays for the Patriot and Ivy) are explosions of matchups and point spread listings and awful band versions of "Rock & Roll Part 2" and buzzer-beaters. Teams jostle for position in their conferences and divisions. And for the most part, the games are good and evenly matched.

An intended effect of playing in a conference is that you are presented with the same competition every year. Familiarity does breed contempt, it's true. In league play, you don't need the geographic proximity of Tobacco Road to form a great rivalry—just look at Oral Roberts and IUPUI, Utah State and UC-Irvine, Manhattan and Niagara.

So I'm offended by the notion that the period of time between the Super Bowl and the NCAA Tournament is marked as some kind of sports black hole. Some people think it's so boring that women falling out of bikinis is the only way to hold fans' attention. While I'm certainly a fan of the effect, I don't like the cause.

But I do understand it, to an extent—conference games do require an attention span that may exceed the limits of the hibernating brain. You can put Duke and North Carolina on ESPN every night, but as long as nothing is on the line other than tournament seeding, many will choose to curb their enthusiasm.

When February turns to March, two months' worth of work have added up to a single number, a seeded dance card to the conference tournament.

Most leagues set up shop in a neutral arena, drawing busloads of fans and cheerleaders and dance teams and bands to their temporary hoops meccas. Each game eliminates a single team, and when the week is through, there are 31 tickets issued to the Biggest Dance Of All. Many of these schools are known only to folks in the 100-mile radius and mid-major freaks, and they've brought glory and unmitigated success just by surviving their leagues.

Then, just like that, it's Selection Sunday, the holiest day on the college hoops fan's calendar. A secretive bunch of suits in Indianapolis fills out the brackets and chooses worthy "at-large" teams—and let's face it, they're usually right about who gets to go. The next three days are the longest, waiting breathlessly for the tip-off of the play-in game while sad, dispirited teams play out the opening rounds of the NIT.

And in four quick days, 64 become 32, 32 become 16. Ten-seeds beat sevens, and every once in a while a feisty teen will slip through. One or two wins for a small school will cement the squad in their fans' hearts forever, and the eventual and inevitable loss won't hurt a bit. In the end, this event belongs to the big boys.

A deep breath, and it's another weekend dedicated to the tough work of narrowing the field. Elite Eight, Final Four, National Championship, and finally a true and deserving winner. It's the most exciting and pulse-pounding event in American sports, and nobody can deny it.

It is the most beautiful of sports seasons—rambling and undulating, slightly flawed, yet offering perfect dramatic structure. The season quickly and effectively winnows hundreds of hopefuls down to one champion (one must only pass a fleeting glance to our college football brothers to see exactly how hard of a task this really is). Four distinct stages in rapid succession, each played with quickening pulse and shorter breath.

So let's begin.

PART I

ESSAY SEASON

THE BIG PICTURE

NOV 1, 2008

It's not supposed to work out for the best, and the system is designed to anticipate failure. On March 21 in Birmingham, the four lower seeds wore their extra digits like anchors, eliminated one after another at three-hour intervals marked with the chiming of buzzers. I watched from a corner seat as American University, South Alabama and then Boise State, and finally Saint Joseph's had their weaknesses cruelly exploited by superior competition, crushed and crumpled on live high-definition national television.

Each head coach ascended to the press-conference dais with two dejected and downcast players, briefly explained to the assembled reporters how those things that worked so well for five months just didn't seem to click on March 21, how things had misfired so badly. And then they disappeared, shunted aside, back to their buses behind the BJCC Arena. By the time the weekend was over, Butler was gone too.

Only fitting that I came out of that first-round quadruple-header to discover a car with a broken alternator. In this game, our game, it's the weak links and the missing pieces that do us in, the things that end up defining the journey. The teams followed here in this space are built possession by possession, win by win, through a succession of upward steps... but it's what falls apart, what doesn't work, what isn't present to begin with, that's what gets carved into March's gravestones.

Nine days on, I was sitting second row courtside in a packed stadium in Detroit. Davidson, yet another of the schools often followed here, was down by two to the eventual National Champions of college basketball—holding possession, 16 ticks and 94 feet away from the Final Four. To this day, I have not seen that final missed shot. When Curry awkwardly handed the ball off to Richards, I reflexively shut my eyes... when I opened them seconds later, it was clear which team was going to San Antonio and which was not.

There are no more than three times in the college basketball calendar when everything makes sense, where the past and future are clear, when there is no confusion as to where we all stand. One comes in mid-March, when the 65 survivors of the regular season are slotted on a rigorous grid, their missions and their challenges laid out on a simple map. All true red-blooded Americans can read that, from the crustiest old head coach to the most temporary of office secretaries. The second moment arrives three weeks later, when one of those teams has amassed six victories and is declared the ultimate winner, with the other 64 left behind.

This, right now, is that other moment. Over 320 teams are all suspended at zero wins and zero losses, each with a theoretical shot at the title Kansas currently holds. Each of those squads is a collection of strengths and weaknesses, or experience and lack of same, a living organism whose true value and resilience will be fully known over four months from now. Each one is capable of greatness, and each is capable of abject failure.

Of course, there are those teams that have resources, conference affiliations, facilities, high-paid coaches, television exposure, and time-tested success formulas that attract outsized expectations. History bears many of these expectations out—in 2007-08, teams from the eight richest conferences beat teams from the 23 poorest 89 percent of the time. And this time every year, certain schools are ranked in an artificial preseason chart of perceived performance.

Take the University of North Carolina, for example, the consensus No. 1 team. The experts expect that team to be 100 percent perfect, and the majority of critical analysis over the course of the season will be concerned with everything that's wrong with them. The difference between UNC and, say, UNC-Wilmington, is that one is forced to spend the year playing against ghosts, chasing a theoretical team Number Zero. The other is a sum of its admittedly meager parts.

So from this vantage point, it's easier to see the common bond between programs like Boise State, Saint Joseph's, American University and South Alabama. Each are defined at this moment by their question marks, not their exclamation points. Only one of those schools is perceived as a favorite to return, but A.U. will spend its season working hard for respect again in the Patriot League. This stands in stark contrast with the teams that eliminated them last spring, all of which can only play themselves out of NCAA tournament bids.

This is what all teams on our side of the Red Line have in common (yes, even Davidson). In a way, it's what ultimately binds us all together in a single, unified, indivisible league. These 225 teams that make up our Mid-

Majority are built from the bottom up. None are inheritors of unshakable legacies that simply self-perpetuate. Every season, teams from the Atlantic 10 on down fight to keep and pay successful coaches, lure and keep talented players who'd have greater chances to be on television and catch scouts' attention in higher-profile leagues. And, through all of this, they find a way to win enough games to achieve postseason berths.

We are bound together by our common, yet unshared restraints.

During this season, in particular, the challenges will be greater. With more teams coming into Division I, the "guarantee games" offered by power-conference teams, six-figure checks that provide important financial lifelines for fledgling programs, are an increasingly finite resource fought over by a larger market. Cuts in media budgets mean that small-college coverage is the first to get the ax, if it were ever a tree at all. Travel costs are up—athletic directors and commissioners across the country have recurring nightmares about being sent to Hawaii for BracketBusters weekend.

But this is what this site, in its better moments, is all about: a study of struggle. For the past four basketball seasons, The Mid-Majority has attempted to chronicle the process of assembling successful basketball programs despite disadvantages, the conundrum of how to win March games that logic dictates shouldn't be won. As we move forward into a fifth year, TMM will concern itself more with the commonality between the programs that work, building projects that sustain postseason pressure, the ingredients that lead to signature victories, and ultimately, the problem of sustaining a level of breakout success.

And when it's over five months from now, perhaps we'll have a better idea of why carefully-built programs break in March, and maybe we'll be better able to posit more advanced theories as to how to prevent that from happening. At the very least, I'll be able to test the limits of that new alternator.

GOLIATH

NOV 2, 2008

This being the first Sunday of The Mid-Majority's Season 5 (and a Daylight Savings-adjusted morning upon which thousands of churchgoers will miss their services), it's as good a time as any for a Bible story. Today, we'll be reading from the Old Testament, the first book of Samuel.

No tale is as carefully tied to our regular basketball business than one which appears in the midst of that book. 1 Samuel 17:49 is read verbatim during the greatest two minutes of American sports cinema, the second in a devastating emotional triple-apex within the championship-game locker room scene from *Hoosiers*. Preacher Purl steps forward before the team and intones meaningfully,

> *And David put his hand in the bag and took*
> *out a stone and slung it. And it struck the*
> *Philistine on the head and he fell to the ground.*
> *Amen.*

Now, about that amen part. That's not the end of the story, not by any means. David's post-slingshotting career, a life of complex morality, is one of the most fascinating character arcs in all of recorded literature. After he sliced off Goliath's head with the giant's own weapon a couple of verses later, Israel violently ran the Philistines off the land (with swords, it should be noted, not slingshots), and the victorious king ended up betraying the young hero in a jealous rage. While in exile among the Philistines, David engaged in some double-agency and later deposited himself in an adultery scandal, before ultimately fulfilling his destiny as Israel's great king. Oh, and he ended up having an esteemed writing career too.

But back to the moment that sent David on his trajectory. It's quite a scene to imagine, perhaps embellished a bit for the purposes of drawing the action in extreme and simple relief. After an odd declaration (1 Samuel 17:9) that absolutely everything rides on this single mano-a-mano conflict, two warriors and their implements face off in an staging space, the interested parties standing in rapt attention on opposite sides of the arena. Why, it's the first sporting event in Judeo-Christian history.

Which is why its lasting power as a sporting metaphor is dependent on its being plucked from context, and why its distilled essence is most potent when limited to that single passage. Large and imposing force on one side; small, smart and crafty upstart on the other.

David v. Goliath carries a disproportionate weight in the United States. This is, after all, a country that owes its existence to a rag-tag bunch that in the 1770's used cannonballs for stones in order to bring down the giant British Empire. David's slingshot is woven into our flag, installed in our hearts, shows up on our x-rays. It's in our essential nature, in our national soul, to root for the underdog. In fact, it's widely thought that the term originated here during America's adolescence.

Here, in its entirety, is a poem distributed in newspapers around the country in 1859, commonly considered the first-ever print appearance of the word "underdog."

The Under Dog In The Fight
by David Barker

I know that the world, the great big world,
From the peasant up to the king,
Has a different tale from the tale I tell,
And a different song to sing.
But for me, and I care not a single fig
If they say I am wrong or right,
I shall always go for the weaker dog,
For the under dog in the fight.
I know that the world, that the great big world,
Will never a moment stop --
To see which dog may be in the fault,
But will shout for the dog on top.
But for me I shall never pause to ask
Which dog may be in the right.
For my heart will beat, while it beats at all,
For the under dog in the fight.
Perchance what I've said I had better not said,
Or 'there better I had said it incog.
But with my heart and with glass filled up to the brim
Here's health to the bottom dog.

Interesting historical time, that. In 1869, a year after "David Barker's" thoughtful meditation appeared, a soft-spoken political underdog gained the White House, and before Abraham Lincoln could settle into his new home, the southern states had taken up arms and staged an unsuccessful assault on the mighty Union. While some may conclude otherwise, that any sentimental attachment to the Stars and Bars a century and half later constitutes a fondness for the slavery days, my own travels and conversations lead me to believe that the majority of old Confederates simply cling to the romantic notion of being the bottom dog in the fight.

Within a generation of the Civil War's end, popular academic theories tying physical activity to healthy minds—along with the effect of the world-wide Olympic Movement—led to a rise of organized sports in America. At last, a country that has always had an uneasy relationship with power had a non-violent outlet for its urges (and later a bottomless well of metaphors when it did end up engaging in life-or-death battles around the world). As the 19th Century became the 20th, professional leagues formed around various rule books. Colleges and universities drafted teams that played baseball, American-style football, all manner of pastimes.

As with in any arms race in recorded history, those with more resources to apply to athletic artillery built great dynasties with areas of influence greater than their own backyards—the New York Yankees and the Montreal Canadiens and UCLA. Over and over, challengers rise to face imposing favored forces, in arenas with color-clad supporters on each side, that tiny sliver of 1 Samuel played out over and over again in safe simile. In the final accounting, nobody dies, and the scoreboard is reset back to zero afterwards.

Since we Americans stopped turn on each other in armed conflict over a century and a half ago, this is how our primal aggression is channelled now, state and city versus neighboring region. If Northwestern State defeats Iowa that's the end of it, it's not an open invitation to class warfare. Two years ago, the streets did not run red with the blood of Hawkeye fans, the Demons did not march to Iowa's campus, set it on fire, or even steal its spot in the Big Ten. It was just a basketball game, amen.

Moments like that, when the powerless defeat the powerful, resonate deep within us and unleash the spirit of revolution that lies at the historical center of our very Americanness. They speak to an essential facet of our human condition, the reason why David appears as a figure in the Christian tradition, the Hebrew Bible as well as the Qur'an. Our souls are designed to strive upward, no matter what forces press down upon us.

And drawing that connection into sharp focus, between the internal yearning and the detached external event, can help us get to the tangle of untruths at the center of this greater lie, the Hickory High fiction, the apocrypha that is the original story of Goliath's defeat.

First and foremost, the sheer disposability of modern Davids. When Northwestern State, or George Mason, or Butler, or Davidson lose their giant-killing power—as they will eventually or have already—they are no longer useful to the multitudes who stole from them brief and stirring reminders of Who We Are. With modern television, it's possible to sit as a passive observer and receive multiple jolts of that Goliath-killing feeling, and that makes these moments of magic as pedestrian as the common orgasm.

Another key problem is simple underdog politics. When a sports David wins an inspirational but ultimately meaningless contest, it's an exception that simply proves the exception, not the rule. It's a self-perpetuating illusion that the "little guy" has a chance to trade marginal effort for success if the stars align correctly, the same dynamic that drives American Idol, the same one that sends the destitute and despondent to casino slot machines and pick-4 tickets. When David wins, a surviving Goliath scores a greater yet more invisible victory—the core reality of a looming power structure has been acknowledged, a reminder that true parity is as mythical as it was the day before.

It's easy to be a champion of the underdog, a cheerleader for the low seed, a grandstander for the little guy made good—it's a potent message that sells extremely well. But not here, and not anymore. From here on out, those messages will be saved for other venues and other audiences, the ones that ultimately fund our efforts in this space. There are many more of them out there, with shorter attention spans and weaknesses for string sections, than there are of you. These programs covered here are what they are, competing for resources in a crowded landscape, playing chess without a full set of pieces, trying to combine strengths in such a way to bury the weaknesses. That's poetry enough for us.

Indeed, few have patience for the whole story. This site is about the chapter, not the verse... the book, not the brief passage. With the luxury of extended long-form, bridging across miles and state lines, years and seasons, The Mid-Majority is about the long, hard and often endless road. In the big picture, the moments of glory are more powerful when set against a backdrop of monotonous, endless struggle. But, by God, that's what makes the victory all the sweeter.

CONDUIT
NOV 3, 2008

New technology always takes time to find its proper place, to soak into the mainstream. Over three centuries passed before the printing press changed from a luxury item for the powerful into a tool of the people. There were 50 years between "Watson, come here, I want to see you" and the Model 102 that brought simple telephony to the masses. It took nearly 100 years for television to go from early and halting experiments to worldwide acceptance.

The cycles are getting shorter, though. In just 25 years, a global web of interconnected computers grew from a defense communication system to a limitless, bottomless information and multimedia network for consumers. One particular use for this internet contraption is the transmission of sequential packages of information, presented most recent first. Sometimes progress works faster than careful labeling techniques, so the generally accepted and unfortunate term for this mechanism is and always will be "blog." (Which is just as unwieldy and incorrect an indicator as "mid-major," if not more so. At least "mid-major" hasn't yet devolved into a verb.)

Despite that speed, blogs still encountered the entrenched status quo that greets any innovation. There are cold-dead-hands adherents to the previous way of doing things, industries inherently resistant to change, and, frankly, old people. Blogs, much like the new technologies that came before, are the sexy racing vehicles of the young. But another key dynamic that slows market penetration is the simple fact that bright new minds usually have no idea how best to use their own inventions properly, or they start out by using them in misguided and myopic ways. The history of blogs proved no exception.

I started my first blog in 2000. I used it to present my problems with girls as wide-screen epic adventures, and to rewrite my own personal history in a way that made me the Protagonist of Everything. Not surprisingly, the few readers who stopped by via Altavista or Netscape searches didn't find what they were looking for (usually some manner of obscure pornography), and I was lucky to get 20 hits per day. That collection is not something I go back to read again... since it's all been pretty well scrubbed from the indexes, few others can either.

Online diaries, ends unto themselves, were a dead end indeed. Screens with no links to elsewhere invited swift extinction. There had to be a take-away, a reason to keep going. No surprise, then, that the people involved in pushing the arc of this format's maturity in recent years were aggregators and distributors—Jason Kottke, Glenn Reynolds, Anil Dash, Mark Frauen-felder's Boing Boing. Each gained massive readership by standing between an endless ocean of scattershot information and like-minded recipients, fil-tering the world into beautiful order by showing only the interesting parts, leaving out the rest. For their efforts, these bloggers are trusted like true friends by their audiences.

More recently, as the old paper-based order begins to fall away, this for-mat has grown to include a different type of key conduit. Seasoned writers and reporters, with press passes and access to public figures, with familiar names and representing familiar outlets, fire off public missives about cur-rent events in a format more immediate and efficient than any paper-based vessel could ever be. The contract between them and their audiences are similarly built on trust, a level of warm comfort, and results in a better and more immediate understanding of the covered issue. Some call this the "reported blog" (as poor a term as "super mid-major"), and the current United States election cycle has cemented its power as a communication tool.

The "sports blog" hasn't quite reached the level of maturation as the "polit-ical blog," but serious gains are being made. Specifically here in the college basketball sub-genre—there are thoughtful and intelligent sites springing up every day, many with multiple contributors and a national focus, pop-ping up too quickly to properly include all of them in any complete linkroll. Which is a relief, because 2006-07 truly was the dark ages (most of the pre-dating survivors of that season, it turns out, have been kindly rewarded with jobs and cash). In the past year or so, there's been an increased premium on intelligence, intellectual curiosity, the furthering of arguments with sta-tistics instead of baseless (and presumably drunken) claims of historical supremacy.

And that's the way forward. The new generation of sports bloggers who will go on to make a career out of this will build bridges between audiences and a better understanding of the games they cover, which will bring them legions of trusting supporters. As newspapers continue to die, those with press passes and an understanding of this new reality will have an increas-ingly important job to do, and our own responsibilities will grow. In the coming years, the "reported sports blog" will be the choice of informed audiences. The future looks a lot more like Joe Posnanski's site than A.J.

Daulerio's, and thank heavens for that.

The result of the first blogging shakeout is that navel-gazing exercises were safely cordoned off in facebooks, myspaces and livejournals. The segment of the market that runs on dick jokes, ill-informed rants and anonymous jackassery is in the process of sealing itself into a separate corner, creating its own self-fulfilling dead end. Blogging as a medium is growing up, and those who refuse to do so themselves will be left behind. After all, it's happened before.

AMBITION

NOV 4, 2008

If you're just now dropping by and don't know what this is all about, this site is all about going to mid-major college basketball games. A lot of them. I attended 117 total games last year, and I've been to 508 over the past five seasons. I'm still married, in case you're wondering.

As I travel around the country visiting mid-major arenas from Big South to Big West, I notice a lot of common elements from venue to venue. The national anthem is played or sung or piped in before every game, the rims are always 10 feet above the court, games tend to be 40 minutes long and the shot clock never, ever reads 36 seconds. But the most striking similarity is the stock character I keep running into from sea to shining sea.

The mid-major beat writer.

In a lot of cases, the only two people on press row are the mid-major beat writer and myself (mostly due to lack of local interest and Associated Press cutbacks). So I spend a lot of time with them... or rather, "him." Most wear the official uniform, an untucked collared shirt and a pair of jeans, a few days' worth of stubble, and questionable posture. After weeks on the road I can be easily convinced that it's the same person, just following me around as I go.

Most approach the games in the same way—with near-total detachment, spending more time checking ACC or NBA scores than watching the game, managing instant-message popups, browsing threads at SportsJournalists. com, or fielding cellphone calls about which bar to meet at the second the game ends.

Their reports, whether in the newspaper the next day or... okay, I peek sometimes... are usually bored boilerplate recap, or columns about every-thing the team is doing wrong, written in the popular current style that makes use of a lot of one-word paragraphs. The team lacks "toughness," or can't "finish games," and certain players aren't "stepping up." Lots of future coaches in this business.

Is this an overgeneralization? Sure. But this script repeats itself over and over, uncannily so. Walk a few thousand miles in my shoes, and you'd see it too.

There are certain exceptions, of course, and I don't want to embarrass anybody by naming names. They know who they are, because I go out of my way to personally praise their work and tell them how much I respect their efforts and dedication. These are the writers who won't and can't shut up about the teams they cover, who can discuss the SoCon or Southland or Horizon League for hours on end, who have well-formed opinions about recruiting, 15th men on rosters, conference politics. These are my heroes in this business.

But in the rare instances when the MMBW returns my attempts at friendly conversation, it's usually to look at my nameplate and ask if "ESPN is hiring," whatever that means. I hope my stunned silence comes off as less rude than what I'd actually say out loud. But I guess this is what passes for ambition in some circles—that this is all about catching "breaks," finding the people whose simple roles are to smile and hand over the secret code to the castle door, or point the way to the golden career escalator.

Which is why I find that doubly offensive, the idea that somebody would or could ever be rewarded for slapdash reporting on a subject they have no respect for to begin with. The idea I have held all along, and the concept this site has attempted to push forward for the past four years, is that it's okay to work hard at this, and it's perfectly acceptable to take this seriously.

Power-conference basketball is important because a lot of people have agreed it's important, and efforts here begin and end with the idea that mid-major basketball is important too. Every game is connected with every other game by separating degrees, every team is a complicated puzzle worth studying. Every possession can unlock a new facet of this game of basket-ball, can offer a lesson about countervailing forces.

That message doesn't register with a mid-major beat writer who's biding their time before fulfilling their destiny as a power-conference beat writer. Which is fine, I guess, because there are those others that "get it" without my intervention, and did so long before I ever showed up.

In my short career as a paid chronicler of college basketball, the business side of things has been good to me. I'm lucky to make a good living at what I do now, and I've somehow been able to make more good decisions than bad ones. One of those moves, which dates back to just over a year ago, was to spin off a large portion of this website to a new home called Basketball State. It's been quite successful, more so than I would have ever imagined.

Starting later this month, once the season begins, Basketball State will begin publishing regular features from a tremendous group of talented writers. We'll have a few medium-sized features a week, all freely available and safely outside the subscription wall. Not all of the contributors will cover our side of the Red Line, but what each has in common is a keen commitment to quality. Each possesses an internal compass that points to interesting and informative work. Most of the names will be recognizable to those who like reading about basketball.

As we move forward with this project, I'm hoping to increase the use of that site as a way to recognize true ambition among those that cover mid-major basketball. I want to offer good writers an outlet where they can act as good conduits, where they can earn a decent rate—more than a blog can pay—in return for copy that treats this level of our game with the respect it deserves.

My primary issues with the common mid-major beat writer are the presumption, the lack of hunger and imagination, and the unwillingness to respect their subject. They're not doing their own careers, or the schools they cover, any good. If they aren't taking this seriously, there's no reason for their readers to take it seriously either—and this is a major reason why the public at large doesn't take this seriously. I'm just hoping that, going forward, we can help distribute the antidote.

BIAS

NOV 5, 2008

In case you haven't heard, our great nation recently concluded a long and protracted and polarizing popularity contest that decided, among other things, our heads of state and guiding ideologies for the foreseeable future. It was often marked by severe disagreements that pitted American against American.

Voters in this election had real choices, not only in political parties and candidates, but in information sources as well. Thanks to a wide array of television outlets and a million-website universe, people had no problem locating and latching onto the message they were looking for. Republicans, for instance, had their Fox News and their Drudge Report and their conservative radio hosts and commentators; Democrats could huddle around their Air America, trade Daily Kos journals, and—in a brilliant example of profitable media positioning—nod in agreement to MSNBC.

It's a level of choice unprecedented in media history, thanks to postmodern technology. In 2012, there will be an entire media complex for the independent middle-of-the-road undecideds, which will view all sides with a shopper's eye, revel in the constant wooing and catering, then not bother to show up for election day by suspending coverage the day before.

In the future, we'll be able to float through their entire lives in agreeable and segmented bubbles, hearing only and exactly what we want to hear. "News" will truly mean "what you already know and believe to be true." Technology will lead America to this great victory, outstripping the promise made 230 years ago by a simple Kansan poet. In the future, never is heard a discouraging word.

That sports journalism has followed the same path as political coverage in the past decade or so seems to advance the theory that, with unlimited choice, most consumers will automatically choose in favor of agreeability and against the intellectual challenge. All around, bland communities of yes-men who rail against the common enemy and play us-against-the-world. (Deadspin, after all, was an empire formed by people who weren't getting what they wanted from ESPN anymore.) Your favorite team has fan blogs, message boards, and, increasingly, its own high-powered media-relations propaganda arm and maybe even its own internet TV station—it's the center of the world.

Analysts, where they exist, get more reaction from armies of like-minded drones than they do from those who praise their work at face value. In an environment where media outlets measure success by the number of "comments" a piece receives, bias becomes a market force. Hack analysts, where they exist, engage on confirmation bias—a pre-fabricated notion, supported by a line of facts that support the thesis, all in the name of generating reaction. That's not being a proper conduit between information and audience.

But there's plenty of reason to color and shade, because the new world dictates that it's profitable and career-advancing to do so. It's easy to consume that material, and many do, but I urge you to maintain a detached intellectual curiosity about the process. Was this written to stimulate a specific emotional reaction? And why would they want to do that?

For my part, this site's part, I realized after a few years that maybe I was going about all of this the wrong way. My own school, Drexel, has a basketball team I'm fond of, but my own fractured relationship with it—some work my company did with DU a decade ago ended badly for everyone, and they pulled a financial aid loophole that soaked me for tens of thousands of dollars—keeps me from being a homer. When I started the Mid-Majority, instead of being an apologist for every team below the Red Line and making everyone feel good about themselves, I made the tactical mistake of blindly praising success when it came.

But glory at this level comes and goes, and fans of down-cycle teams that were, at a time, the toast of the site (Wisconsin-Milwaukee, Bradley and Holy Cross come to mind) didn't get what they wanted from me after a while. I went from being a genius to an idiot, from being quoted extensively to the subject of e-mail carpet bombs. While some enjoy the attention, adrenaline and controversy, I find it tiresome, and dealing with it gets in the way of the work.

There's a price for all of that selectivity, and it's niche alienation. If you've been reading this site for four-plus years, which is one full college cycle from matriculation to Senior Night and plenty of rises and falls, it's likely that you're more interested in the anthropological overview of the landscape than any specific portion of it. And there's a good chance that we've swapped e-mails or talked on the phone. There aren't many of you out there.

Which is why this site will always be a loss-leader for me, yet will always remain as my greatest love among all the projects I'm involved in. Readers will come and go when I say something positive or negative about their favorite teams, but this site is not for them. It's our semi-private conversation.

So, for you, I promise to continue this project with the focus it deserves. I'll travel around the country and tell you what I find. I'll attempt to find the common threads between what builds success and summons failure in mid-major college basketball, and invite you to come to your own conclusions about the results. Above all, I'll try to report on all the stories that can't be written ahead of time.

PACKER

NOV 6, 2008

Here in early November, we're still at least a month away from the non-stop barrage of "Year In Review" specials, all those bow-snapping recaps that attempt to impose order on a loosely-joined, selectively-selected group of events. But after 11 months, one thing is crystal-clear: 2008 has been a horrible year for old white guys.

Old white guys are shriveling before our eyes, falling increasingly out of step with the times, their power and majesty collapsing, judgement and senses slowly taking leave of them as they drift into history. To the younger generations from failing hands they fumble the torch; be ours, indeed, to hold it high. From John McCain to Jerry Lewis to Ted Stevens, off they go into the cold night of history. And then, of course, there's Billy Packer.

On July 14, the college basketball voice of CBS was carefully extricated from the business, left at the side of the road of progress by his employer after 27 years. The news interrupted my placid and serene summer, a reminder of storm clouds in my sun-dappled reverie. I was idly taking in a weekday afternoon minor-league baseball game in New Britain, Conn. when the news came in, beeping and ringing by voicemail, tweet and text. Everybody wanted to be the first to let me know, to join in on the celebration.

I am, after all, a "mid-major" person, and Packer was most decidedly not. The 68-year-old sportscaster was once a 21-year-old star guard for Wake Forest, helping the Demon Deacons win the Atlantic Coast Conference twice and in 1962 achieved a place in the event he was later to be synonymous with, the Final Four.

In the years that followed, he was an outspoken defender of college basketball's power structure, questioning top NCAA seedings given to Indiana State in 1979 and Saint Joseph's in 2004, then blasted the selection committee two years later when at-large spots were given to low-resource teams like Bradley and Wichita State and George Mason, and not power-conference with long CV's like Cincinnati and Florida State. He didn't feel the CAA or MVC had done enough in the past to merit any consideration.

The 2006 Final Four in Indianapolis was the only time I ever encountered Billy Packer in person. At George Mason's open practice the afternoon before the national semifinals, I saw him sitting by himself in the second row of the long, plastic-covered press row tables in the cavernous RCA Dome. He was carefully studying a computer printout, and there was a tall, sloppy stack of literature in front of him. I maneuvered my way into the seating area for a closer look.

From a seat two chairs away, I could better view Packer's reading selections. A George Mason media guide, a xeroxed clip file of Washington Post stories about the team, statistical breakdowns and box scores. All the homework he hoped against hope that he would never have to do, before the Patriots' wins over Michigan State, North Carolina, Wichita State and Connecticut forced his hand.

Just then, a prominent and well-known print journalist sidled up between us, wearing a tight red sweater with an embroidered golf-club logo over the chest, wielding a small wire notebook. He leaned in close to the grizzled sportscasting veteran, asked him what he thought of what he saw.

"John," Packer said wearily, rubbing his face. "Wake me when this mid-major shit is over."

It's a story I've told only sparingly over these last two years, partially because it's nothing more than an affirmation and fulfillment of a perception most people already have. In the collective consciousness, Packer is a curmudgeonly and divisive figure who loves power-conference teams and throws cold water on mid-major accomplishments.

He's never tried to show himself as anything more complex than this cartoonish WWE caricature, and so any NCAA upset is not only a victory on the court for the "little guy," but a needly fork in Packer's bare arse as well. When the CAA and MVC proved him wrong in the spring of 2006, Packer uttered the following cryptic mea culpa: "I'm often wrong, but never in doubt."

Bad literature, and sorry attempts to project a cheap good-and-evil narrative on the sports world, need clearly-drawn heroes and villains. It would have been an even less gratifying storyline if Packer had come out after the 2006 NCAA Tournament with a newfound appreciation for schools that start with nothing and build towards greatness. It would have been ridiculous if he had pledged never to second-guess a mid-major team again, in a stream-of-consciousness monologue about seeing the light. Billy Packer knew his place in this world, and embraced that role with everything he had. It was better than the alternative.

I like to think I understand Billy Packer. To hold opinion close to the heart and deny doubt, even in the face of mounting facts, is its own self-contained and greyscale-free world that is always more safe and comfortable than the swirling debate outside. The stability of a power structure is easier to cling to than the anarchic chaos that upsets the balance. Knowledge acquired and collected in ages past is always preferable to any new reality that questions it, that threatens to shake it to its core. When you're old, you don't want to have to do any more learning.

And though the man himself has moved on, his career obituary written a thousand times already, his spirit lives on. We're not rid of him yet. Within every recalcitrant statement on an internet message board, Billy Packer is there. Every pundit who takes a top-down approach to college basketball, who sees us as invaders and pretenders to the throne, carries his message forward.

Every time a commentator or fan chooses conventional wisdom over intellectual curiosity, lazy perception over rigorous research, they unleash his indomitable spirit. From on high, Billy Packer is smiling in the moon, unleashing that big, ugly laugh of his, his cackles echoing across the expanse of a cold and dark midwinter college basketball night.

SPORTSGUY

NOV 7, 2008

For a nation that takes its freedom so seriously, we sure are confused about it. Our society is rigidly segmented and specialized, everyone must find their place. From parental career projections to college "majors" to printed titles on business cards, American life is a series of restraints. To break out of the cycle requires upheaval, doubt, expensive retraining.

Culture provides a series of mixed signals about all of that. Nearly every feel-good Hollywood movie ever made concerns itself with a protagonist busting out of a prefabricated life, finally becoming what they truly want to be at the end, overcoming odds to become what they truly are despite a power structure's insistence of obedience. At the same time, there are high-profile dire warnings about the consequences of destiny-smashing: Don Johnson's singing career, Michael Jordan's flirtation with baseball, and more recently, Mariah Carey's acting.

Maybe it has something to do with the American idea that there's a military solution to everything, this invisible insistence on lock-step. Over the past century or so, the major sports in this country have conformed their rules and customs to become grey, cold variations on human chess. American football, for instance, is the worst. One's size and IQ determines what their job will be, and when an alternate theory comes along, purists act as if the communists are overrunning the game. In our lifetimes, baseball has evolved from nine positions to 20—on every pitching staff, you'll find a setup man for the setup man.

And in our beloved game of basketball, pure creativity diminished the moment that three-point arc was stamped into every court. Pop in a tape of a game from the Sixties or Seventies, appreciate the danger whenever a player dribble-drives from 20 feet out without the easy option of retreating for a long lobbing extra-point shot. Players didn't have the numbers "one" through "five" tattooed on their souls back then.

With such joyless games as these, modern American fans—looking for temporary escape from their own cages—require value-added content to keep their attention fixated on them. Into this world stumbled the right man at the right time. His real name was William Simmons. He came to be known, simply, as the Sports Guy.

Whether he carefully calculated the formula beforehand, or stumbled upon it by trial and error, there is no question that modern sportswriting on the internet owes Simmons not only a debt of gratitude, but royalties for life. He is the father, son, and holy spirit of the sports blogging movement. Over the past decade, virtually every sports blogger stole his template—the fan's eye view, the bar-buddy familiarity, and the steady stream of pop-culture references that can give dull and endless regular seasons meaningful simile. But none figured out the secret to his success: the thumbnail-sketch biography that quickly and easily made the Sports Guy a known quantity. Nobody cares who you are, or what you have to say, unless your entire being can be distilled into 25 words or less.

When I was starting out with The Mid-Majority four years ago, slowly building my audience from nothing, the comparisons started coming in. You're like the Sports Guy back when he was good, one might tell me, or more often and likely, Stop ripping off TSG's shtick, you loser. I made a point to correct anybody and everybody who said it to my face. "No, you don't understand," I'd tell them. "I'm building something different here."

And it's true that we have some things in common, he and I. We now both get checks with Mickey Mouse in the top-left corner (his are for considerably larger sums) for doing roughly the same thing, which is to write about sports on ESPN.com in column and chat form. We're both on the all-time SportsNation marathon chart—me at six hours, he at 7:04 (this was before Rob Neyer blew us both out with a Ripken-like 10:56 on baseball's Opening Day this year). We both have squeaky voices that keep us from ever being SportsCenter anchors. We both grew up in New England idolizing Larry Bird, and we both went to tony prep schools. Both he and I attended mid-major colleges, and we've both tended bar to pay the rent.

But, and I hope this is the case, that's where any and all similarities end. I've never crossed paths with the Sports Guy, never swapped e-mails with him, and the closest I've come is the (possibly apocryphal) story about how I was issued the last ESPN credential to the 2006 Final Four, the George Mason one, the credential he would have used. I've never reached out to him, it's not something I need to do. He's got enough friends.

Instead, while I admire his work and everything he's accomplished, I use his career as reverse inspiration. I ask myself, "WWTSGD?" Then I do the opposite. I don't do mailbags, I take myself out of columns, I use movie references only one or two people will understand. I try to keep from antagonizing others, and I constantly tell people how grateful I am for the opportunity to serve the machine. The Sports Guy is the reason why I have made a point never to use the first-person in an ESPN piece, a promise not broken since 2006, when an editor spliced in an "I." There was nothing I could do about that one.

I'm serious about staying out of the way between subject and audience, from being a "Mid-Major Guy" who stands in the camera shot's foreground, while the schools and players that aren't getting enough coverage anyway play in the background. It's nowhere in my nature. I take to heart what the great David Halberstam once said: "By and large, the more famous you are, the less of a journalist you are." I want to be a conduit, not a short circuit.

Being the Sports Guy means constructing theories and definitions for others to view the world through, submitted for acceptance or rejection. It means writing things to elicit reaction, not broaden understanding. It means telling people what they already think they know.

When he was given the chance to appear on West Coast Conference basketball telecasts in 2007, the Sports Guy ranked his newfound WCC expertise "among the most useless talents I've ever had." (Never mind that he witnessed the initial architecture for the breakthrough three-bid year that came just a season later.) This past summer, he declared tennis a dead game before Wimbledon displayed the true and unquestioned beauty that

all competition is capable of. This incident prompted legendary internet conduit Jason Kottke to mutter, "If you're a sports columnist, it helps if you're,
you know, interested in sports."

I have no idea how much of Simmons' output represents what he truly
feels, and how much comes out of a perceived need to pander to a large audience with a certain set of expectations. But if there's any difference between
the two, then this much is clear: "Sports Guy" is a prison, as much of a
ironclad cubbyhole as "Utility Infielder," "Middle Linebacker" or "Small Forward." While a master at any of these positions can find fame and success
and great riches, I prefer a different road. I choose independence, anonymity
and relative poverty. I choose freedom.

BOOK

NOV 8, 2008

Since the invention of the printing press and discovery of binding, it's been
the dream of everyone who strings words together to write a book. A long-
form work of 80 or 100 thousand words that can be touched, held open,
smelled, stacked on a shelf and command a reader's undivided attention for
hours on end—there's a lot of power in that. And it doesn't stop there. When
you as a "writer" become a "published author," bulldozers will clear out a
forest for you, machines will pulp the trees and stamp your sentences on the
flat, double-sided end product. The whole process is a victory of human
ingenuity over nature itself.

This April, when the season was over and I'd recovered from Detroit, I
was approached by two outlets interested in distributing my work. One was
a "digital publisher" that wanted to distribute my travelogue series from last
season. I didn't think those entries were as good as I wanted them to be,
certainly not good enough to receive payment for—so I said no thanks.
Besides, they were already in digital form. The other company was more for-
ward-thinking—it proposed a project about the 2008-09 season, a behind-
the-scenes chronicle of the efforts of several mid-major teams to qualify
for the NCAA Tournament, the Big Dance. Sprinkled in amongst, stories of
struggle and season survival that would draw the stories of champions in
important relief.

At last, someone with large printing equipment was reading my mind.

I said yes before negotiating, I was excited. I'd get an advance of several thousand dollars on submission of two chapters, and it was arranged that an excerpt would run in a magazine over the summer of 2009. I'd do a reading tour, flog the book like any author, and embed sales pitches in every single blog post and chat session during the 2009-10 season. The contract was minimally restrictive, except for a non-compete clause that stated that I could not offer another publisher a college basketball manuscript until the fall of 2010.

I signed the contract the same night as the "sports blog" discussion on Costas Now, and I wrote about the feeling of starting as an accidental blogger turned first-time author-to-be. "After that ridiculous TV discussion show on Tuesday night, I'm more proud than ever of the internet," I noted. "The internet made me. None of what's happened to me is possible without a 'blog'—that horrible little word splinter that's come to represent irresponsible reporting, tit jokes, parents' basements and anarchy."

Sports Publishing LLC started 20 years ago as a small specialty press in Illinois, was once named as Publisher's Weekly fastest-growing independent publisher and has a number notable titles to its credit. SP distributed Michael Phelps' first bio and published the autobiography of one of my heroes in this business, Dickie V. I was proud for the opportunity.

But the difference between large publishing houses and those that don't become large can sometimes be measured by the quality of their business acumen. The company had a history of odd lawsuits, and I found few first-time authors that had good things to say about their experience with SP.

I didn't care. For one, I knew that my book about mid-major basketball would never make me a millionaire. I wanted my name on a book. I just wanted to do the best job I could, make a book I was proud of, one that would make the authors I desire acceptance from to look at me as more than just an "internet writer." I just wanted to get on Amazon.com and into the Library of Congress. I know too many authors with day-jobs and adjustable-rate mortgages to ever believe that a book would be my ticket to riches, and I could afford to take a bath on billable hours.

In September, in amongst a larger American financial crisis, Sports Publishing LLC teetered on the brink of a savior sale before falling into Chapter 11 bankruptcy. The employee list was whittled down to two, creditors barred the door to their warehouse, and the company's tattered financial books were put on display. It was revealed that the company owed Michael Phelps over $57,000 and his co-author over $49,000. A bank seized all SP's assets, including my contract.

As the company melted down over the course of the summer, many writers were, as the president put it, "stuck in the middle." My project was dead, but I hadn't written a word or accepted a cent. Many hard-working writers with projects of their own were placed in horrible positions, having invested hours and days and months into their manuscripts. Some of those authors were forced into pennies-on-the-dollar settlements, and many were, understandably, angry. I know how hard it is to come so far and be denied at the end, that's the key recurring story of mid-major college basketball.

For my part, I went through the stages (anger, denial, whatever), thought about it for a couple of weeks, and consulted with counsel. Finally, after much deliberation, I decided to go ahead anyway, to write this book. Three programs had promised me full access with which to work, and I wasn't about to give up that opportunity.

The first question, though, was distribution. Here's the plan for now, which is subject to change. Once the manuscript is complete and independently edited next summer, I will release it one chapter at a time, in PDF form, for free. If you want a copy with a nice color cover that you can hold in your hands, that can be arranged (thanks to a DIY digital outfit that prints one-off copies) for whatever price you feel is worth it beyond print costs. It's an idea inspired by monologue-heavy sci-fi author Cory Doctorow, and it's the loophole in the fall 2010 clause of my contract. I've joked that the working title of the book will be "In Mid-Major Rainbows."

As for those three schools, the list is secret for now. Those inclined to tease out the details will be able to do so, the places on the map that I keep visiting will offer clues to the riddle. But I won't mention them as a group until the season is over, to keep from presenting the appearance of preferential treatment. Obviously, I have an interest in their success, but I want to make sure that doesn't have an impact on my work here, or with ESPN or Basketball Times.

And finally, a special message to agents and publishers (even the "digital" ones) out there. This book is going to be good, there's a defined audience that will buy it, and it's available for pickup if you're willing to take a chance. The initial publisher is a dead company that cannot enforce the deadlines set out in the contract. The odds of a holding company enforcing a two-year non-compete are very slim, and if you have a legal team with a workaround for something like that, I'm all ears. That clause, right there, is the only trap standing in the way between this book and the public. I'm willing to talk, you know where to find me.

NEXT

NOV 9, 2008

I have no Wikipedia entry of my own, not even a stub. If I understand the process correctly, you have to be either rich or a character on The Simpsons to get one of those. Being neither, and therefore not sufficiently notable, it's up to me to write my own encyclopedic biography.

I was born on May 19, 1972, of German and WASP extraction. I grew up mostly in New Hampshire and New York, and attended a prep school called High Mowing (a year behind action hero Judson Mills of Walker, Texas Ranger fame). When I was 18, I changed my name because I found a better one. I went to journalism school at the University of Oregon, took a two year design degree at nearby Lane Community College, and moved back east to Philadelphia in 1997. Since then, I've never been out of debt. At Drexel University, in the collapsible bleachers, I discovered mid-major college basketball.

Since 2004, when I got a crazy idea in the upper east stands of The Palestra, I've been curating a website called The Mid-Majority. It's about two things: mid-major college basketball and travel. Over the past five years, I've been to 508 games from coast to coast and in between, sleeping and showering at truck stops when I've needed to. I run a number of websites—one's about the Olympics and one's about sports transactions and one's about internet scraps—but this is the only one that's ever landed me a job. The thumbnail bio-sketch I talked about the other day is this simple: mid-majors, truck stops, ESPN.com.

I live in Pawtucket, Rhode Island, where I'm writing this now. I have a spouse (known in these pages as The Official Wife of The Mid-Majority), no legitimate children as of yet, and two cats. There are few things in life I would have done differently.

Here now, a day away from a new season, it's a chance to plan, to lay out the blueprint that will be measured against the regrets of tomorrow once it's time to write the epilogue. It's an opportunity to make the promises that you, gentle readers, will hold me to, those that I will strive mightily to fulfill. As with any of the teams covered here, it's a game of expectation management.

Some things will change from Season 4. Weekday posts will be differently presented, for one. We're retiring The Boubacar, because the original inspiration for the concept has himself "retired." Boubacar Coly, 6-9 former defensive force of the Morgan State Bears, forewent his final season of eligibility and has apparently dropped off the map. Instead, your A.M. hours will be filled with Good Morning Hoops Nation, the fun and frisky morning show that mid-majordom never had. Each post will feature links, scores, analysis and video clips, focusing on what you need to know. It'll be like Morning Joe on acid.

There will, of course, be a Game! Of! The! Night! every weekday, as always. Features will generally be anchored to their regular days. On Mondays, the Mid-Majority Baller of the Week (MMBOW), a tradition that dates back to the beginning. Starting again in late November, the State of the Other 22 (1/2) will be posted on Wednesdays, a computer index based on the Basketball State rankings. And a popular sporadic happening will go weekly this year: every Tuesday, TMM will post a contest of some sort, the prize being the intensely prized stuffed Bally. The entry window will close Friday, and winners will be announced the following Tuesday along with the new contest.

You've probably noticed the new scoreboard up top that will keep track of mid-major scores, as well as my mileage and games attended and next stop. Also included is a running percentage of "mid-major upsets," defined by teams below the Red Line beating those above it (two exceptions: Gonzaga is considered above, and A-10 teams' wins only count if they're against the Big Six). You can also get notifications of upsets in your e-mail with the "upset club" list, found in the right-hand columns.

Another new wrinkle will be the use of Twitter, the "social networking tool" that forces participants to channel their inner Hemingways and keep things to 140 characters. Recent posts are on the right of the screen, and you can follow along if you have an account yourself. Most of the updates will be about road food and in-game updates. ("Stephen Curry: good at basketball" is a potential preview.)

Every so often, there'll be a new Bally cartoon. And, of course, photos of our small orange friend from all across the country. And speaking of sporadics, a product of this past election cycle has inspired and pointed the way to a new method of traveloguing—check out the Road to 270 at FiveThirtyEight if you didn't get a chance to. Instead of yammering on about myself, I'll be starting up something called Mid-Major America this year. We'll periodically talk about a region or city and its small schools, investigate what mid-major basketball has meant to these places, share some stories and take some pictures. (My photos won't be very good, though.) It'll be like Charles Kuralt on acid.

PART II

EARLY SEASON

SILVER SHOES, AND AN INVITATION

NOV 13, 2008

CARBONDALE, ILL.—I'm breaking out a new gameday uniform this year, which I hope will be the kind of gimmick to shed my "Mid-Major Guy" thumbnail bio, without actually yielding the territory to competitors. I'm upgrading my look from the standard shirt and tie of years past to a full suit... and a pair of silver Nikes.

Initial reviews have been positive. The UMass beat writers couldn't stop talking about them. When I was at Duke the other day, climbing over the media table to the floor at halftime, a young African-American Cameron Crazie standing nearby in the sardine-can crush called out for my attention. "Hey, where did you get those shoes?" he asked, his eyes wide. I have to tell you, as pale and rhythmless as I am, a black dude complimenting me on my kicks is the sweetest feeling in the entire world.

The silver shoes were a birthday gift, from The Official Wife of the Mid-Majority™. Back in May, we went up to the Nike Outlet store up the road in Wareham, Mass.. I was tagging along, this was her shopping trip. She was due to be deployed within the month, and the Navy required running shoes with non-marking soles for physical training ("PT"). It took her a half an hour to find the perfect pair, so I browsed around.

In the running section, there they were. A single pair of brilliant and shiny Air Max sneakers, and they were in my size—fourteen. Anybody out there with giant feet knows how difficult it is to find shoes this big, and long-time brand adherents how Nike stores generally keep just one pair of every style in 14, which touches off a massive cutthroat competition amongst us. I slipped the silver shoes on, admired their bounciness and light weight, and went over to where my wife was trying on pair after pair.

"Look at me," I said, mugging and vamping. "I've got shiny shoes!"

My wife rolled her eyes. Then she smiled at the sheer goofiness of them. She asked me if I wanted them for my birthday, and I put up a front, but we quickly came to a resolution.

"I'll get them for you only if you'll wear them," she said. "I can't imagine what kind of situation calls for silver Nikes, though."

I plan to wear my shiny shoes to every game this season, all 125 or so that I attend during 2008-09. It's not some kind of symbolic gesture, like a yellow ribbon or a rubber wristband that's supposed to stand for a cause. I miss my wife dearly, and often find sleep difficult and addled with nightmares, but there will be no Silver Shoes Movement to bring our troops home from Iraq. There are other avenues for those emotions.

When it comes down to it, I wear these silver shoes because they're superfly.

I initially got the e-mail in truncated BlackBerry form while in Carbondale traffic yesterday afternoon. "Mock Selection," the subject read. There was some talk about brackets and select writers inside, and I thought it was another of these insider journalists' bracket pools with 25 years of history, a funny name ("The Gerald" or whatnot) and the opportunity to wear some sash around for a year that will make all the other dyed-in-the-woolleds have to buy you drinks. At which time people actually know who I am, they'll stop sending me these invitations—I have on-the-record recorded opinions about this practice.

When I scrolled down, the signature bore the mark of the National Collegiate Athletic Association. It turned out that I had been picked to join the 3rd annual mock selection process held by the NCAA in Indianapolis this coming February.

Since 2007, the NCAA basketball committee has chosen 15-20 basketball writers to take part in a crash course in the real Bracketology, a one-day seminar that strives to replicate the four-day selection process. Writers are asked to take the roles of selection committee members, and are asked to complete a bracket that follows all guidelines, using the same equipment and information that the real SC will have. My ESPN colleague Andy Katz was the first virtual committee chair last year, and Pat Forde joined in too. Everybody who's been through the process has come out of it with a deeper understanding and newfound respect for the committee's job.

I will be one of those writers three months from now, and will be holed up in a conference room at the Westin Hotel as we attempt to hammer out a 65-team Dance card. I'm overwhelmed and humbled at the opportunity. The NCAA does a lot of things wrong, but this is something that's very, very right—an exercise in transparency that brings about greater understanding of a process that's nearly impossible to understand from the outside.

It should be pointed out, once again, that I started in this business as a blogger. I was a computer systems analyst five years ago. In a lot of ways, I didn't inherit the opportunities that I continually receive, and I've tried to work hard enough to deserve them. This is just another example, and I may be the first non-traditional basketball journalist to take part in this mock selection process. I am fairly certain I'm the first non-member of the U.S. Basketball Writers Association, a back-slapping mutual-appreciation society I've vowed never to join. I'm also not a bracketologist—there are plenty of those.

But I go into this as somebody who wants to learn all I possibly can, and I take this very seriously. I'll bring a file folder full of persuasive arguments for the mid-major teams that deserve recognition, but I'll also be leaning on my power-conference friends beforehand to fill me in on what I don't know. I want to know and understand, and will try my hardest to honor this process.

I also want to pass along everything I see in there to you, so that you can go into Selection Sunday as informed and enlightened about the process as possible. There will be 10,000-word blogs, Q and A's, tweets and chats, and I will answer each and every question that's brought to me, from fans and bracketologists alike. That's my job, after all.

DREXEL'S ROLLOUTS

NOV 19, 2008

PHILADELPHIA—This blog has been involved in several pet causes... heck, this entire thing is a pet cause. But TMM is getting involved in a new charitable campaign that strikes to the heart of what's important in Our Game. This is all about getting Drexel students to adopt proper rollout procedures.

The rollout is Philadelphia's second-greatest gift to college basketball, between the Palestra (No. 1) and streamers (No. 3). Crepe cascades after first baskets are long gone thanks to no-fun rules and technical fouls, the Cathedral may not last another century, but rollouts are forever. Drexel (which is "my school," after all) had a wonderful epoch-making win yesterday morning, and several of the students' fledgling missives were very good ("If Ben

Franklin was alive today, he'd be a Drexel engineer" was devastating enough to leave the Penn section calling back meekly, "Dre-xel High School").

But the execution was downright embarrassing.

Yesterday, the long paper rolls were unwrapped along the front row of a section, then passed upwards and backwards over the crowd. Once in the back row, the endline section did the right thing and tore it up into a million little pieces (good). But the sideline section moved the rollout over the rest of the crowd as if it was a crowd-surfer at a Pearl Jam concert. At one point, I saw someone roll up the rollout after a few minutes. I couldn't believe my eyes.

I was able to buttonhole one of the organizers, and I made a hand gesture indicating that rollouts, like bodies in motion and apples, tend to follow the rules of gravity—they go down. "We do it a little differently here," came the reply.

I've rarely been this red-faced at a basketball game. I wanted to impale myself on a souvenir William Penn statue.

I've noticed in the last 24 hours that Philadelphia is a much friendlier city than it was during the seven years I lived here, and I'm attributing that to a.) the world champion Phillies, and b.) "Phillies sex," which I guess occurred around the city that night when the World Series was clinched, the end of decades of internally-directed sports inhibitions in what used to be called the "City of Losers". With all that in mind, I'm sure my old friends in West Philly are more open to friendly advice.

The art of the rollout has been perfected for years in the Palestra, the Fieldhouse, (the?) Pavilion, even that new place at Temple that serves beer. There are reasons why certain things are done a certain way, and it's because they make sense. Bad ideas and broken pieces are removed from a mechanism over time, and Philadelphia rollouts are no exception.

They begin at the top and end at the bottom because when they're held by the front row, then TV cameras, players and other fans can read them better. If it's in the back row, the people in the second-to-last row are in the way of easy reading. If rollouts go from top to bottom, the rollout obstructs the view of the fans in that section for fewer sections. And when they're ripped up in the front row, it makes it easier for the cleanup crew to sweep away the pieces.

Look, I hope Drexel fans keep doing rollouts, and because the number of city games will decrease thanks to Bruiser Flint's demands that the Big 5 play the Dragons home-and home, I hope that there are more during league games.

It's one of the few ways that Drexel can put a Philly stamp on the CAA, and the wit is there. Now it's time to honor the city by doing it the right way.

MADISON SQUARE GARDEN
NOV 21, 2008

New York City—Madison Square Garden IV, indeed the fourth venue to have had this name, is a layer cake built on the corner of 7th Avenue and 33rd Street. It opened in 1968, four years before I was born. By the time I started going to games there, in the mid-1980's, its internal workings were as stained and dysfunctional as those of a 60-year-old lifetime chain smoker.

The "blue seats" in the ring farthest from the floor, in particular, were in the worst shape. I learned a lot of things about human nature up there in the ten-dollar obstructed-view seats during Rangers games, where the dockworkers would drink and yell and vomit and piss in the aisles. Folks would come down from Harlem or in from Queens for Knicks games, and I saw more than a few instances of hand-sex up there in the 400 level. I don't recall many people sitting up there for the NIT or Holiday Festivals or Big East tournaments, unless Saint John's was playing. Then it was hard to find a seat.

Even when the crowds were thin, Madison Square Garden maintained its status as the capital of college basketball. It's always mattered to play here, a feeling that's survived the building changes as well as the generations that have passed since the NIT stopped meaning anything. New York City is the place where the original championship was decided, before the NCAA stole the idea. In sepia-tone days, cigar smoke would create a cloud above an arena floor full of set shots and chest passes, scratching and clawing and blood in the post. New York City is the crucible out of which college basketball started to matter, before it was polished and buffed and packaged for mass consumption.

Between the time I moved to Oregon for college in 1990 and the time I returned seven years later, MSG had undergone a complete makeover. Much like the rejuvenated Times Square just six blocks north, the World's Most Famous Arena was suddenly its sparkliest. Proper lighting was installed up in the 400 level, and the seats were changed from blue to a soothing aquamarine. A ring of luxury boxes were installed. They painted the stairwells and the aisles and put up tan-colored stucco everywhere. When I would drive the two hours up from Philadelphia to see the Rangers or a college hoops tournament, I'd find an expensive "fan experience" in a place where "life experience" had always been free of charge.

I'd go to the Big East tournament every year, and I remember the fans from around the country reacting to the big city and the gleaming facade of the arena more than I remember the actual basketball. Once I discovered the joys of mid-majordom, I'd come to the Holiday Festival and root against Saint John's, hoping Hofstra or Canisius or Columbia could pull off an improbable upset. I miss Big Saturday, the quadruple-header held in early January that would bring together schools from the NEC and MAAC, give them a taste of the big stage. I loved the players' reactions when they'd look up for the first time, and see that roof, that famous roof.

But at the same time, things changed for New York as a hoops mecca. Starting at the top of the food chain, the Knicks are as relevant in the NBA as the Oklahoma City Thunder, and signs around the arena now insist that fans should be excited about somebody named "David Lee." (John Doe wasn't available.) After a string of scandals and disastrous years, Saint John's can't draw at the Garden anymore, and play games at their old shoebox gym. Manhattan and Fordham, battling over the Bronx once again this very weekend, are stuck in down cycles. And neither Long Island or Saint Francis, the NEC's two Brooklyn entries, have made a dent on those leagues in years.

Last night, I went to the Garden for possibly the thousandth time in my life for the Coaches vs. Cancer semifinals, but this time I was a real actual reporter. For a half, I got to sit in the long press box between the 300 and 400 levels, the one that I sat behind when I had a partial Rangers season ticket in the late 90's, wondering what kind of royal treatment was afforded the vaunted New York media (final answer: an $8 media buffet). I took in the late game between UCLA and Michigan in the same way I used to watch games as a younger man—stretched across three random seats, with a beer in one hand and a container of criss-cut fries in the other (total and final price: $13). The whole night was a real sentimental journey.

But one thing really struck me. Using my yellow badge to move past the security barricades and descend into the backstage areas after Southern Illinois' loss to Duke, I felt drawn into a two-decade time warp. Past the black curtain, in the tunnels, is MSG how it used to be. The same cracked white paint, dull copper-finish signage and general neglect that I remember from the old blue seats is still there, underneath the fancy veneer that was painted on in the 1990's. The interview room, a dingy closet with strange stains on the walls, looks just like the bathroom behind the 410 sections where I once saw a fat guy squeeze out a crap in a urinal.

There's no doubt that Giuliani and Bloomberg did right by New York, that steps needed to be taken in order to keep Manhattan from becoming Gomorrah. (I was mugged once in the old Times Square, on a block where there's now a theme restaurant centered on wrestling.) But too much prettifying stifles the true soul of New York, the soot-stained, cum-encrusted heart that Lou Reed keeps singing about, the deep spirit that despises strangers and dies for friends. The niceness has even spread to what used to be the city's proudest export, basketball.

Maybe it's time for New York City basketball to generally get back to basics, peel back the layers, and return to the beautiful ugliness of old. To return to the roots, to the same blood and shit and piss that Our Game came out of. It's all still there, I saw it myself.

CONFERENCE PLAY

DEC 10, 2008

BALTIMORE—Last Thursday, I saw my first conference tilt of the year. It was at the Truman-era art deco palace known as Memorial Auditorium, one of my favorite places to see a game, and the Badlands Conference clash featured the home-standing UMKC Kangaroos hosting the Oakland Super Golden Crisp Grizzlies. Oakland won.

I love conference play, and so does Oakland head coach Greg Kampe. Where our opinions diverge slightly is on conference play in December. "I hate it," he said after collecting his 400th career win. "One minute we're out playing in the Las Vegas Invitational, and the next we're playing two games that are life and death."

The Mid-Majority's official position is for anything that makes December basketball meaningful—no disrespect intended to the vaunted LVI, whose champion will live on in the halls of history forevermore (remind me, who won that again?). In lower-RPI leagues like the Badlands, the Atlantic Sun and the SoCon, every pre-Christmas conference game is one more day you're not getting your brains beat in at some power-conference arena.

What I have a problem with, and this is substantial, is the way the schedules have been set up. Ever since Major League Baseball went to an imbalanced division-heavy schedule and didn't adjust interleague play at all, regular-season records have been absolutely meaningless. If you're a second-place American League West team that drew a strong NL division, and you're in a wild card battle against an AL Central team that pounded on a weak bunch of NL teams in May and June, you're basically screwed. There's no fairness in that, and it's a mentality that's seeping into Our Game.

The issue is that December games are not being meted out evenly. Take the Atlantic Sun, for example. Six of the 11 teams have played two league games already, and congratulations to Jacksonville for jumping out to a 2-0 mark. Campbell, which was busy getting run off the floor at VMI last night, hasn't played an Atlantic Sun game yet, and won't until Saturday. Same in the NEC—Wagner hasn't played a league opponent yet, but eight teams already have two in the books. Sacred Heart is 2-0 there.

This is wrong, because it forces teams to transition into conference-play mentality at different times. Teams that have to make that adjustment early, especially ones that are working in new players or a new coach, are put at a severe disadvantage. In a one-bid league, or a campus-site conference like the NEC, one game could mean the difference between home and away in the tourney, a bye-day off, or a more advantageous quarterfinal opponent. To start the process towards March with a staggered start is a disservice to those who have to begin early.

The answer is easy: do what the MAAC, the CAA and the MEAC are doing. Start on the same weekend. If you're a conference with an odd number of teams, like the A-Sun or NEC, set three dates close together and play two games... you know, just like in January and February. Put them down in stone, and don't let AD's jerk you around. If you're not available to play, you get scheduled and you forfeit. League schedules are serious business, and the process should be respected.

POETS AND GEEKS
DEC 11, 2008

NEW YORK—I don't read my website traffic stats, and I strongly encourage any self-respecting blogger to do the same. If the traffic is too low, there's no incentive to post something that nobody will read. If it's too high, it becomes a game of giving increasingly pleasurable pander-jobs to your audience in an attempt to boost your PageRank. Either way, your soul dissipates.

But with a decade of web-tech experience, I'm very sensitive to site load, and its effect on site uptime and performance. In the past week and a half, the number of bytes transferred in and out of this domain have spiked considerably. Having ruled out hacker attacks and Digg, there can only be one reason for this. The traffic upswing coincides with the launch of a daily statistics feature.

Now, as I'll tell anyone who asks, the Mid-Majority was started in 2004 as an information site. The first incarnation of TMM was a grid of start times and scores, and its reason for being was that the big-time sports websites didn't bother to tell you when Drexel or Southeast Missouri or UC Irvine was playing, or whom, and a lot of mid-major schools were just getting their stuff together on the web. The blog was started as a side-dish, the 100 Games Project as a gimmick, but that's what visitors gravitated towards. I had captured the small-school struggle in a way that hadn't been done yet, and I used literary references and song lyrics when I needed to.

I remember one post that I wrote, which is somewhere in the archives... but it was a defense of the SWAC, showing that despite its horrid RPI, the conference led Division I in close games that year. Readers, who had been sending in literary references and song lyrics of their own all season, were outraged. Numbers? Who do you think you are... Ken Pomeroy? I was advised, as the soothsayer warned Caesar, to beware the statistical asides of March.

We have kept certain factions away from this site, and have done so by simply not giving them what they want. For frat boys and all those who wish they were, a demographic Deadspin locked up years ago, there's nothing to see here. The gamblers all left for Basketball State when that was spun off last year. Coaches and "insiders" are better served elsewhere. What TMM is left with is two groups that have been waging cold war on college campuses for centuries: poets and geeks. Forget jocks v. nerds, that's high school stuff. Poets and geeks battle in the ivory towers all the time, facing off over funding scraps for their fighting robots and Shakespeare festivals.

I had the poets on my side for a while, the college basketball versions of the "thrill of the grass" crowd that revel in the romance of the ol' ball game and the boys of summer. Poets love stories of the open road, the uphill struggle against The Man, and 1000-word essays. But policy shifts (like cutting down on oversharing) has chased most of them away. I knew this when my "conceptual" Bally contest about Drake U'u only brought in 12 entries, and this week's research question about conference winners yielded (and I am not kidding here) 163. And now, this with the traffic surge after the new daily stat feature.

There are many more geeks than poets (and not enough who are both to fill a room). And the geeks will always, always win. I wish this wasn't the case, but it is.

DEMAND DETAILS

DEC 12, 2008

CHICAGO—Flying today is going a lot better than the last first flight of the season. Almost missed my air ride this morning out of rainy Providence, though—Joan as security woman ran my wallet through the X-ray three times, before she finally found the Victronox Swiss army card with the three-quarter inch blade that's far better suited to picking toejam than murdering stewardesses. She had to check with her supervisor, but I let her have it as a reward for her mad CSI skills. It was something in the way she said, "A-ha!"

Now, safely laid over and watching the planes land at Midway's A concourse, I contemplate my status as a member of the final generation to smoke legally on a commercial jetliner. It makes me a little past due, like Don Draper is going to feel in season six of Mad Men if it ever gets made.

I'm also remembering a conversation I had yesterday afternoon. Someone I met once at a game and gave my business card to called to chat (after this, he probably won't do so ever again). He noticed that DAVIDSON, NC is listed as my next stop. So, naturally, we talked about Stephen Curry, about how he's Iron Man, the Punisher and Hellboy all in one man.

Then came the glamorous traveling-writer talk, at least what some people might imagine it to be like. Was I staying in the Charlotte Marriott he had stayed at once, how about that CLT airport. I explained that I'm flying into Indianapolis, driving 600 miles south and crashing at a truck stop on the way. If I'm lucky, I won't miss shoot-around. Well, that doesn't make any sense.

I might have explained that I'm also going to the Wooden Tradition next Saturday in Indianapolis to see Davidson again (as well as Saint Mary's and Southern Illinois—it's a mid-major bonanza) before turning the car back in on Sunday the 21st. In the interim, I get see five other games. Instead, I listened to a unsolicited business plan for a recruiting website that's really going to be great. I mean, really awesome. It's going to have everything.

I've come into contact with a number of people who have wasted my time with their big plans. In my old job as a dream enabler, they balked at the cost of making them come true. I guess I didn't lose my internal entre-preneur magnet. Somewhere over Syracuse this morning, I realized I have completely lost patience when it comes to dreamers. Seriously... don't tell me what you're going to do, tell me exactly how you're going to do it. Trust me, I have the patience for that—I can get 600 words out of a layover.

Plans and goals might fit on bumperstickers, but what sticks them to the vehicle is complicated polymer adhesives that require patient explanation as to how they work. Too often, glue is taken for granted.

Basketball, like website management, is a profession full of idea-men and true architects, and it's just as difficult to tell them apart. Chances are that your school has, at one time, hired a new head coach who preached "tough defense" and "getting after it," then proceeded to recruit Best Athlete Avail-able and turned the program into more of a chaotic clusterhump than it was before he arrived. That story usually ends with the coach getting fired, and wondering why. Or maybe he's still there, and maybe you've been wasting quality time calling for his head on a message board. You could have used that time to change the world.

All I'm saying is, demand detail. Better yet, insist on beautiful, intricate, Sistine Chapel detail. If you don't have the patience or attention span for it, take a yoga class. Life's too short for short answers.

PERSPECTIVE

DEC 17, 2008

CLINTON, S.C.—What's the value of a score? The market has it much less than the 1/1000th of a cent that manufacturer's coupons are worth—interested parties expect to get them for free, that a score should cost the same over a computer network as it does transmitted from mouth to ear.

Is "Tennessee 80, Marquette 68" any more valuable than "Savannah State 53, Kennesaw State 49"? One is more rare than the other, but the former is of interest to more people. Neither piece of information, however, is actually worth anything on its face.

If I told you that Toney Douglas of Florida State had 28 points and hit nine free throws against Tennessee Tech last night, then told you that Chicago State's Petras Balocka double-doubled with 21 points and 10 rebounds against Hawaii early yesterday morning, which would get your attention? Neither? A fair enough answer, because you've probably never heard of either player, and the statlines are presented completely out of context of wins or losses or NCAA futures trading. But still they sit there side-by-side in the Basketball State database, taking up the exact same amount of real estate as North Dakota State guard Ben Woodside's 60 point performance from last weekend.

Going back to those two games, though. The Tennessee-Marquette game generated many more stories, analysis and blog entries than Kennesaw-Savannah, because the market has dictated that descriptions and accounts of one are worth immeasurably much more than the other. There was probably one beat writer present in Savannah, if there were any—I've been to a lot of games like that. And in this tiny world, we don't give a rat's ass what happened with Tennessee and Marquette. This is why I'll never be famous.

The Kennesaw State sports information office, good people, published a five-paragraph game recap on its website. How much is this worth? How much is any game recap worth, those AP stories that bounce around the wires minutes after final buzzers? Increased technology has forced down the value of these, too—fans expect them to be as free as scores. Or boxscores, for that matter. An aggregation of millions of bits of data is worth something if aggregated and packaged in a pleasing fashion—I know of at least a few thousand who think that's worth 20 bucks a year.

If the AP stringer's account of a game, or the SID's, isn't worth anything on the open market, whose account is? The local beat writer's? That of the national one? What about the young blogger? Does it matter if the game was viewed from 10 feet away or 1000, or through the filter of television?

The difference is perspective and research. Perspective doesn't require access (but it helps), you just have to put in your time. A gamer can be written by a boxscore-parsing algorithm (and if the scared writers I talk to are correct, budget cuts will lead to the honing and perfection of the RecapBot). But add a few trendlines, some adjectives, a thumbnail sketch of a participant, what it looked and smelled like in the arena, a story of what happened 10 years ago... and suddenly there's life and vitality there.

While I love all my blogger brothers and sisters, as well as a few of the columnists, a lot of them are going about this the wrong way. Sports value is not measured in entertainment, or quick-hit jokes, or egotistical reminders of who's bringing the information to the people. Value is measured in perspective.

After four-plus years of doing this and over 500 games attended, I'm still getting by on charm. I will fully admit that I'm faking the funk. My mistake was choosing to cover a giant swath of college basketball—over 230 teams in 23 conferences—and taking no shortcuts. This Mid-Majority is so wide that I can't cover the breadth in any single season, despite my best efforts, and so deep that folks don't remember my name on my second visit.

Someday, though, I'll do this landmass justice. In five, maybe ten years, I'll know what I'm talking about. In the meantime, thanks for sticking with me.

MEDIOCRITY

DEC 19, 2008

GREENVILLE, S.C.—Mediocrity is a touchy subject around here, generally because the word mediocre shares the same Latin root as mid-major, which confuses people into thinking that basketball at our level is just, you know, meh. (That's what the Atlantic 14 would have you believe, anyway.) We've spent the last five years hijacking the word, removing it from the tyranny of wins and losses, and recasting it as "to have less"—mostly because the hyphenate was already in general use, and this route was easier than creating and selling a new word. Besides, we still haven't thought of a good replacement yet.

But there has to be a word or phrase out there somewhere that adequately captures "to have less" and "to give great effort." Struggling suggests a ceiling, the yuppies ruined upwardly mobile... maybe "endeavor" is the best we can do with our incomplete, patchwork language.

You can find plenty of disadvantaged complacency at our level. Part of the frustration of loving the MEAC and SWAC, or sizable portions of other low-RPI conferences, is that many in these places truly don't care about moving beyond their station. Teams show up and play out their strings, pick up their guarantee checks, and move like ghosts through Nietzschean basketball landscapes. It's hard to assign value to something that doesn't assign any value to itself.

There's nothing about a lack of imagination or endeavor that deserves praise. When presented with true mediocrity, and you know it when you see it, it's often a challenge how to respond. Ignore? Mock? Attempt to instill a sense of self-worth?

But there's a special place in hell for the brand of mediocrity that demands attention and love for just showing up. The reason I hate NCAA mascot J.J. Jumper so much is that he will dance more spasmodically, pander and preen when the audience inevitably finds him detestable. There are no efforts to improve the act, become better, question the approach—all mortal insults to endeavor. Last night at Furman, watching a stock 1970's character named Fro Bro attempt to work a stunned crowd with bits stolen directly from J.J. Jumper (the fake ref gag, the broken jukebox), I felt that same burning, uncontrollable hate rage in my soul.

Which makes those instances of true endeavor found here so profound and satisfying. Often they're hidden. Take, for example, the events last night in Cheney, Wash.. With a foot of snow on the ground outside, Eastern Washington made sure that its game with visiting UMKC went off as planned, even though it would be easier to just cancel what many would consider a meaningless early season tilt.

And a few hours earlier, North Florida (which we profiled this week) came into that game with Furman having lost its first 45 Division I roadies, more for lack of talent and skill than effort. Despite a "curse" that weighed heavy on their shoulders, despite an opponent that spent the last four minutes attempting to open their greatest weakness (foul shooting), despite Fro Bro, the team held onto its lead and won 77-66.

The players hopped around the bench like idiots, and their coach clenched his fists and roared, "The streak is over!" before carefully cradling the boxscore printout so it wouldn't get folded—he was going to frame it and put it up in his office. The last time I had seen any team so happy to win a game was nine months ago at the NCAA Tournament.

A lot of fans find it easy to make fun of teams like North Florida, which is the equivalent of frying a bug with broken legs through a magnifying glass. I think these people are failing to make the important distinction between those that struggle and those that don't care, or those that think their very presence affords them automatic respect. Last night, I was reminded once again that there's a line between those you make fun of, and those you don't.

SPECIALIZATION
DEC 22, 2008

NATCHITOCHES, LA.—I can't prove this, because it came out of one of those directionless garbage-time conversations amongst us proud folks who refuse to leave any game early. But one of my most brilliant ideas ever was The Sportswriter's Thesaurus, which would give sportswriters all the material they need to write decently on deadline. For example, there are lots of ways to describe the distance beyond 20"9': 3-point land, downtown, behind the arc, etc.. Anything to keep from using the same noun or phrase twice in a paragraph, which I just now did on purpose to illustrate how bad it reads.

Much of sportswriting language is that of the people, that is to say the people who don't have much time or energy to accept new ideas. One of the most common ways to convey the quality of action is to lay it over a temperature scale. "Hot" is good, while "cold" is bad. Sadly, what separates the AP stringer and the well-heeled columnist is usually the ability to spot points on that spectrum—icy, lukewarm, torrid, frigid, blazing. I hope I'm not giving away too many trade secrets here.

But it's undeniable how close to home the weather hit this weekend, if you look at things from our perspective. On Saturday, we personally witnessed the tragic collapse we hinted at last week—triple-superhero Stephen Curry's 5-for-26 shooting night against Purdue on free national television, which unleashed a wave of mid-major backlash and ensured that it will be a long while before the coaches and writers will allow the Davidson Wildcats back into their special Top 25 club with the doormen and the gold-plated washrooms. We, on the other hand, left fascinated about the future, wondering how this team will adjust to overcome its omissions and weaknesses. We saw it as a cautionary tale told in feature-film length, a fable about the endeavors of a red-colored organism, one that foretells the harsh equation many Americans will find themselves living out next year.

In 2009, specialization equals fucked.

But walking outside Conseco Fieldhouse on Saturday night was stepping into a sports metaphor. It was minus-10 with windchill, the kind of cold that buckles steel and crumples internal organs. Gusts that carefully guided pedestrians to the worst glistening ice slicks, a calculated and coordinated war by nature against man. And this was just the tail end of it—for the second time in a week, elevations in the Northeast were raised higher over sea level by feet upon feet of thick snow.

And so it was for The Mid-Majority. High-flying teams like Miami of Ohio were frozen stiff by power-conference opposition like West Virginia. Proud A-14 teams like Xavier were iced over by the likes of Duke. Dreams were chilled at the last moment, like those of Belmont (as well as for our distant cousins Gonzaga). Zags aside, this was the worst weekend of the year for teams in conferences under The Red Line that separates haves and nots: after weeks of hanging around the 14 percent upset mark, the bating average has slumped to .128. That's just a percentage point better than it was last year.

To add insult to injury, which is a phrase often carelessly thrown about in sportswriting, our Sunday flight to Texas was delayed by ice on the wings of connecting planes in Chicago. When Dallas was achieved, it was 30 degrees. It's colder here in Louisiana, which is technically in the South and supposedly immune to this.

But it's cold out there, Hoops Nation. Real cold.

GOING TO UTAH

DEC 29, 2008

LOGAN, UTAH—Whenever I travel to this part of the country, the Tetris-stack of states that makes up the intermountain west, I feel a great sense of unease. This goes back to when I lived in western Oregon for seven years, and would occasionally come further inland, but my advancing age allows me to better articulate the feeling.

It will take this nation at least a thousand years to fill up this time zone. The earth will spin into the sun before there's time enough to attach houses to cliff faces, or to string enough long-distance irrigation to turn deserts into magic valleys. A proud line of Colorado mountains, a wide Utah desert, either is enough to force any human being into their proper miniature scale. Disappearing into these vast landscapes would be effortless (even less so after a trip to a Wal-Mart Supercenter for sufficient supplies). Places like these invite loneliness, as much as they demand it, enforce it and amplify it in equal measure. In that open space, there's a lot of time to think about one's relationship to larger things.

So it's never been any mystery to me why these lands have been a magnet for those with a religious bent, why Brigham Young said that this was the place and not, say, Laguna Beach. A place of cosmic loneliness inspires higher thought, as much as it compels people to draw closer together into communities and ensure that they continue in the most efficient way possible. Look, I've seen "Saturday's Warrior," and I didn't poke fun. I've been here, I know that zero population is not the answer, my friend.

But an outsider like me needs to learn the rules of passage, and quickly, even if they've changed slightly since the covered wagons came across. But Law No. 1 is still this: help is not on the way. Crossing these areas requires careful forethought, and errors can be devastating and costly. I'm reminded of a long passage two seasons ago, sidling north and west to Spokane airport, straining to catch a morning flight after a night game in Pocatello. The 560 miles through a snowstorm was manageable enough, but finding a service station on I-90 open at 3 a.m. was a different matter. Finally, after exits full of darkened signs, I filled the 12-gallon tank of my rental car with 12.1 gallons of gas. As the low-gas light burned for nearly an hour, my hands were shaking, I was terrified.

To live here, anywhere along America's backbone, requires faith, and it requires patience. I clearly don't have enough of either, so this could very well be the perfect place for me to spend some time.

PART III

CONFERENCE SEASON

SPORTS INFORMATION DIRECTORS

JAN 6, 2009

NASHVILLE—A lot's happened in the past 48 hours. I've driven 1,450 miles through high Colorado mountain passes, endless Kansas, Oklahoma hailstorms. I've watched Southwest Airlines' careful domino-stack of hourly gate departures collapse under the weight of a weather delay, into a maelstrom of screaming passengers. I've changed into a suit in a cramped airport bathroom stall, then made tipoff by three minutes... only because of a late-ending women's game.

But the moment I'll remember most is flipping idly through my cell phone address book during a two-hour stay in a Dallas departure lounge, cleaning out ancient names and numbers. These were people I'd exchanged business cards with over the years, a gesture that's often used as a quick excuse to end a conversation prematurely. It struck me that most of these people were sportswriters. Then it stuck me that after five years of doing this, I don't have many sportswriter friends.

Sportswriters tend to travel in packs: going to bars together wearing brown sweaters, posting on specialized message boards and joining specialized sportswriter clubs. The only purpose of the U.S. Basketball Writers Association is for writers to give each other awards, and I've already stated many times that I will never, ever join that particular society of mutual adult pleasure.

Since I don't drink or smoke or have much to complain about, I tend to hang out with the sports information directors. There are a lot of SID's on my Christmas card list, and zero sportswriters. SID's, by their very nature, have to be poets and geeks at the same time, and they don't get bylines. They're in this because they love it... it's certainly for not the money, or for the ego tripping.

On the other hand, sportswriters are a big part of America's sports problem. Last year, Neal Pollack wrote a smart-bomb of an opinion piece for Slate about the 2008 NBA MVP "race." "It's the ultimate circle-jerk of sports-guy self-regard," he wrote in April. "Sportswriters can't affect the outcome of the games--only David Stern can do that--but the MVP race is theirs to decide, and it's the most thrilling part of their season."

It's probably because he ran into a word count wall, but Mr. Pollack only scratched the surface by skewering invisible horse-races and arbitrary rankings. You can find sportswriters' desire to grab power, to place their opinions high above the everyman's, everywhere you look. In our game, we have an Associated Press writers' poll, and cheap web space gives individual writers the opportunity to have their ballots viewed individually. In the sport of collegiate American-style gridiron, the system is set up so that a team can't be national champion without the scribes' general permission. And the pinnacle of doughy hubris is the Hall of Fame... in baseball, it's the writers' last line of revenge against decades of hurt feelings. Just ask Jim Rice.

Young people ask me all the time how they can follow their dreams, ask me to provide tips on how to enter the corridors of true sports power, the pantheon of flab that passes judgement on all aspects of the passing parade. I figure that anybody brazen enough to ask me for tips on how to displace me is enough of a jerk to make it as a passive-aggressive sports scribe, and that they'll succeed just fine without my help. I just tell them to burn all their brown sweaters, because they make press rows ugly, and all the customers behind them didn't pay to look at the asses of fat white guys who shop at TJ Maxx.

My true, heartfelt advice for anybody who loves sports and writing and statistics is to become a sports information director. They are the true conduits, those for whom acting as intermediary between sports and the public is its own reward. They have my highest respect, and always will. There's a reason why there is no running weekly college basketball poll with SID's making up the panel, and that's because most are too humble or busy to participate.

Plus, that poll would always be dangerously and devastatingly accurate, and that'd be far too much truth for the public to handle.

ARENA HITS

JAN 7, 2009

ATLANTA—One of the upsides to spending so much time in basketball arenas is that my connection to popular music remains simple, true and direct.
In this atmosphere, with athletic competition on the floor and fans demand-
ing two hours' worth of entertainment, organized payola can't find purchase. If a song comes over the P.A. system that sucks, the reaction is
immediate and awkward.

Down here, there's no preset Jock Jams playlist like you'll find at the
cookie-cutter "NBA Experience." In mid-major college basketball, the set list
is usually handled by an assistant SID, work-study or volunteer, and each
is an individual study in what works and what doesn't for any particular
crowd. Not surprisingly, most places play a lot of hip-hop during warmups,
time outs and halftime. As far as the popular form goes, it's a genre that ran
out of ideas years ago, and as such it's become as much benign background
noise as Muzak.

In the age of iPods, some DJ's are more adventurous about getting off the
script. A couple weeks at Furman, the crowd got to hear a set of straight-up
Freedom Rock—imagine getting fired up for a game with the opening licks
of "Sweet Home Alabama." A few places in the Ivy League bust out some
indie rock from time to time. At Quinnipiac a few years ago, before they got
the new arena, halftime meant time to chill heads with some Aphex Twin
and Massive Attack.

There is enough similarity around the country to build a mid-major pop
chart, however, and there have been songs that have dominated seasons. The
first year of the Mid-Majority (2004-05) was all about "Yeah!" by Usher. During 2005-06, everybody was playing Chris Brown's "Run It" (There's a man...
on the floor...) and in the following season, "We Fly High (Ballin')" started
in the MEAC and SWAC with united crowds miming a jump shot during
the money moment, and the song flowed outward into the white colleges,
displacing Fall Out Boy as No. 1.

In the last few weeks, I'm getting the feeling that "Let it Rock" by Kevin
Rudolf is the song of the season. "Let It Rock" has enough infused adrenaline to be used in warmups, and is hard enough that you can see the brothers
nodding their heads a little. Besides, that moment in the refrain with "I'll

make you come... alive" is, without a doubt, the best multiple-entendre since the white rapper Snow ("Infor-muh") named his album *12 Inches of Snow.*

I've taken a lot of heat for this stance in my family, in Twittercasts and on press rows across the country, but I think "Shake It" by Metro Station is the only other pop song from 2008 worth anything resembling a damn.

Since MTV doesn't play videos anymore and I don't have a teenage daughter, I'm blissfully ignorant of the packaging or the posing associated with it. I just know that at face value, it's a phenomenal production that always gets asses out of the seats when it's played during a timeout, whether it's played in Pennsylvania, South Carolina or Utah. And it's one of those songs that's amazingly self-aware of its own quality—that part at the end when multiple voices join in is like passing the microphone to an audience that's been singing along for two minutes anyway. If you were to release "Shake It" at any point in the past 25 years, it would be a hit. I'm convinced of that.

But anybody who listens to terrestrial radio knows that pop music is horrible right now, which isn't really anything new because pop music is usually horrible. A big reason why is that there's no direct accountability for what the radio plays, and music charts can be just as manipulated and hype-polluted as the AP writers' poll. But over a PA system, with thousands of people in attendance, the truth comes into harsh focus. The market is always right.

AMERICAN FOOTBALL
JAN 9, 2009

Birmingham—This is a wonderful morning here on The Mid-Majority, as dawn breaks on one of the three high holidays of our local calendar. We used to celebrate Football Independence Day when the professional turd-tossing season came to a close, but that's become more a public exercise in defiance. Last year, we made it all the way to Tuesday, Feb. 6 without knowing the score. (Thanks, Valpo.) This time around, we're gunning for Thursday.

I've been approached several times by cunning, whip-smart entrepreneurs about extending the Basketball State brand to include a college gridiron edition. Here are a few things I'd rather do instead of spend a summer thinking fake gladiator combat for 16 hours a day: gnawing off my toes one by one without novocaine, injecting lye in my urethra, and renting out the Hollywood Bowl with my own money for a 20th anniversary showing of "C.H.U.D. II: Bud The Chud."

American-style football is the worst game ever invented—it's violence without violence, a dim-witted celebration of the kind of career specialization that's killing our nation's competitiveness in the global economy, and a sport with more rules of conduct than Communist China. At the risk of repetition, we've made our definitive sound-bite statement two years ago. "At its very core, football is a game for confused, maladjusted, passive-aggressive sissies."

But before the college season disappeared once again, leaving fans confused as to what actually happened and who the best team was, the 2008 American university football season exacted one last measure of revenge on us. Last night's game between Samford and Furman was moved up two hours in order to accommodate folks who wanted to rush home and watch the BCS title tilt, despite the fact that the only thing local about the contest was that Oklahoma shares the same time zone.

This is a slippery slope. First, they move basketball games. Then Americans start taking the day off. After a while, the corporate community will get involved, marketing around BCS parties and BCS-themed products. Soon, it'll be just as big as the Super Bowl or Christmas. We can't let this happen.

We had received a press release about the Samford-Furman time change a few weeks ago, but I'll be the first to admit that I spaced it. So it wasn't until yesterday afternoon, when I was making a routine check of the game slate, that I noticed the game sticking out like turf toe on the schedule. Crap. I abandoned the article I was working on, got in the rental car, drove like Jehu, and made it to the Pete Hanna Center with a half-hour to spare. Damn you again, American-style football, damn you to hell.

POP CHARTS

JAN 12, 2009

BOONE, N.C.—I'm going to get into my grandpa rocking chair and tell you what's wrong with pop music. I'm sorry that you had to get this from a basketball writer, but that's just the way it worked out.

Most music specifically released for public consumption is far too dependent on context and reputation. At their worst, 21st Century pop songs are built around a 10-second hook that can be resold as a ringtone, and thematically oriented towards a very specific script that suburban 14-25 year olds supposedly live out on a regular basis. But if stores were organized by theme (hurt-hearted breakup songs sung by gravelly-voiced "rock dudes"; countrified female vocals about old-fashioned romance; pattern-validating shout-outs to single females who like to go to clubs), that would keep people from spending time browsing.

At their very worst, modern pop songs are just too specific, mini-movies that make it difficult to understand how a population segment larger than a few thousand people could latch on, much less stand for 20 or more listens. This is why I appreciate "Let It Rock" and "Shake It" so much. Sure, they're both about dudes trying to getting laid, but 95 percent of the best pop music is about trying to get laid—everyone, even kids, can understand that concept. Both songs have enough general appeal to register on a wider basis.

Consider all the current niche tunes that require readily-available backstory to understand, something that listeners 200 years from now won't have the luxury of having at their disposal. If you were to encounter "Love Lockdown" without knowing what Kanye West has been through personally in the last year, would you consider it anything other than repetitive, tedious piffle? Would it be on the radio if anybody else had recorded it? How about Britney Spears' "Womanizer"? All I know is that when they play over a basketball arena PA system, people sit inanimate. Out of comfortable context, neither could be considered "pop."

Don't worry, this relates back to the topic. The college basketball polls have just as much accountability and connection to the marketplace as the traditional pop charts do. Both types of standings are easily manipulated by outside interests, and both products—pop songs and college basketball teams—require constant promotion. Work in the back channels can get your song extra spins on the radio, or your conference extra spins on cable. In both worlds, a lot of money changes hands.

And both types of charts are exceedingly irrelevant in the 21st Century. I'll bet you couldn't name the number one song on the Billboard Hot 100 right now, and even if you could, there are many other rating systems that serve the same purpose—iTunes, Amazon, Last.fm and the like—that will give you a different answer. With iPods, XM radios, a trillion MySpace band pages, social networking and file sharing, we don't need people to tell us what to listen to anymore. A song with a very targeted demographic message will hit its intended mark, and there's no reason for anyone to shove it down the general earhole.

Our game's Top 25 is just as outdated as the Top 40. The AP writers, and the assistants who fill out their bosses' coach-poll ballots, are given ultimate authority from November to March, just for watching the same ESPN as you do. In fact, you're probably more informed than they are, reading blogs and evaluating tempo-free stats and poring over charts of national numbers. In all likelihood, your level of intellectual curiosity is far beyond theirs, and you're more open to new concepts and different teams and unconventional thinking. Where's your ballot?

Don't hold your breath, it's not coming. Your only recourse is to stop talking about the polls. Ignore them. Don't use rankings when talking to friends, don't go over to check the rankings this afternoon, don't use them to win arguments as to which team is better. Make your own chart, rank the teams yourself, post it on your blog, contribute to the atmospheric static.

The AP and ESPN/USAT polls are only powerful because we pay attention to them, and if we try hard enough and work together, we can diminish their significance. We won't rest until that little number to the left of the school name is eradicated forever, when "No. 1 team" means just as much as "No. 1 song."

LESTER HUDSON

JAN 13, 2009

NASHVILLE—I'll be honest with you: I don't know which time zone I'm in, what time it is, what I'm doing here, who I am or who I work for. After last night's Davidson-App State game, I drove 340 miles west (with two hours' worth of sleep, in 30-minute increments, taken in rest areas), back to Nashville to drop off this rental car and go on to the next episode—which is a flight into snowbound Cleveland and a week in the MAC. I had difficulty explaining myself to the ticket counter agent, so I'd have an even worse time putting together coherent paragraphs for you here today.

So we'll resume tomorrow—I had a big followup to Monday's post planned, and we still have to crown the winner of last week's Bally contest and start another one (hint: it's a research project that has nothing to do with stats). Today, we'll dispense with the normal routine and share a wonderful mid-major story from our inbox, about a wonderful player, his wonderful mother, and a wonderful place (in this very state) that we've visited ourselves.

Take it away, Ben from Cincinnati.

Good Morning Kyle, This is Ben from Cincinnati with a great story for you.

As you might recall, I mentioned on Friday in the ESPN Chat that I was traveling to Tennessee-Martin to see Lester Hudson play on Saturday, and you said that I was 'in for a real treat'. Well, you weren't kidding about that. I got to the Elam Center early while the women's game was still going on. Being a relatively small school in the middle of nowhere, I wasn't really sure what to expect.

At the small ticket booth in the dimly lit hallway just outside the court, I ignorantly asked for the best seat available. I was pre-sented with a ticket that said 'General Admission—Good at any 2008-2009 home game'. Surprised, I walked down a little further to the concession stand, (er, table) to find that the options consisted of popcorn and beverages that were served from 2-liter bottles. I asked one of the ladies working behind the counter if they sold any programs anywhere. Her reaction was priceless; though she only said "no we don't have any", her underlying tone was more like 'who the hell is this guy, looking for a program? To a Martin game? Ha!'

I proceeded into the arena with roughly 10 minutes left in the women's game. I saw that there were only a couple of people sitting behind the T-Martin bench. I couldn't believe that I had arrived early enough to secure a bleacher seat directly behind the bench!

I went down and secured my spot, camping out there during the entire 25 minute break between games. I would have gone to get something to drink, but didn't want to chance someone taking my seat. While the stands somewhat filled up, to my surprise, I was the only one sitting in my row 10 minutes into the game.

There were so many empty seats. (The official attendance was 3,736, but I assure you there weren't nearly that many people there—I have the pictures to prove it). While sitting there, still in disbelief that I'm actually sitting this close to Lester Hudson, watch-ing him rack up almost another quadruple-double (30 points, 10 boards, 7 assists, and 8 steals), I couldn't help but wonder why the stands weren't full.

Doesn't everyone know just how good this guy is? Do they know what they're missing out on?

Now don't get me wrong, I've been to small venues before (IUPUI), but I suppose I didn't expect the same from Tennessee-Martin, especially when you have the second leading scorer in the nation and a future NBA player. With roughly 5 minutes left in the game, a lady sat down next to me in the first row. I hardly noticed her. When I took a picture of Mr. Hudson, she turned and engaged me in conversation.

She asked if I was taking a picture of 'Les', and when I said yes, she said that she was his mother. I laughed at first in disbelief, but when I looked back at her, she looked just like him in the face—it really was his mother. She wore a T-M vest and a ball cap with an airbrushed Lester Hudson #5 on it. When I told her how I had traveled from Cincinnati to see Les play, she was shocked. After talking with her for just a few minutes, one of her daughters came down and pulled her aside.

She came back and said how her family thought I was some sort of recruiter or a scout for Les, and they were worried that she was hurting his chances by talking to me. I assured her that I was nothing more than just a fan that wanted to see him play before he graduated. I proceeded to have a conversation with her for the rest of the game.

We talked about everything from Les' home life growing up back in Memphis, his time at "Southwest" (SW Tennessee Community College), his time at T-Martin (he has his own apartment; no roommates), and his future in the NBA. She must have asked me on 10 occasions if I really thought that he was going to the NBA. I don't know if she really wasn't sure or if she just got enjoyment out of hearing someone tell her repeatedly that he was.

When the game ended, she asked if I wanted a picture of her and Les together. We went out on the court and I took the picture. She then asked if I wanted a picture with Les, so we did that too. Then, she said, "how about a picture of you, me and Les".

So after the picture, I turned and introduced myself to him. I told him how I traveled from Cincy to see him and how I read a lot about him through ESPN writer Kyle Whelliston. I then told him how he was the player of the week last week and asked him if he knew that. He smiled and said that he did know and said he appreciated the support.

Before leaving, Lester's mother attempted to give me her vest as a souvenir (as Les had given it to her) or even her hat. I refused, but she insisted that I take her telephone number. I'm still not exactly sure why she did as I have no reason to ever call her. But she insisted that I call her anytime to talk about Les and she made me promise that I would.

She again said "Do you really think he is going to the NBA?" At that point, I said "I'll tell you what, on NBA draft day, when Les gets drafted, I'll give you a call and say 'I told you so'". We then parted ways. I left the Elam Center with an amazing experience and made the 5 1/2 hour drive back to Cincinnati.

KULEE BABA
JAN 14, 2009

INDIANAPOLIS—In 1980, Steely Dan released *Gaucho*, a seven-song album full of disco-jazz pop songs about getting laid and drugs and revenge, all set in Los Angeles. All three are popular enough themes that the record went double-platinum. Due to various production problems, the album took the group three years, 11 engineers and 42 musicians to record. After the album was released, the band was discontinued, but nowadays the reunited group can be found performing expensive casino shows for rich burnouts.

One of the songs that has never been on the setlist is "Kulee Baba," one of a large number of Gaucho-era demos that was never polished completed, many of which ended up on illegal "Nice Price" CD's. It exists only in stripped-down piano/keyboard demo form, and it remains my absolute favorite Steely Dan song. I can't find a better example of their mastery of the five-minute musical short story format, as opposed to the general reputation as lite-jazz godfathers they ended up with. Predating the Discovery Channel by many years, this is likely the only tune ever recorded about an exploitative remote-location TV host. And since the beginning, it's been the reverse theme song of The Mid-Majority.

My nom d'voyage is McSwain
I carry the proper papers
I've seen the primal rhythms of the bush
I preserve great moments as they come
I'm sure this must be one

It doesn't become obvious until you try it yourself, but tone and approach is of the utmost importance when discovering an existing world and repackaging it for public consumption. After five years, I still struggle with getting that part exactly right, and still fail from time to time. I can't tell you how easy it would be to present mid-major college basketball in a condescending or archeological way. As I've continued doing this, I've seen competitors attempt to do just that, and I've had no problem openly mocking them. Each of our past targets has moved on to something else, and this site is still here.

More subtle—and more difficult to navigate around—is Marshall McLuhan's old notion. The song's protagonist has no problem inflicting personal judgement on the material ("cruel, primeval") or jumping into the frame in his green suit. The idea that his presence and presentation grants the subject lasting importance—that's makes him an asshole. When the show's over, it's on to the next one: more, more, more content. As I go from game to game, I realize that's an easy trap to fall into.

Or at least a fine line. Sometimes when I'm sitting there on press row in my suit and silver shoes, I feel a lot like McSwain, a cheap grandstanding huckster breezing in from out of town. Truth is, I'm still trying to figure out how best to balance professionalism, fun, and respect for the subject, and not come off like a complete jerk in the process. It might take me a few more years to get it right.

People ask me why I'm so adamant about not using the first person in my ESPN articles, why I twist sentences into knots to avoid it and why I get so angry when editors splice in an "I" (something that hasn't happened in three years). Others ask why posts on TMM lapse into the royal we (it's not a tribute to Will Leitch), or the real reasons for the no-radio rule. I just want to stay out of the way of the story, be as good of a conduit as I can be, but that's just part of the answer.

The full answer is "Kulee Baba."

THE SPORTS BUBBLE

JAN 16, 2009

INDIANAPOLIS—We are on the cusp of a wonderful new chapter in American history. Our great nation will once again be a place of logic and reason, a country where simple answers don't cut it, where perpetual double-digit percentage growth is no longer expected nor demanded, where an enterprise's true worth is measured by its value to the marketplace instead of its ability to be subsidized. At least we hope against hope that this will be the case.

I write this to you in the literal shadow of a true icon of America's Nonsense Era. Lucas Oil Stadium, home of the 2010 Final Four, rises up next to the Indianapolis skyline like a giant Monopoly hotel. It's a place where American-style football is played eight times a year. The regular tenant pays its employees millions of dollars each, paychecks funded by VIP tickets sold to the very same advertisers and companies struggling to explain themselves in the new logic-based economy. Working fans were priced out of the building before it was even built, and they can stay home and watch the games on free television anyway.

Does all of this make any sustainable sense to you? Doesn't this strike you as completely fucking ridiculous? Big-time American sports is just another bubble, with as fragile a meniscus as those of the dot-com boom or the failed, suburban house-as-ATM movement.

No part of the Sports Bubble, not even the attached layer of media soapscum, is immune to structural weakness. Just under a month ago, while staying in this very city, I was given advance warning that ESPN.com is planning 50 percent cuts to its college sports coverage, and I was put on notice that my contributions would likely be halved in the new year. Earlier today, I was notified that beginning in February, I will indeed be cut in half—writing and chatting every other week instead of weekly.

Now, if I know my audience the way I think I do, I know what you're thinking. ESPN is not "screwing mid-majors." These were cuts ordered by faraway men in suits who have bottom lines and share prices to protect, and this situation is not unlike the ongoing bloodbath at Sports Illustrated. I'm not the only one affected, and I'm fortunate enough not to be cut completely—a fate that will befall others.

Let me make this perfectly clear: I will never engage in any Worldwide Leader-bashing, even if I'm gone for good at the end of the 2008-09 season. I consider those writers whom have taken that route the lowest form of tactless vermin, and I have no respect for them. Those put in the position of actually making these cuts and delivering the news are good people with consciences and families and mortgages, and I can confirm that the day-to-day operations in Bristol—despite rumors to the contrary—are handled by actual human beings, not soulless robots.

If you're looking for the sole reason why this site is what it is now, it has four letters. The 100 Games Project was regional and provincial, and ESPN gave me the chance to visit mid-majors from coast to coast. And they don't pay for my travel 99 percent of the time, since I'm not a staff writer, so it's been a zero-sum and zero-profit equation. (Although, in retrospect, this probably wasn't the right year to dissipate Basketball State's margins by hiring a full staff of contributors. But I'll never regret that.)

This also didn't happen because I'm a "bad writer," although there are plenty of people who let me know every single day that they think I am. Nobody who's ever been successful has ever spent time worrying about what people think or defending their work to the peanut gallery. But if you've ever seen your favorite rock band dissolve after being dropped by its record label, you know that "good" and "commercially viable" are mutually exclusive, and ever more will be so. This has nothing to do with subjective "quality."

Suits work in calendar and fiscal years while we operate in "seasons," but there's no denying the awkward and horrible timing of this. I'm in the middle of a season-long road trip that's already been planned out, and halving my incoming funds means I simply can't stay on the road. It would mean the book project is dead, and I'm already working without an advance because my publisher went out of business last fall. I'd also miss the Mock Selection in Indianapolis next month, something I was lucky enough to be picked for. Instead, I'd spend my days sitting at home doing phone interviews to play out my 2008-09 string.

But you know and I know that this site, and this journey, has never been about watching games through a TV filter. The Mid-Majority has always been about the open road, risk, struggle, and sleeping in truck stops. Since the site opened four years ago, I've attended 484 games from coast to coast. If I can't do this the right way, I'd rather be doing something else.

I'm consumed by an unbearable lightness, however, because I'm in a much better position than a lot of other writers. I have thousands of yous. So I'm just going to place this hat here on the ground, and slowly tip-toe away.

This isn't the first time for that hat, and there was some real mixed-bag success with donation drives in the early years. But none was as big a drive as this one. In order to stay out on the road for the rest of the season, taking into account my 50 percent cut in ESPN income, I'll need $4,000 in additional funds. I don't expect any corporate sponsors to swoop in—the tight, devoted fanbase means it's a bad branding investment (as evidenced by a .03 percent clickthrough rate on the Google ads). I was out on the fundraising trail last summer, so I know people are scared and hurting and hesitant to take their wallets out. I also know that there are plenty of "investors" out there who want to be a "guest writer" or have me otherwise lick their ass. So my expectations for this are low.

But I draw faith and inspiration from recent events. Wikipedia just raised a gajillion sawbucks in a donation drive, and donors received the same old collection of Battlestar Galactica episode recaps they'd had beforehand. We elected a president who spammed American inboxes and raised zillions through a web form. And more germane to the situation at hand: a beautiful young redheaded reporter, left out in the cold during the presidential campaign when her magazine went under, raised enough money through a PayPal link to stay on the trail. And she was covering a candidate who'd already lost!

All I can offer you is more of the same—perhaps greater transparency with my travel plans and finances as well. And, of course, an acknowledgement in the book, whenever that comes out. If you need a thumbnail sketch or a rate card, $5 buys me a Veggie Delite sandwich at Subway, $10 is a truck-stop shower, $20 for a tank of gas (at Jan. 16 rates), $40 for my once-a-week three-star hotel from Hotwire, $200 equals a Southwest plane ticket, and $400 is good for a week's worth of rental-car wheels. (If you'll allow me a single moment of presumption, any overage or unused funds will go to Samaritan's Feet, which we'll discuss more on Monday.)

If you can't afford or are unwilling to give, here's some free advice: it's time for all of us to ratchet back our reliance on corporations, and fly or die on our own. I've been living off the Sports Bubble for so long that I've lost touch with the actual value of what I do, and I have no tangible idea if this operation would survive with a lessened subsidy. Nobody asked me to start covering mid-majors this way, nobody demanded it at any point, and the market didn't require a smart-ass traveling reporter who talks as much about losing as winning, who posts more about philosophy than basketball. It seemed like the right way to do it, so that's the way I do it.

Believe me, there's a certain calm in knowing that this can only continue if it makes logical sense for it to continue. Ventures like the Mid-Majority will only survive if they are supported by their audiences, and those that are not directly accountable to the people—or overly reliant on the teats of Big Commerce—will be prone to sudden and catastrophic failure. That's right in line with our nation's new Obama-era reality.

But I'm not above soliciting donations from those who are still safely inside the Sports Bubble, somebody for whom a Mid-Majority bailout would be like tossing a coin in the fountain. Kyle Korver? Jason Thompson? George Hill? Are you out there, can you help a brother out?

INAUGURATION DAY

JAN 20, 2009

WASHINGTON—In the next several days, you're likely to read many accounts of these days by special columnists (even some sportswriters) who have spent the last few days being whisked from inaugural ball to celebrity gala, who've worn tuxedos to fine restaurants and will sit in special boxes watching the swearing-in—so close to the podium as to see the pebble-grain pattern on the Bible. You will be treated to first-person stories written expressly to help you live this historic moment through their privileged eyes.

None of these will include sleeping two hours in a truck stop in Maryland, then sitting in four a.m. traffic among a sea of cars with license plates as far-flung as Oregon, Florida and New Mexico (honk, honk—hello, Rhode Island!). Very few will mention the Greenbelt Metro station, heat packs, sharing Nutri-Grain bars with strangers, buying goofy XXL Obama-head t-shirts for the folks back home, or watching history unfold on a Jumbotron with 2 million new friends.

And that's all well and good. There's a long history of sending representatives from the hoi polloi into high society to send back missives on they've found, and a history just as long of those reporters becoming drunk on their own power of the press. But this time, the whole cycle feels incredibly inauthentic. That wasn't the way this moment was put together. Like a successful mid-major basketball team, this was built from the ground up, with no silver spoons or legacy or reputation to fall back on.

But we're not here to talk politics. All I know is that as of 12 noon Eastern time, there will be a basketball player in the White House. This wasn't something we could miss out on being a part of.

EVERYTHING THAT HAPPENS

JAN 21, 2009

PHILADELPHIA—It was written nearly 30 years ago, but "Once In a Lifetime" remains the most concise four-minute statement on modern humanity that rock musicians have ever come up with. There are two mantras and a zen koan within it but at its lyrical heart, it's an absolutely terrifying poem. The song descends from order to chaos as it goes forward—it moves from a simple survey of existence to spiritual queries about the architecture of a life; as the onion-layers are removed and too many questions are asked, truths are revealed. It's all random, it's all meaningless, none of this means anything—an unstoppable and angry array of forces, nature and death and time, will tear through our constructed bubbles and wash everything away in the end. Same as it ever was.

On Monday afternoon, during the 73rd and final edition of my ESPN.com chat, a gentle and loyal reader from Michigan reminded me of a different song. I realized that evening on the Washington Metro, with my beautiful iPod, that this is in many ways a reverse bookend to "Once In A Lifetime," written three long decades later. At first encounter, it's entirely unremarkable, full of small fears and desires and dreams and heartaches and snapshots, glued together only with rhyming words. When the chorus comes in, deliberately placed at the very end for maximum effect, it stitches the world together instead of tearing it asunder. In a world full of live human beings, everything is possible—and while seemingly random, there's a great and simple beauty in this vast sum of parts.

> *Everything that happens will happen today*
> *And nothing has changed, but nothing's the same*
> *And every tomorrow could be yesterday*
> *And everything that happens will happen today*

There was a large concert at the Lincoln Memorial on Sunday. I didn't go, but I hear there were songs of hope and renewal and change, and that everybody knew the words and sang along. But for me, no set of 32 bars captures this moment like these. And no refrain has ever rang more true on Tuesday, a day upon which everything did happen. In large and global ways, as well as small and personal ways, we have been transformed by the events of January 20, 2009. But the order of the universe, and our capacity for opportunity, remains unchanged from January 19, 2009.

This is why I am at peace.

———————————

Some things have indeed changed since yesterday. For one thing, the number of expressions of support in my inbox has increased exponentially after my sudden firing from ESPN.com. I appreciate each and every single one, and the emotions contained within them have been very potent. While I have some extra time in which to respond, I won't be able to write a proper response to all. If I'm not able to write you back, please know that I have read your words and that they have touched me.

At the current pace of fundraising (as of this writing, we are over the three-quarter mark), the pledge drive that started it all is clearly headed for a successful conclusion—the orange bar will soon be at 100 percent, perhaps possibly even within 24 hours. I'm not going to ask you for more in light of recent events, I will cut back where I have to in order to make the funds fit the timeframe.

Also, just a few technical followups. I'm not going to answer your questions, or do interviews about this. I'm also not going to respond to vitriol in any fashion. I appreciate the offers of bed and board along the way, but you don't want that—there's a strong streak of anti-social A.M. jerkiness in anybody who is accustomed to writing five hours a day, something I fully intend to continue to do. And I won't need tickets to games. I write a monthly column for Basketball Times, a magazine more than a quarter-century old, so I can get credentialed pretty much anywhere and I can still talk to coaches. Your offers of help are all very, very appreciated, if not occasionally unnecessary.

Finally, I'd just like to address a sentiment that's appeared in many of the messages: "Don't give up." That's a powerful phrase, and the late former head coach of Bucknell and Iona made it an important rallying cry for cancer survivors before succumbing himself. But I often think of the limits of those three words (or four, when you add "ever").

Back before I was a sportswriter, a job that requires a lot of sitting around (and jerkiness), I ran marathons to stay in shape. Judging from the massive and growing crowds at marathon starting lines across the country, perhaps you've done that too. There were times when I ran badly, or fought cramps, or wanted to stop and do something else. There was a little voice inside my head that said, "Don't give up." A lot of times, especially around the 22-mile mark, I always had an answer for that little voice. It had a simplistic message that appealed only to starting and stopping, and as such it was easy to trick.

The reason why I didn't give up, why I have never dropped out of a marathon or stopped a run shorter than my previously intended length, is another little voice. It has a more powerful message: "Don't be afraid." It's a phrase that has resonated through organized religion, philosophy and politics, and is imbued in every speech and physical action of our new sitting President. Those three words, when taken to heart, calm and heal and restore any wounded soul. I can tell you right now, in this time of intense personal and professional upheaval, that I am not afraid.

THE NJIT BLUES
JAN 22, 2009

EMMITSBURG, MD.—They call them the blues because of blue notes, those tones hidden in between the in-between places there on the pristine straight streets of the music scale. Each one of us has had the blues at one time or another, stuck in the gutter, the ditch, the rut, been down soooo loonnnggg... Maybe that's why those non-notes resonate so deeply within us during those times, especially when emitted by wailing harmonicas, out-of-tune guitars, oboes, sad singers, baying hounds. Those blues get us, too—it's totally symbiotic.

What I've never understood, though, is why the language settled on that particular color, and I don't know if the people making these decisions were in the proper emotional state to make such important choices. I mean, you know, blue. When I've had the "blues," it's never been blue. I'd liken it more to the grey of soggy newspaper pulp clinging to a drainage grate in a pouring rainstorm at night, mixed with the yellow beer vomit and piss of hopeless transients, and maybe there's the mottled browns of dead wet leaves in there too. Been down soooo loonnnggg...

What I do know for certain is that an important stage after these so-called "blues" is getting over feeling sorry for oneself, and confronting the pain and loss and woe and desolation head-on. I don't think there's any debate on the color of that—it's red. We're human beings, and if you scratch and rip deeply enough you're going to reach a level that's crimson, whether it's the metaphorical shredded heart or the literal blood protected and enclosed by complicated systems. We've all had the reds.

And last night, the reddest, sorest, bloodiest college basketball team in the country had its long-overdue moment of sweet relief. In an over-lit gym in Newark, N.J., a place that quickly fell through Division I's wide cracks since joining the top flight in 2006, the New Jersey Institute of Technology beat Bryant 61-51, to close a losing streak that stretched back all the way across a season and a half. There were 51 losses since a victory at Longwood on Feb. 19, 2007, and two more since the Highlanders last won in front of their home fans. Only 424 souls, some of which were undoubtedly invented by NJIT's sports information department, witnessed the event. There is plenty of evidence, however, that this game really did occur the way it's been reported to have played out.

I wasn't there, but I was fortunate to have recently seen the end of another long streak, when North Florida's 54-game road losing skid ended at Furman, giving the Ospreys their first-ever Division I road win. I've seen the weight lift, the joy on the faces, the relief at the removal of an invisible stone from progress' door. And I know, from experience, that these moments are just doorways to patterns, and that is why they receive wider recognition. The second victory, and the fourth, and the 17th, will each be less notable and more normal.

So with an event like this, ordinarily a basketball game amongst basketball games, it can be a time to make note of and study the contrast between winning and losing, happiness and despair, joyous gold and painful red. The next time you're down in the dumps, when you've been down soooo loonnnggg..., when you finally move past the blues and take stock of your burdens, think of the New Jersey Tech Highlanders. Nobody's losing streak lasts forever. Their time done came along, and so will yours.

THE BIG LEAD: NEITHER

JAN 23, 2009

> *"Like many Web sites that traffic partly in gossip, The Big Lead's information is not always correct." –SI.com, March 2008*

CLEVELAND—What is the truth? The truth is one part fact, one part perspective, and zero parts perspiration. The truth is the vessel, the conduit that carries it, and it cannot survive without a fixed context. The truth is a woman... except for the times when it's something else entirely. The truth has no temperature or consistency or weight; life would certainly be easier if it could be picked up and examined like that.

Speaking the truth is never a mistake, especially when spoken in one's own defense... or in the defense of one's dreams. The truth will set you free, but it may end up costing you everything.

Sometimes the truth is hidden, secret. Sometimes one chooses not the divulge the truth as a matter of principle, which is a shade of difference removed from not telling the truth. There is a painful consequence to silence, however. It allows for others to insert their own details, to fill the spaces in between with opinions, to fulfill tiny agendas. If these versions are broadcast far and wide enough, many might simply accept these unchallenged third-party distortions as the whole truth.

And indeed, the truth is relative... absolute truth collapses, absolutely. Every war ever fought by human beings has centered around a clash of competing truths—while this method has been effective in redrawing maps and consolidating power, very few have ever truly murdered an opposing version of the truth, or exterminated every last true believer. You may be able to kill me, but you'll never kill my five-eyed Lizard God.

I think that one of the great unexamined elements of our culture is its use of sports to fill a void where no absolute truths exist. No matter what religion you subscribe to, no matter your ideology or political affiliation, everybody has to accept what the scoreboard says. You can niggle about perceived superiority, or the minute details of "why," or who's the "best ever," but you can never question 68-59 or 65-42. Those numbers will never change. When there are rules and referees and countervailing forces in a controlled arena, indisputable winners and losers and facts are possible and real.

Eventually, the game ends and it's time to leave—too much time in these careful confines can result in an advanced stage of mental infancy. But we'll linger here a few moments more, before we swing wide the doors and continue attempting to navigate the scary and chaotic morass of moral relativity. Together.

THANK YOU

JAN 24, 2009

OMAHA—Every so often, I'll get a long note from one of you detailing exactly when you found The Mid-Majority, the post you first discovered, and occasionally you'll remind me of something that I completely forgot I wrote. I'm always taken aback, floored and flattened by these letters, mostly because I'm too busy working on the next giant long post to remember what I've just posted. I'm just trying to present this complicated 225-team world in a comprehensive yet digestible fashion, and I never feel like I've done enough.

My strategy, and this has developed over the years, is to write long— thick paragraphs tend to scare away the people who shouldn't be here in the first place, and invite true friends to stay for a while. Over the past week, I've had to accept that this also invites selective readings and partial quoting from drive-by readers, and I've developed an enormous multiple-personality problem I never knew I had.

Some actually believed I had no clue about the risks of posting this essay, or that I was surprised or angry or ashamed at the final outcome. (Huh? What? Really?) It's been more frustrating than I thought it would be, dealing with these message boards and blogs and various Web 2.5 ephemera, but I am inspired by these great words from a great dad: when you're fighting an enemy with no attention span, wait five minutes.

You couldn't have pieced this scenario together the wrong way. You know what this is about, you have since you first arrived. You also understand the homebound alternate reality that would have unspooled had I not written that Bubble thing, I don't have to spell that out for you again. Above all, you understand this site's goals: respect for our subjects, recognition of the uphill struggle that comes with no start-line advantage, new adventures in truck-stop philosophy, and enough stupid jokes to keep things from getting too drippy. We have an understanding, you and I, or you'd be among the trillions doing something else.

You're one of us. And I always knew I could count on you when the chips were down. That's why I knew the risk I took last week was 100 percent worth it... and you came through! I am so overjoyed and proud, and okay, just a touch smack-talky. Find me a non-charity website that's been able to quickly raise an operating budget just by asking nicely.

It took less than a week to raise just over $4,000 to keep this operation on the road. A total of 147 of you donated, despite an economy in which non-essential things are increasingly non-essential. Some gave a lot, and some gave a little, but everyone gave what they could. I'll take that kind of loyalty over 10 billion "hits," because I'd rather talk directly to the right people than a vast and random public.

It's vindication, it's a stuff-you to the critics, and it's proof that a website can sustain itself through simple generosity. We're still vastly, vastly outnumbered, but this victory is a justification of the principles discussed last week. The Mid-Majority makes perfect logical sense as an independent entity, and it will once again continue until the very last mid-major has been eliminated from the NCAA Tournament.

Each of you who donated will receive a small token of appreciation sometime in the next few days, which you all must cherish and keep close to your hearts, and by that I mean don't put it in your trash folder. And you have voting privileges now—once the BracketBusters matchups are announced, you'll receive your ballot with which to pick the one I'll go to. And starting next week, we'll talk a lot about preparations for the third annual NCAA Mock Selection, which I'll be attending in Indianapolis on Feb. 12 along with 19 other writers. I'll make sure you see everything that I see.

IN OMAHA

JAN 26, 2009

OMAHA—You know what I don't understand? Hubris. How anybody could believe that they're the center of the universe, or better than everybody else, or the owner of unassailable opinion, has always been beyond my comprehension. Walking the world demands humility, and is full of reminders why our lives are anything but charmed.

Take this past Saturday, for example. I made it to Cleveland's airport by 5 a.m. for a 7 a.m. flight to Omaha, confident that I'd be able to make tip of a Creighton-Drake game at 1 p.m. CST. I made it through security on time, the plane left when it was supposed to, the transfer at Chicago Midway went as scheduled, and the arrival was timely as well. But one of my bags wasn't on the baggage claim carousel at Eppley Airfield.

This happens every once in a while, sure. I spent an hour in a small office as they unravelled the mystery—it had fallen off a cart in Chicago and would catch up with me sometime in the late afternoon. By then, I'd realized that I'd checked the most important part of my trip—the Missouri Valley "golden ticket" issued to journalists that's helped me through my frequent journeys to the midwest. I can tell the sports information director that I don't need for them to print me a credential. It's also good for the environment.

Which is what I did for this game, and once I had strapped on a suit in an airport bathroom and arrived at Qwest Center 20 minutes late, all the lady at will call had for me was parking passes. I tried calling into the arena a few times, but Creighton SID Rob Anderson was busy with the game. So I did what I did before I was a credentialed journalist, when I did this from the seats, and I stood in line.

Sold out.

The Qwest Center is a huge facility, larger than just a basketball arena or a concert venue worthy of Celine Dion. It also contains a convention center and restaurants, and is the crown jewel of not only Omaha, but all of eastern Nebraska. This weekend, the building hosted the Midlands International Auto Show, and so I bought a ticket.

I skipped the "Dinosaur Revolution" and the classic cars and the new Corvette. Instead, I stood slurping an empty fountain drink, staring at a American economy car that had apparently had its front end beaten with an ugly stick during production. Its lights were set as high rectangular ovals like sad eyes, with black speaker-grill venting interrupted by long, thin chrome bands. It was the worst-looking car I'd ever seen, and I was transfixed. All I could think about was how many times Avis or Hertz will issue it to me in 2010. Then I went to see a matinee of *Frost/Nixon*, and later picked up my bag.

So that's why I didn't go to a basketball game, the first time in over a year I haven't spent a winter Saturday in a suit and tie, sitting in the front row at an arena. Instead, I spent the weekend enjoying a pleasant state of ordinariness.

DAVID BERMAN NEVER WROTE A SONG ABOUT BASKETBALL

JAN 28, 2009

CEDAR FALLS, IOWA—Since 2004, I've gone through a lot of different bags, pens, cell phones, cameras, iPods and Moleskines. The only item that I currently carry around the country that came with me on trips four years ago is a taped-together copy of "Actual Air" by poet and songwriter David Berman, a book of obtuse modern short verse that I open any time my writing gets too stagnant and repetitive.

Two days after I was fired by ESPN.com, Mr. Berman announced on a message board that he was leaving the music business and disbanding his group, the Silver Jews, to devote his life to the fight for justice. With the luxury of retrospect, I realize I took this news harder than any other last week, probably for the same reasons that a few of of you might have had if I completely disappeared. It's hard to come to grips with losing the opportunity to enjoy somebody's creative output, and in some cases it allows for reflection about the absurdity of talking about live people in the past tense. Our art will survive us, no question.

I remembered three years ago, the first time I put that gig out on the line. I skipped out on preparations for the Mid-Major Super Bowl and drove up from D.C. to Baltimore to see the Silver Jews play at a small wall-hole, one of the very first times in a decade that the band had broken its strict no-concerts policy. Berman hid behind a lectern the whole night, fumbling through a stack of his own lyrics and delivering them in a quavering voice— just another reminder for me that writers don't need to be rock stars. Then I spent the next morning explaining why I hadn't covered practices.

David Berman never wrote a song about basketball.

FREEZING FOG

JAN 29, 2009

CHARLESTON, ILL.—Being an East Coaster with a family tree that only extends thin branches into the midwest, freezing fog is definitely a new experience. Yesterday morning, driving the long straight Interstates of Iowa headlong into the sun, the sky was thick and golden, just like heaven would probably be like. In perfect asphalt solitude, with the soft hum of the Japanese engine, you'd be checking every few minutes to make sure your skin was still there.

Just a few hours to the south and east was pure hell. A thick line of storms ripped through our nation's midsection, leaving behind dead people and broken trees and cold houses without electricity. As evidenced by the list of "Ppd." entries on last night's scoreboard, it also erased several mid-major college basketball games.

I spent most of the day yesterday in Cedar Falls with Missouri Valley commissioner Doug Elgin. At Creighton the other night, he convinced me to swap out Missouri State-Southern Illinois for Illinois State-Northern Iowa, noting that he'd heard there was a good chance that the game in Carbondale wouldn't go on as planned. It didn't; both MSU-SIU and Evansville-Drake were moved off until today to accommodate for the storm and its cleanup. The commish was trying to figure out the last time conference games had to be rescheduled like this, and he finally guessed it had been nearly two decades.

At our level, postponing a game isn't as simple as crossing it out on the calendar and penciling it in somewhere else. Teams can't just tell the pilot of their private planes to hold back the flight for a day. And when you're dealing with conference rivals looking for each and every possible advantage in their quest for a lucrative NCAA bid, it's difficult to get anybody to agree on anything. When it was clear that there was no way the games could be played on time, Elgin spent the day on the phone with athletic directors and coaches, acting as mediator, arbiter and psychiatrist.

Pushing games back meant scuttled charters that had been purchased months in advance, unexpected bus rides through treacherous weather, lost practice days for the next opponent, and countless ideas of how to reparate. Tempers flared, nobody got exactly what they wanted, and the commissioner was forced to miss a good portion of the best game his conference has had to offer so far this season: UNI's tight and exciting win over Illinois State that built a unexpected two-game lead over the rest of the Valley.

As for tonight, when Evansville plays at Drake this afternoon at 4 p.m. Central (a game up here safely north of the storm line), keep watch over the scoreboard. Know that the Purple Aces left a city without power, to bus nearly 15 hours overnight across storm-wracked Illinois... and then afterwards, they'll have to turn around and return home for a Saturday homer with Southern Illinois.

It was a long day, and at 10:15 p.m. Central the exhausted commissioner and I were at a Cedar Falls Starbucks. Halfway through the ordering procedure, his hand slipped and sent my grande Pike Place Roast all over the counter, soaking the stack of free iTunes cards and the tip jar.

"This is so going in the blog," I deadpanned. He laughed, for the first time all day.

AMERICAN FOOTBALL REDUX

JAN 30, 2009

INDIANAPOLIS—Every once in a while, I receive a hit through the feedback form, written in a language I don't understand. Sometimes these are in French, or German, cast in a Cyrillic alphabet or rendered in simplified Chinese. I'd like to think these are messages of support, and they indicate to me that I'm serving an important role of bridge-builder, bringing the message of Hoops Nation around the world. One person at a time, we're building a Hoops Universe. Together.

I'm sure some of these kind folks are wondering why all this hubbub, kerfuffle and hoody-poody is going on in the United States this weekend. It all seems so exciting! So as a proven ambassador to the world, I'm going to take it upon myself to explain our strange and wonderful tradition to them. Thanks to Google's translation powers, this website is available in Chinese, Dutch ("Den midtnordiske Flertal"), Japanese, Hindi, and many other languages.

"American Football" is a game played on a large field marked by lines and numbers. There are 11 players to a side, and the object of the game is to propel an ball past the opposition, an orb which resembles human excrement in both color and shape. Many of the rules and procedures were stolen from older and more violent European games, but we've added full-body gladiator armor, endless layers of middle-management, and have assigned it false religious meaning. The only thing in American culture more important than American Football is Jesus.

This sport represents the only true prism that captures what this country is truly all about. Only in American Football can you find short bursts of action punctuated by long meetings about how to proceed, a testament to the inactivity that has allowed every other country on earth to surpass us in productivity. This game also teaches important lessons about one's place in society: everybody has one small job, assigned by body weight and intelligence level, and the thinnest and prettiest employee gets paid the most. Everyone has a preassigned number, and if one is caught doing something that is not in that number-holder's job description, penalties are assessed.

There are a lot of different penalties in American Football. This is because there are a lot of wrong things you can do in America. We are a nation of laws... a whole bunch of them.

This weekend is the ultimate pinnacle of the professional American Football season: the Super Bowl. Two teams, each of which have been playing once a week for many months, will square off in a sanitized bubble full of money and entertainment on Super Bowl Sunday, as hundreds of millions of Americans watch at home because it's the thing to do. There have been 14 days of laser-focused buildup to this, each one generating more and more trivia and uselessness. Super Bowl Sunday is a celebration of our national ability to be excessive.

And oh, the Super Bowl Parties. No screen is large enough, no couch wide enough, no amount of food sufficient. This, right here, is America's last vestige of female subservience, as wives serve tray after tray of nachos and hot dogs and hamburgers to their obese husbands, hiding gritted teeth behind broad smiles. In their $200 replica jerseys, the men gorge and barf and argue about who's the best ever.

Then, when that touchdown is scored, the party devolves into a homoerotic orgiastic Man-Caligula, lubricated by nacho cheese sauce and lite beer. Nobody involved will ever want it to end.

I hope this clears things up for our international audience.

———————————

So anyhow... once again it's time to commence a tradition that stretches back over two decades, and became a Hoops Nation-wide phenomenon last season when I made the mistake of going public with it. I will be the last person in America to know who won the Super Bowl. After Creighton plays Missouri State on Sunday, Bally and I will be retreating into our zone-cone, and will do everything I possibly can not to become infected with the hideous knowledge. This means no phone, no e-mail, no satellite or terrestrial radio, no television, no newspapers, no Google Reader. I will be an American hermit. My goal is to get to Wednesday, which as far as I know is the U.S. record for holding out (me, 1988).

This year will be a lot tougher, though. I have a Monday morning flight back home to Rhode Island, and it's going to be nearly impossible to get through an airport without seeing a USA Today, or a stupid fan in the winning team's jersey, or an overhead TV with highlights. This could end up being the greatest challenge of my lifetime.

But if I survive that, and get home without failing, I'm home-free for a while. No games Monday, no games Tuesday, sealed in my abode. It'll be the last time I'm there before the season ends, and I have a bunch of chores to do... no time for TV or sports websites or idle chat with neighbors. If I can just make it to Wednesday, I have a shot at busting through. That will all depend on if I can get through a basketball game without somebody telling me.

That didn't work out so well last year.

I won't tell you where I'll be next Wednesday. If I can get through that airline gauntlet on Monday morning, I'm going all the freaking way this time. I will refuse to be informed. I'm going to erase that 1988 mark, because this is my time. But the little "next stop" indicator at the top of this page, which will automatically flip over after Sunday afternoon's game, will betray me—and I know the people there will be ready.

I'll be ready for them too.

THE LAST MAN IN AMERICA TO KNOW WHO WON THE SUPER BOWL

FEB 2, 2009

CHICAGO—So much of modern life is blocking, filtering, limiting. There is so much information coming at us every day that we must become fighters of information, lest it overwhelm and submerge us completely. We battle back with fast-forward buttons, delete keys, spam-guards, RSS news-readers, trusted conduits, earphones. We achieve small victories, but never truly win.

Some information is so large and pervasive, like a noxious cloud that hovers over and consumes everyone. The identity of the winning team in the national professional championship of fake gladiator combat, and its final scoreline, are two such pieces of data. I've made it my goal every year to hold out as long as possible. Every year I find it's harder and harder to hide.

One place not to hide from the Super Bowl is a truck stop (unless that truck stop is in Southern California). At 5:30 p.m. Central yesterday, typing away at a Flying J restaurant booth in Effingham, Ill. I heard the grunts and squeals from the nearby driver's lounge. That was my cue to pay the bill quickly and exit; after driving around the cluster of roadside businesses for a few minutes, I found a lonely Starbucks with a pretty girl behind the counter. This was a safe place for the duration of the evening.

Another safe place is a hotel in Meadville, Pa. (the second spiritual capital of The Mid-Majority), where I drew the blinds and lurked in the darkness for two long days one year ago. Another is a car, hurtling down the back roads of Missouri under a spattering of stars, with the radio off. Each of those, though, is a temporary haven, and each has a definite checkout time. There's only so long that room service and fast-food windows can keep one fed... at some point, humanity has to be faced.

Then to the airport, with hat pulled down and coat drawn tight and sunglasses on, white earbuds in to ward off the idle chatter I so often am drawn into. I walked across the terminal, head down except for quick glances at directional signage. No eye contact, no walking past newsstands (Monday is always the toughest), and yes, a very suspicious appearance. A mental checklist of incidents most likely to cause failure: the baggage check-in line, the wait at the gate, the ticket handover. The TSA checkpoint is designed to be as sterile and same as possible; that's the time to let down the guard and take a deep breath.

Check, check, check. Each test passed with the precision and accuracy of a true expert, one who's mastered the art of Super Bowl information blocking. My confidence surged, my heart floated. For an hour, I sat facing the corner, peering down at my unanswered BlackBerry blinking red in my shirt pocket. I knew my inbox was full of jokesters wanting to be the first to deliver the news I so longed to avoid. Just like last year.

As we passengers boarded the Southwest plane, I shuffled down the aisle, head down, earbuds full of a death-metal playlist as to completely block out any and all coversation amongst the crew or other passengers, who were perhaps discussing all their favorite plays from the Big Game. I moved to a seat in the far back of the half-full 737, peeking above the chairline to make sure there were no protruding newspapers. I slunk down, my spine fully coiled.

Then, as per federal law, I removed my earbuds and turned off my iPod, as it's on the list of approved electronic devices not approved for use during the pre-flight announcements.

"Our flight to Chicago Midway will be one hour and five minutes," the peppy flight attendant chirped into the handheld microphone. And then, "Do we have any Steeler fans on board?"

"Whoo!" cried out a couple of male passengers.

Fifteen hours, 52 minutes. That's all I could manage this year. The record, which still stands at three days (Wednesday), will have to wait until 2010. Next time, I'll know not to fly... the only way to become the Last Man in America to know who won the Super Bowl is to go underground.

BRACKETBUSTERS

FEB 3, 2009

PAWTUCKET, R.I.—BracketBusters pairings are out, and we're temporarily reunited with our own bed and desktop computer, so it's a good time for a game reset. Who am I? Why am I here?

Seventy-five percent of what The Mid-Majority is about during the regular season is analysis. There are check-ins on league races, five Game! Of! The! Night!s a week, weekly rankings, things like that. What we do in these spaces is not designed to make you, the alumnus, feel good about yourself and your life choices. The object of our analysis is not to give drive-by shout-outs to your school and get links on cubicle-powered message boards. Those things fulfill the intentions of general-practitioner national columnists who are trying to appear well-informed, by recognizing the struggles of the "little guys." Through a microscope, of course.

No, we attempt to identify the teams most likely and best-positioned to kick power conference ass in the NCAA Tournament. When we talk about emerging programs, it's an effort to find the ones who will do it next year, and the year after. Imagine if the upsets stopped altogether, which would give the NCAA all the reason it needed to split Division I college basketball into a big-bracket series and a "championship" subdivision. Don't be a myopic pretender, this could be just a few chalky years away.

And because of this, we may have slightly different perceptions of what BracketBusters is about, you and I. This event has two main components. On one hand, it's an invaluable sparring match for a handful of teams that are preparing to kick power conference ass in the NCAA Tournament. (At SIU-Butler two years ago, we knew exactly what was playing itself out.) For everybody else, it's a filled schedule hole next year (with the return game)—so they don't have to get bought by an SEC team in yet another money game, or play a worthless D-II opponent. Who's on TV, and who isn't, doesn't matter. "Conference respect," whatever tangible meaning that has, isn't worth a thing outside these walls.

BracketBusters is about preparing a select few teams for the battle that's coming all too soon. We want well-rounded, disciplined teams that can play at different speeds, possess an array of positive basketball attributes, and have enough scoring options that the star doesn't get double-teamed at the Dance, resulting in the 111-44 blowouts that we're all accustomed to seeing over the first two days. This is why we demand more of Davidson than Stephen Curry, why we recognize the multiple strengths of Utah State behind the weak schedule, why we see more potential in Butler 2008-09 than we ever did in Butler 2006-07. If you can recognize this as Siena's most important game of the year so far, you're on our wavelength.

In past years, when I was in league with the WWLIS, I'd be consulted on possible matchups that would look good on TV. I'd argue for certain pairings, and once in a while my argument would win. This time around, a number of mid-major conference executives who were on last week's planning calls were on my phone and in my inbox looking for input. "Who are the good teams?" they asked. This was a question more in line with this site's mission. So I went ahead and told them.

Butler-Davidson doesn't require any analysis, it's the two best teams this level has and its two brightest hopes for deep March runs. But the top-line game RPI-wise is Northern Iowa-Siena, which is simply a masterstroke of scheduling. These are two teams that are iffy for March play, but both were given the only chance to work on their respective weaknesses, a truer battle than they'll get in their respective down leagues. It's swift (Siena) against deliberate (UNI); each team will test the others' defense in the way the other needs to be tested. Utah State-Saint Mary's features two teams that are evenly matched and could make the Round of 32, given the right circumstances... as we've been using them in the same sentence for months, they were probably destined for each other.

Then there's a group of flawed second-tier teams for whom any excessive travel will be offset by positive TV exposure. A note regarding the CAA: the league couldn't get anything done in non-conference, and has a lead pack that would need extremely fortunate March matchups to win at the NCAA's. Save your boo-hooing and your hand-wringing.

As for Northeastern, which was sent to Wright State, I've been frank about their chances all year. I've seen them play multiple times, and haven't bought in. I told everyone in a suit who asked that Mason's the best team in that league and that despite the current standings, it's wise to short-sell NU. The Huskies can't rebound, turn over the ball too much, and don't really have plans in place to overcome those weaknesses other than to limit games to as few possessions as possible. Judging from the RPI disparity in this matchup, they might have listened to me. But the Raiders, too, slow things down to hide their considerable set of shortcomings... should be a great game.

I think that this slate of 51 scheduled games represents the best bal-ance of quantifiers of any in BracketBusters history. I commend everyone involved with balancing the need to toughen second-weekend contenders, putting attractive matchups on television, and accounting for the travel requirements of smaller schools. Off the top of my head, there are only two or three pairings that didn't work out so well for all involved, which is defi-nitely an all-time low. Good job, folks.

MIDSEASON FIRINGS

FEB 9, 2009

BATON ROUGE—When the ax started falling in the SEC last month with midseason firings, the thought around here was that it was kinda cute. Four such severances in four years seemed like another indication that the pressures of BCS basketball were getting to be more in line with those of the pros, where seven coaches have been fired so far in 2008-09. The power conferences were getting increasingly like the NBA, we thought, and the next logical step would be 48-minute games or shoe deals for individual players. Didn't figure that this bad idea would hit our level so soon.

On Friday, Tennessee State embarrassed Cy Alexander by firing him 12 games into the OVC season. The reason given was the need for a "new direction," the same phrase we've been hearing for years at the higher levels when an NBA team gets out to a poor start. From everything we saw and heard at the OVC tournament last March, this would have been done last summer if the Tigers hadn't come out of a seven-seed to make the title game against Austin Peay. The school was just waiting for the right excuse, and a 6-16 overall record was good enough.

Alexander, who's coached for 24 years, deserves better treatment and more respect than this. He took South Carolina State to five NCAA tournaments, won three coach of the year titles in the MEAC, and is still spoken of as a living legend around that league. In the OVC, which honestly isn't a much higher level of basketball (and plays almost just as many guarantee games), Alexander was eight games under .500 in league games since 2003. The very least TSU could have done was let him coach until the end of the season.

Obviously, this isn't the pros. There's no trading deadline, and players have to wait a year if they want to go anywhere else—which is 365 days longer than schools have to wait to alter course with coaching changes. Either way and in any event, TSU would have to wait until summer recruiting to start on this "new direction." With the intricate systems the NCAA has in place, few things could be more disruptive than a midseason firing, or a more blatantly indicative of executive ego.

Unfortunately, we're going to see a lot more of this going forward. Here in the mid-majority, we really thought we were immune to this kind of nonsense... but like the off-court player issues that have become part of leagues like the WAC, WCC and America East, this has become a much less enjoyable pursuit.

MOCK SELECTION

FEB 13, 2009

INDIANAPOLIS—The NCAA Tournament is played out over 10 days: four full 12-hour 'thons to break 64 down to 16 over the first weekend, followed by Thursday and Friday evening regional semis, four standalones over two weekend days, then a Final Four and a final game. All told, that's roughly 78 hours of action. To build the bracket, the Selection Committee spends roughly five 16-hour days convening in an Indianapolis hotel room leading up to Selection Sunday.

Now, I want you to take a step back, consider and digest the following concept, something you've probably never even thought of thinking about before.

It takes just as long to make it as it does to play it.

Granting at-large bids was a devil's bargain all along. Moving away from a tournament of champions, and yielding that certain conferences had more than one title-capable team grew the bracket was the first step towards this mess. Then the gigantism kicked in when the NCAA realized that it had a money machine on its hands.

Most of the people who were responsible for making these decisions back in the 1970's and 1980's are either retired or dead. The bracket is now so complicated, so convoluted, so intricate that it requires logician/geniuses like Greg Shaheen and David Worlock to beat it back into submission with an endless list of rules, regulations and standards. Both are brilliant men, king minds of the highest order. They've created the antidote for a disease the NCAA invented for itself three decades ago, when it made itself sick by eating too many octopi.

The selection exercise was the most eye-opening, incredible experiences I've had in my relatively short career as a member of the sportserati. It was a glance into the overwhelming responsibility that these 10 people have every March, with millions of dollars and the interest of an entire nation on the line. But be sure of this: there was very little basketball in that room, and even less poetry. For a game that features the pure simplicity of propelled ball up into a raised goal, followed by the placid swish, that's plenty ironic.

Another thing, this time about the prediction industry. I've been pretty low on office pools to begin with, but this experience has cemented an intense dislike for "Bracketology" in all its forms and variants, where before there was a cold ambivalence.

The biggest takeaway from the 11 hours in the mock selection room is that selection, seeding and bracketing is a team event, subject to the laws and policies of any flawed clusterhump groupthink. It's definitely not a sudoku puzzle. In order to properly replicate the process, the prospective bracketologist is invited to find nine other like-minded people and spend five days locked in a room hashing it all out (daily ice cream deliveries optional). The "science" as it's currently practiced, the pre-filled bracket, is not too far removed from the preference-based form submitted in Wednesday's initial balloting. You've only just begun.

Further to that point, any and all references to "The Committee" as some kind of mind-melded entity (a wholly misguided one, most likely) are wasted words. I think it's an error in human wiring that we're capable of putting the acts of collectives on par with those of individuals; many are comfortable considering the decisions of groups as coming from a single granular point, and not from the complex internal-debate engines they really are. "Congress," for instance, or the "shareholders of Ford," or the "Pawtucket City Council."

Or "ESPN."

This is the imperfect process we have to live with, and I'm happy I saw the compressed reality-show version up close. Knowing what I know now, when the bracket comes out on March 15, I'm not going to spend time trying to figure out why Team X is included, why Team Y isn't, or cavil over seed lines or shake my fist to the heavens over a perceived lack of fairness. I'm going to shrug, get back in my rental car, and try like hell to make Dayton by Tuesday.

BRACKETOLOGY
FEB 19, 2009

MORAGA, CAL.—I've come to avidly dislike "bracketology" in all its forms, I don't make any bones or excuses about that. I can't stand bubble watching or seed projecting. I respect Joe Lunardi for combining computer power and over-the-top braggadocio to single-handedly ignite a cottage industry, and I think Cort Basham's approach is great—he gathers a group of friends every March to create an actual mock committee to hash out a bracket. Everybody else is masturbating into a washcloth.

I don't think that characterization is too far out of line, especially since we're talking about "fantasy sports" here. Bracketology and tournament pools are part of a larger trend that includes fake baseball and pretend football. This fantasy is a dream of executive force and power over an uncertain future. I'm not so sure what any of that has to do with sports.

Fantasy sports seem like a response to a secret powerlessness. Average Fan, priced out of the arena and forced to watch through a TV filter that adds its own value-added storylines, wants his precious control back. Doughy and unathletic from the products hawked during the commercial breaks, Average Fan seeks to commoditize the very entities that alienated him. Overwhelmed with choices and cable channels, recasting the sports universe in his own image must seem like the only remaining option; the others are boredom, dissatisfaction and ADD.

There's a thin line between guessing and wondering, and I try not to cross it. Me, I love watching sports, and I'm happy to take them at face value. Sports provide studies of countervailing forces with wide arrays of variable attributes, a giant conundrum that continually solves itself, and that'll always be good enough for me.

It's getting more difficult to find kindred spirits, though. I once completed a circuit of all 30 Major League Baseball stadiums (and have the framed ticket stubs to prove it), but I haven't been to a MLB game in two years. Not because of steroids, an issue I'll leave to the Judgey McJudges, but because I can't find anybody to go with who will shut up about their fantasy team(s). If I go alone, there's always somebody nearby who's agonizing about either cheering for the home team or rooting for the WHIP he needs to overcome the Quahog Stewies for first place.

During the NCAA Tournament, listening to people bleat about their busted brackets is bad enough (and somehow my overwhelming urge to kick them in the nuts makes me the jerk). I don't know if bracketology will become prevalent that "I have them in as a West No. 5" is as common as "I'll never forgive George Mason for 2006." But since there are people actually making money at this, chances are good.

Besides, Average Fan needs something to do in February. I maintain that this is the second-best sports month of the year—college basketball conference races, and once every four years there's the added bonus of the Winter Olympics. Watching hundreds of teams jockey for March position is the most fun I can think of. I know that I'm in the clear minority on that, because February is deemed a dead period in the American sports calendar. This is how bad it is.

Bikini babes in magazines are our last defense against widespread bracketology. I can live with that. But American sports have become so abstract a world, such a huge gulf exists between consumer and product, that distracting fantasies are necessary to keep folks interested. If I better understood the history of how and when this happened, I'd work harder to turn the ever-advancing tide.

As it is, we still have simple and unadorned sporting pleasures, like mid-major college basketball—chaotic and strange at first appearance, but every completed game points towards something bigger, later. It's a 225-piece puzzle that may be just as sexy as the Springbok brand jigsaws of European churches that your great-grandma used to put together, but it's the way sports should be, used to be, and still can be. I'll save you a seat if you want.

VINCE LOMBARDI
FEB 24, 2009

LYNCHBURG, VA.—In the late stages of a Sunday flight from Raleigh to Nashville, after the announcement about portable electronic devices, I did what most people in need of an info-fix do: page through the Sky Mall catalog. It's only in those 20 minutes at the end when full-size Lord of the Rings swords and adult footed pajamas make 100 percent perfect sense, and I'm sure they'd sell a lot more if phone calls were allowed before the thud of the landing. It always breaks the spell.

One item I noticed, and lingered on, was an expensive framed shadow-box print featuring a speech by Vince Lombardi. He was a famous coach of American-style football before having his name placed on the best service area on the New Jersey Turnpike. It's a famous speech, delivered to his team one time, and historians and marketers have given it the title, "What It Takes to be Number One." It ends like this:

> I believe in God, and I believe in human decency. But I firmly believe that any man's finest hour, the greatest fulfillment of all that he holds dear, is that moment when he has worked his heart out in a good cause and lies exhausted on the field of battle—victorious.

Seriously? Are there people out there who believe this garbage to be true, relevant or inspirational? The part that's missing here is that time doesn't stop, and there's no happily-ever-after or The End with a great victory. Nowadays, as Lombardi's battle-man lies expended, agents will pick his pocket, and sportswriters will demand endless repeats of the performance for the sake of "validity." Then, some guy's liable to come long, pull down the hero's pants, and take a picture of his schwanz for Deadspin.

Number 1 has to come back and defend the title, over and over. Unless this great and noble warrior keeps winning, stays in first place forever, maintains a pure and perfect Johnny Champion image, the story arc always points to the same place: loser. With all due respect to Vince Lombardi, losing is not a habit, it's the default state of the universe. There is as much room for second place as there is for first, and a whole lot more room below that. To defeat enemies, expectations and the passage of time in equal measure is impossible, and nobody goes undefeated.

Vince Lombardi died of colon cancer several years after giving that speech.

I'm not a great coach, and as famous former colleagues have rightly pointed out, I never played the game at any level beyond high school. But I do know about losing. I see it every day after every contest, and I get to see the emotions it brings out: flashes of anger, somber regret, numb acceptance. No team that I've ever covered won at the end in March, and it always ends in a loss. The true subtitle of this website is A Chronicle Of Loss Management, not Truth, Justice and College Basketball. I've lost nearly everything I've amassed since I first began it, and have almost nothing of what I owned when I started.

The most profound type of loss is the inevitable and looming defeat. In basketball, this manifests itself in the wide and unbridgeable deficit: down 20 points and sliding backwards. There have been plenty of pop-culture attempts to sell certain sports as "life" and the rest as mere details, but nowhere in Our Game is universal truth more revealed than in the inglorious blowout, when each small advance is met by three or four emphatic responses in kind.

I've seen it in the struggle of North Florida's 40-point loss at Clemson, and on Cal State Bakersfield's own court. I see it at NJIT and Hartford and Fordham and Maryland-Eastern Shore, teams with wins in the single-digits, Division I's walking dead. I've seen the broadcast switch away to a game that's invariably more interesting to more viewers, and I've seen people leave with 10 minutes to go. Watching these games play out, it's a wonder why the team on the losing end doesn't just quit playing altogether and, for all intents and purposes, walk off the court. I've seen that happen too.

To know you are overmatched by forces too powerful, and to continue to stand up and fight anyway: that to me is true inspiration, the ultimate measure of a human being. To have lost before the game is over, and to never give up, that is spirit and faith and love of the highest order. With apologies to the late Mr. Lombardi, I firmly believe that any man's most important fulfilled test is that moment when he can stand erect on the field of battle, defeated by superior forces but also an honorable survivor, thankful to God just for the opportunity to participate and compete.

BOOK REDUX

FEB 27, 2009

INDIANAPOLIS—Though nobody has time to read them anymore, and the economy's so bad that folks are burning them for heat, writers aren't really considered "writers" until there's a stack of dead tree scrapings covered with their scribblings available for general purchase. Especially since writing has moved increasingly online, and into real-time, being able to string 80,000 words together is more a test and a feat of mental strength than a profitable exercise. It's the ultimate marathon experience for people who sit around a lot.

A standard greeting colleagues have offered this season is, "How's the book coming?" or "Can't wait to see that book!" or "Can I preorder on

Amazon yet?" It's been a project with its ups and downs, dating back to the smug initial announcement last May, then through a summer during which it became obvious that my publisher was careening towards Chapter 11. Even though I had a restrictive contract, I vowed that I would continue the effort, to chronicle the seasons of three squads as they attempted to return to the NCAA Tournament after at least a year away. I was granted locker-room access as well as everything I needed to tell the stories correctly.

The "November" section was going to be hopeful and promising: everyone starts 0-0, the beautiful season, etc. etc. Each of the three teams had some early success, building momentum and announcing their intention to build something special. Each fell off in "December," which I initially saw as an easy way to build dramatic tension. Sure, they were being blown out by 30 on national television now, but could they turn it around after Christmas break? Stay tuned, keep reading!

Unfortunately, "January" turned out to be even worse. Season-ending injuries, player departures, team dissension, coaches being tuned out. The losses mounted, and people were less willing to spend a lot of time talking to somebody who was chronicling The Worst Season Ever. The realization set in: this book was dead and getting deader.

On January 16, ESPN.com published this feature story I wrote, about the Samaritan's Feet charity that aims to put shoes on millions of impoverished children around the world. It was the beginning of a whirlwind weekend. Two days later, on a Sunday, I was in Columbus, Oh. mulling another uninspiring performance by one of my book teams when I received a return call from Emmanuel "Manny" Ohonme, the founder and CEO of the organization. He wanted to know if I would be willing to help with a project.

Mr. Ohonme had been talking to the other principals of the charity, and they all really liked my article—they felt that it hit on certain aspects and details of the mission that others of the many features on Samaritan's Feet had missed. He told me that he'd been looking for somebody to assist him with an autobiography and history of the organization. Folks were asking him if he had written a book... after all, everybody does need one these days. So he asked me if I'd be interested. I told him I was working on a book already, but that switching projects would be like being moved from a last-place team to an inevitable pennant-winner.

Another two days later, I was fired by ESPN for writing "The Sports Bubble." The Samaritan's Feet article was the last feature I ever wrote for them.

Samaritan's Feet is headquartered in Charlotte, and it just so happened that my donors voted overwhelmingly to send me to the Butler-Davidson BracketBuster game just a half-hour north. During halftime of that game, Mr. Ohonme appeared at halftime (with a giant sneaker!) to thank the Davidson crowd for raising over 10,500 pairs of shoes for his and Wildcat senior Andrew Lovedale's native Nigeria. After the game, Manny and I spoke for two hours, then sealed the deal with a handshake. As part of the summer-long journey of writing this book, I'll be going to South Africa and Nigeria in late May with Mr. Ohonme and several basketball coaches to experience the process for myself, and to place shoes on the feet of children.

This is a humble man who received his first pair of shoes from an American stranger in his home country of Nigeria, went on to take a full basketball scholarship at North Dakota, and later let go of a high-paying executive career to create and build SF. I'm honored to have the opportunity to have my name appear below "as told to" on the cover of this amazing story. It will be available in October in time for next basketball season.

I don't go into my personal religious beliefs much at all on this site, because I don't believe a goofy mid-major basketball blog is the place for them. But you have to admit, the path from there to here is a beautiful and intricate one which couldn't have been scripted more perfectly. I'll just leave it at that.

For the record, the three teams were Southern Illinois, Miami (Oh.) and Northwestern State. It would not have been a very uplifting book, and you're spared from having to read it.

PART IV

POST SEASON

THE COURT AND THE CONFERENCE ROOM

MAR 16, 2009

CLEVELAND—Lately I've been reading "When March Went Mad: The Game That Transformed Basketball" by Seth Davis, a man I'm privileged to know and lucky to share a bond of mutual respect with. It's a tremendously fantastic book by a supremely talented writer, one that documents the famous 1979 national title game that ignited all this nuttiness. There's only one problem: it's about hoops. The book that's still out there waiting to be written is Please Tell Me What This Has To Do With Basketball: How the NCAA Got Greedy and Turned The Tournament Into a Big Ol' 65-Team Clusterfuck. It's going to be a bag of words about committee meetings, and it's going to be pretty darn unreadable.

Back when I was in college, there wasn't a day I loved more than Selection Sunday. I would sit in front of the television as the details were leaked out, tried to keep up by scratching excited team acronyms and codes on my blank bracket. I felt that euphoria of emotional overload that only comes when incoming information overwhelms the brain's ability to process it. It was a revelation of order from chaos, the bridge between darkness and light, every gift-giving holiday wrapped into one big and glorious package.

Then I went to the NCAA mock selection last month (Seth was there too), and I saw how brackets are made. I saw how 10 people are stuck in a room for five days and are forced to shoehorn today's basketball reality into the monstrous and unwieldy structure that yesterday's bureaucrats created. I saw how hundreds of votes and endless debate and a blur of team sheets turned the process into something as bland as third-quarter sales projections. It was the same kind of flawed groupthink that chased me out of the 9-to-5 world and compelled me towards mobile sportswriting. In short, it broke my heart.

The NCAA made me hate Christmas.

There's a major misconception that some TMM readers have (and in the old days, ESPN readers had it too). Some think that I'm some sort of mid-major apologist, that I go to bat for the downtrodden right or wrong, that this site is some sort of endless underdogathon. This is not true. (If it were, I'm sure I'd have more of a following.) I promise nothing but a point-of-view perspective of what it's like in college basketball's relative shadows, what life is like out here in leagues where air travel is a luxury, and what victories mean to those teams that have to struggle and sacrifice for every one.

But with the same instant readiness of internet publishing that made my career possible, there are plenty of people lining up to be the champion of the little guy. I generally don't read those sites, and am happy to let them micro-divide a large potential audience that likes to root for small and helpless things. I find that approach unrealistic and cloying, and it triggers the same gag reflex that always made me root for Gargamel against the Smurfs as a kid. To oversimplify the story of the underdog is to cheapen the struggle.

I like thinking and logic and philosophy. I also like numbers. I love the clarity that Our Game inherently contains: it provides a 40-minute closed context in which there are always clear reasons that separate winner from loser. The scoreboard is the perfect antidote to votes and compromises and deals, and the basketball court is the anti-boardroom. (Later this week in offices across America, you'll see exactly how much that's the case, once again.)

Well, I suppose you know the raw numbers by now. There are three at-large teams that represent sub-Red Line conferences in this year's NCAA Tournament (Xavier, Dayton and Butler), down from four last year. This is supposed to be an outrage of the highest order, or so I've been told. I'll tell you again that it doesn't matter.

There will always be conspiracy theories, and red flags carried by those who wish to turn this into a Frank Capra movie. People have a lot of time to kill before the games start, I recognize that. I can see how easy it is to turn Committee Chair and SEC commissioner Mike Slive into some sort of cartoon villain, and also how easy it is to forget that six of the panel's 10 members represent schools and conferences on our side of the Red Line. I can understand that it's easier to blame a perceived bias than it is to recognize that Southern California and Mississippi State shrunk the at-large bubble pool. I also know that it's easier to point the finger at others than one's own team, even when it lost its most recent elimination game and was forced upon the mercies of fates.

I used to get a real rush out of skewering the Selection Committee chair, parsing his exit interview for validation of my belief that the process is rigged against the teams I like. Now, I just feel sympathy. He has to sit through a five-day convoluted process, oversee thousands of votes and manage nine egos, then he suddenly has to become Ernest Hemingway and break everything down into three minutes of perfect sound bites. It's a no-win situation. My reaction now is: "Poor guy."

But this is the only outrage I'll ever feel. Say that VMI wins the Big South tourney, that the Keydets dance on the court and are mobbed by their fans in a hot, sticky, sweaty storm. Eight days later, the brackets are announced, and VMI isn't there. When the CBS or ESPN interviewer asks the chairman why, he says, "Well, we didn't like their body of work. So we left them out." When they come for our autobids, that's when I'll fight.

For now, we have a bracket. I hurriedly filled it out last night at 7 p.m. Eastern with little emotion as my room service food got cold, then I filled out my application for the first and second rounds this weekend. Then I switched off the TV, I saw little reason to talk about what had just transpired. Then I went back to sweet 1979 with Bird, Magic and Seth Davis.

The time and relevance for the Selection Committee and "bracketology" are mercifully over, and we are three days away from the Round of 64. The games are what really matter, those are what will be worth documenting later with heroic prose. And judging from the looks of things, there are plenty of combinations and permutations to get six or more small-college teams past Thursday and Friday—that's how we measure mid-major success around here. We'll be talking about that more as the week goes by.

LOOK OUT, THEY'RE BACK
MAR 17, 2009

DAYTON, OH.—Back during a time when the years had smaller numbers than they do now, I went to Drexel University, a fine, upstanding and expensive mid-major school. In my studies there, there always seemed to be fellow students who skipped out on the first eight weeks of class, then showed up for the last two (Drexel's on the trimester system, you know) with lots of questions. Not the hand-raising kind—these were ass-covering queries about chapters and papers, whispered to strangers, the shortcuts that make up so much of what we Americans call higher education.

I don't see much difference between those poor slackers and the millions of college basketball fans who are just now tuning in. You and I have been here all along—taking notes, doing the homework and paying close attention for the past four months. But here comes the crowd whose excuse was that they were focused on football all winter, the folks who didn't come to class in February because the material was too hard to follow. And it's kind of annoying, you know? But the bracket's out, and here they are again. And this is where the metaphor breaks down: in this classroom, they're likely not deferring to your superior attendance record. They know way more about basketball than you do.

I fully understand the importance of casual fans to this process. If it weren't for them, there would be no March Madness as we know it, the NCAA men's basketball championship would have all the cult snob appeal and limited national relevance of the Softball World Series. We need boorish Johnny-come-latelies to yell "That's a foul!" and "That's the worst call I've ever seen!" because it wouldn't be as loud without them, bless their hearts. We need their energy to power this thing forward as it moves into larger and larger stadiums; like any blockbuster movie, the crowd scenes require tens of thousands of extras.

One of the key elements in the growth of the NCAA Tournament over the past 30 years is the low-seed upset. "Cinderellas," they call them, even though this strongly implies the players like to cross-dress. Every year, schools few have ever heard of emerge from the mist and knock off traditional hooping powers. Just the very mention of their names each recalls a flood of memories: Indiana State, Weber State, Hampton, Southern Illinois, Northwestern State, Davidson... George Mason. Casual fans love this, corporate champions sell this, it all taps into dormant American underdoggery that dates back to our fight for independence from the British. So powerful is this dynamic that many March-only college basketball fans feel cheated— cheated!—when the upsets don't come.

Which, finally, brings me to what's done here. For the past five years, I've followed the trials and travails of those otherwise forgotten schools, and have gone so far as to observe them in their natural habitats. A lot. This has made me something as a go-to guy between Selection Sunday and Round-of-64 Thursday—people want me to help them fill out their brackets (even though they ignore my advice otherwise), and they want to know which mid-majors they should "keep an eye on" as great underdog stories in the making. Who's the next Davidson?

In the not too recent past, in years with numbers similar to that of the current one, I had a lucrative gig covering mid-major collegiate basketball for the largest sports website in the world. My least favorite part of it, by far, was this week. I was put forward as a "mid-major expert" with a name not recognizable from television, and my job was to sell the general public on the merits of the low seeds and why they could win. I pointed out the "good stories" so people who hadn't been paying attention could pick their favorite.

It made me feel like a pimp. Not the cool kind in the rap videos with the gold-encrusted chalices, but a dirty street hustler. I was promoting a cheap thrill for a short time at an unbeatable price. Do you like this one, or this one? If a chosen team won its first-round game, it was an unforgettable night. When it lost, became used up, didn't live up to expectations, they could simply discard Cindy at the curbside and move on to the next street corner.

If you've been reading this site for the past four months, you've probably picked your favorites long ago—based on the evidence and rolling backstory provided, and you don't need me to sell you on anything. You have emotions invested in this weekend's events. Or, you simply go (or went) to one of these tiny schools that find themselves still contending for the National Championship, and this is the best freaking week of your life.

I never got to experience that at Drexel—during my time there, we came close... but never could get past that league title game. For those of us who had followed diligently since November, the hurt and frustration took weeks to disappear, and it usually took baseball season to make us forget. We recognized that at-large bids weren't created for schools like ours, we knew our place.

But the greatest feeling a mid-major college basketball fan can have is when the team you've followed during the season, seen play in small gyms with sparse crowds, is suddenly on the biggest stage there is. It's a giant arena, flashbulbs popping everywhere, CBS cameras swooping and circling, and tens of thousands of random people cheering. It's that contrast between the shadows and the spotlight that is this event's true spark, and why this is as special as it is.

Free of previous sales obligations, I'm looking forward to going to Minneapolis and seeing this happen all over again with the long-suffering fans of Robert Morris (I like to believe there's a very happy truck stop worker out there somewhere) as well as the Bison Fever of North Dakota State. The emotions on those campuses right now aren't the disposable kind.

As for the drive-by fans, they're to be merely tolerated until they inevitably leave. They can follow along for a few days, they can "adopt" a team and buy its $35 "Road to Detroit" t-shirt at the official NCAA merchandise stand, but they won't get to the heart of this. Cinderella's not for rent.

GO AFTER IT, GRAB IT, TAKE IT

MAR 18, 2009

INDIANAPOLIS—The year 2006 wasn't really all that long ago. Sure, we're dealing with problems light years beyond those we faced back then, and anybody would trade in total world financial meltdown for another "bird flu" scare. But Nelly Furtado's "Loose" feels like it just came out yesterday, innit? Most current seniors were freshmen. The inaugural World Baseball Classic happened that year, remember? It was a gentler and far more halcyon time.

It was The Year Of The Mid-Major. At the NCAA Tournament, eight mid-major schools won their first-round games, and three broke through to the Sweet 16. And of course, there was George Mason, taking matters all the way to the Final Four. It was an exciting time for me as well, from a professional standpoint. For a brief moment, my chosen pursuit of documenting this world was intriguing, vibrant, relevant on a national level. There was plenty of irrational exuberance about the "little guy" back then, and plenty of idle chatter about the sudden "parity" that existed in college basketball.

I didn't see parity, I saw eight teams with inferior resources that found ways to defeat well-heeled units with superior game plans, coaching ingenuity, heroic performances, solid systems (and yes, ball control). In the week between the Elite Eight and the Final Four, I wrote this column about the importance of money in Our Game, about how nothing was going to change the fact that teams like George Mason spent 20 percent of what UConn laid out for men's basketball operations. I mentioned that things like that catch up over time. It wasn't really what people wanted to hear in the happiness of the moment.

The year 2009, at least so far, has not been The Year Of The Mid-Major. Not a single team south of the Red Line that won on the NCAA's Big Bracket three years ago made the 2009 Tournament—Wichita State, George Washington, Bucknell, Northwestern State, Wisconsin-Milwaukee, Montana, Bradley or George Mason are all simply wishing this time around. Followers of this site, or college basketball in general, will recognize that most of those teams didn't even come close. Of those eight, only George Mason even made its league title game.

I talk about the Red Line a lot. It's a self-made creation, sure, but it is as simple a way as there is to cut through all the constantly shifting definitions, the ones based on winning or analyst expectations or perceived legacy. There are eight leagues with average athletic budgets of $20 million or more, 23 that have less. Twenty-one of those have men's basketball budgets below $2 million (the Atlantic 14 and Missouri Valley are the two exceptions). Gonzaga's results are exempted from either side, because that's a freakshow that can write its own nonconference TV schedule and sell sweatshirts in New York City.

And it can be summed up in one sentence: teams in the richest eight conferences beat teams in the other 23 leagues 87 percent of the time.

I get a lot of letters about the Red Line. The vast majority want me to change it, or they have their own ideas that are based on winning or analyst expectations or perceived legacy. These letters are usually paragraphs and paragraphs long. My response is 18 words long: teams in the richest eight conferences beat teams in the other 23 leagues 87 percent of the time. Then there are the constant questions.

Q: Why don't you go by men's basketball budget? That would put the Atlantic [14] over the line, where it clearly belongs.

A: Overall athletic budget helps take into account important elements like facilities, operations and media relations. The A-14 is a combined 20-37 (.351) against the richest eight conferences this season. By the way, nine of 10 dentists agree that teams in the richest eight conferences beat teams in the other 23 leagues 87 percent of the time.

How about other lines, like one at $10 million? Why don't you define "low major?"

Two guys walk into a bar. One says, "Hey, did you know that in college basketball, teams in the richest eight conferences beat teams in the other 23 leagues 87 percent of the time?"

The Red Line is not a poverty line, or the border where pride ends and panhandling begins. The Red Line is not a red flag, some kind of reminder that wealth should be redistributed. That already happens with the ugly and abominable practice of guarantee games. It's simply the demarcation between those who are given everything that they need to win, and those who have to earn and take every single thing they get. It's not the line between Richie Rich and Oliver Twist, but you know which side each would be on. Conference USA and Mountain West have schools that take football a lot more seriously than they do basketball, but they have all the resources they need to make hoops a priority—if you have 25 or 30 million to spend on athletics, do like Memphis and spend a quarter of it to buy a basketball power. We don't have that luxury of choice.

As George Mason proved in 2006, individual wins can't be purchased... on the other hand, consistency can. Consistency is an invisible thing made out of perks, million-dollar coaching contracts, private jet flights to recruits' games, sufficient bankroll to send the entire staff to Las Vegas for summer-time meat markets, package deals that include jobs for blue-chip relatives.

None of the eight low-seeded small-conference teams that won games in 2006 can afford any of those things. None of the 248 teams that live under the Red Line can, for that matter. Life in this world is a constant blur of com-promises, bottom line-watching and day-long bus rides. Charter flights have to be reserved months in advance, and it's all night on the bus if you miss the departure time (it even happens in the Valley). That is, when you can afford a coach at all. On short-notice trips, you might have to rent three minivans from the airport Hertz and squeeze everyone in. I've seen it happen.

And that's what makes all of us one big mid-majority, and what most analysts and pundits can't or don't choose to understand: to survive and advance from our side of the Red Line is a series of challenges and struggles, and every champion that's made it this far has done so because it kept going in the face of all obstacles. Each of these 25 teams represent the hardest workers and the superior innovators among their peers—not necessarily those with the deepest pockets. Every team of ours that will win on Thurs-day and Friday will do so despite financial disadvantages, and each will take something that doesn't belong to them: part of that precious 13 percent of the pie.

This boldness is also an attitude we all share on this side, because the only other options are mediocrity and failure. I recall something that David-son head coach Bob McKillop mentioned during the throes of the Wildcats' February losing streak that ultimately cost the team its chance to follow up its amazing run to the Elite 8.

After the BracketBusters loss to Butler, McKillop said, "Last year we got to the Elite Eight because there was no sense of entitlement. We went after it, we grabbed it, we took it. At this point, in the last 10 days or two weeks, we've kind of let it come to us, rather than take it."

Davidson took again last night—beating South Carolina on the Game-cocks' own floor in the NIT. And with superior game plans, coaching inge-nuity, heroic performances, solid systems (and yes, ball control), they'll take more in the future. Those teams that will excel and win over the next several days will do so because they, like the Wildcats in 2008, take what wasn't readily offered, and wasn't for sale anyway.

RESPECT, RESILIENCE, JOY AND DESPAIR
MAR 21, 2009

MINNEAPOLIS—Just so we're clear, we don't care about your brackets. We know you want to talk about who you "have," about how three of your eight website entries are totally and thoroughly busted, and how you'll never win that $84.50 in the office pool now. We don't want to hear about how you knew that Illinois was overrated, about how much you know about a sport you were ignoring six weeks ago. (We also don't care that UNC's mission is not to let you down this time.)

This must be a lot of fun for you, this March Madness. It must be pleas-ant to rally behind something until you have no use for it anymore, to adopt and dispose the efforts of a team, to judge its efforts without any real con-sequence. But the idea that your gambling stories are somehow as thrilling as the on-court action is misguided at best. The delusion, however great or small, that any of the participants care who you've picked in your brackets is the luxury of narcissism. It's the same Princess of the Universe mentality that turned a lot of our country into soulless suburbs, each two-bedroom ranch an island unto itself.

Our respect is reserved for those who have invested much more than lunch money or barroom bragging rights. First and foremost, our admi-ration is for the players, coaches and staff members who fought for five long months to win the championship of a lesser-known league and earn a toehold on this Big Bracket. They didn't do it for the sympathies of strang-ers, or for the opportunity to stand in front of a Vitamin Water tank on national television.

We respect the dedication and devotion of those who were there the whole time, who dared to tangle their short-term fates up with those of athletes. The families and fans who spent sleepless nights in December worrying about the next opponent didn't do so with the sole purpose of making a "crazy vid" to help Coca-Cola sell Coca-Cola, they drove long distances to games simply just to yell for their team. For them, the joy of an NCAA bid is the fulfillment of half a year of hopes and dreams and wishes. And for most, because of that diehard adherence to the cause, the losses that have come these last couple of days are emotionally devastating.

North Dakota State's loss to Kansas was sealed by the ultimate symbol of power-conference supremacy: a series of primal-scream dunks by a 7-foot behemoth that a school like NDSU would never have a chance to sign. There was the series of stock TV shots—slumped shoulders, bowed heads under towels... and then the NCAA Tournament, as is its nature, quickly forgot the Bison and continued.

Thirty minutes after the final buzzer, the players and families and fans gathered in a shadow-drawn holding area behind Section 10 of the Metrodome's temporary seating, clutching each other and sobbing. In two quick hours, Bison Fever had become Bison Despair. Some stared into the distance at nothing in particular, the blank look that only comes when you've poured your heart into something that's gone. What do we do now?

To repeat, more emphatically this time: we don't give a flying shit about your brackets.

We respect those who recognize the same struggle in others. The NDSU fans, thousands of them, stayed in the building all day and evening, rooting for Dayton and pleading with Robert Morris in the late game to stay close to Michigan State. We respect the fans of Utah State, who forgot their heartbreak over a one-point loss to Marquette long enough to root on Cornell in the Big Red's failed quest to upend Missouri.

Joy didn't wait for long to resurface, at least in Minneapolis. Dayton is a program that never asked for anyone's sympathy, and has a support base so dedicated that it fills the UD Arena during winning seasons and losing seasons alike. Flyer fans rarely refer to their players by their last names, and are notorious for driving through snowstorms to see their team play. Most among the new generation of students, however, either weren't alive or were too young to know what a basketball was the last time their beloved Flyers won on this grand national stage.

But with a team that embraces and embodies the selflessness and sacri-

fice of their fans, Dayton ground out a first-round win over old (and seemingly unbeatable) nemesis Bob Huggins, and the victory over West Virginia
represented the program's first NCAA W since 1990. While the Metrodome
security attempted to clear the building to prepare for the evening session,
the Dayton red-clads stayed put. "We don't want to leave, we want to stay
here forever!" one fan cried out.

Dayton was soon joined in the Round of 32 by Atlantic 14 rival Xavier,
a program with a clever and resourceful coach, marvelous facilities and an
endless array of available talent. But it's a school that plays in the radio-only
shadows for much of the year, denying it much more than the small scraps
of national respect it receives... this is in stark contrast with a school out in
the northwest with a similar CV of recent accomplishments, one that's given
a gold-plated TV schedule full of marquee opponents every autumn. Xavier
has earned every hard-earned step and has been granted precious little; we
will always respect and admire its unstoppable hunger.

We respect the resilience of Cleveland State, whose postseason hopes
seemed over and done when injury and adversity struck over the winter.
We respect the Vikings' confidence and defiance. In Miami against Wake
Forest, they made clear that they belonged on the court—more so than the
other team. At no point in the game did their power-conference opponents
have control, and this can be added to a long list of similarly-bracketed first
round games that turned the S-Curve into a cat's cradle. Navy-LSU 1985,
Southern-Georgia Tech 1993, Siena-Vanderbilt 2008, Cleveland State-Wake
Forest 2009. The only way to tell which was the No. 13 and which the No. 4
was that the thoroughly outclassed team wore the light-colored jerseys.

Finally, speaking of Siena, the Saints became the fifth team from below
the Red Line to enter the Round of 32. Despite the higher seed, it was a
more difficult assignment: what amounted to an away game at Ohio State.
But after 50 minutes of mistakes, Ronald Moore, a 5-11, 160-lb. guard who
could be kindly described as the team's fifth scoring option (he scored in
single digits in 21 of Siena's 34 games), picked up his teammates at the end.
He sank the two shots that eliminated the richest school in Division I.

So we're down to five. For those who haven't been around at this time of
year in previous seasons, The Mid-Majority ends when there are no more
teams. (Note: we will follow Xavier, but we will not follow Gonzaga, for
reasons described above). It could be tomorrow, it could be next week, it
could be deep into April. In our continuing efforts to replicate the diehard's
experience as best we can, our progress depends on theirs and our season

ends when theirs do.

And, of course, we respect the efforts of yesterday's fallen: Morehead State, Robert Morris, East Tennessee State, Portland State, Temple and Stephen F. Austin. Each remains a champion, and each struggled and succeeded to get here. Even as the Big Dance passes them by, we're proud to have been able to record their journeys.

FEELING MINNESOTA

MAR 21, 2009

With no mid-major schools in the state of Minnesota, there's never been a reason to come here. It's very meaningful for us to be in Minneapolis this weekend, for a lot of reasons. Before I was capable of clear memory, I spent many days in this area, just south of the asphalt slab this site used to be. Being a Minnesota Twins fan all my life instilled early lessons about the importance of being resourceful and efficient beyond one's financial resources, maintaining consistency in the face of all obstacles, and never whining about long odds.

The media dining room is pressed against where the baggie usually is, the same right field patrolled by Tom Brunansky and Randy Bush and Michael Cuddyer in days past. Yet another blue curtain separates it from exposed FieldTurf, and I snuck out to the place where Kirby Puckett made That Catch in Game 6 of the 1991 World Series after he told his teammates, "Guys, I just have one announcement to make: You guys should jump on my back tonight. I'm going to carry us." Chris Wright probably said something like that before he took over yesterday's Dayton-West Virginia game, 300 feet and 18 years away.

There's another important connection, one that I haven't discussed in any great detail—but one I should. Without Batgirl, there is no Mid-Majority.

Batgirl was Minnesota native Anne Ursu, an immensely talented author who has written wonderful books for adults and children, a woman for whom the universe lacks sufficient acreage to contain her imagination. In April of 2004, she started a Movable Type blog about her Twins. It's nearly incomprehensible in an age when "sports blog" means ill-informed opinion and dick jokes, but Batgirl imposed a separate, gentle, superior reality on baseball—a stunning literary achievement in any medium.

Batgirl Photoshopped pictures, constructed Lego re-enactments of key plays, and wrote her own off-field narrative structure (Johan Santana was a volunteer firefighter, struggling fifth outfielder Lew Ford was a comic book nerd). Everybody had a nickname, and the site became so popular that the two realities blurred: some of the real Twins players accepted and used their Batgirl names in real life.

Batgirl always wrote in the third person, and the members of her family and her cats became a supporting cast. She turned a ridiculous oversized milk bottle down the Metrodome's right field line into the "BatQuarters," where they all virtually lived. She always told her readers she loved them, but antagonized enemies mercilessly (Chicago-A.L. was referred to as the "Bitch Sox"). There were contests, Javascript games to play when you were bored at work, and T-shirts for sale. Favorite players were "boyfriends," or in men's cases "man-crushes." As a result of all this fun, tough Twins seasons were suddenly easy to get through. It's the closest to magic that I've ever seen on the Internet.

She also knew when to stop. Three years after the site started, in May of 2007, Batgirl retired. In the weeks and months that followed, her fans left over 500 brokenhearted comments. All of her archives are gone now (well, not really); this history, like anything digital, is fleeting and quickly forgotten by nearly everyone.

I found the Batgirl site within a month of its inception, and became a commenter known by my initials. I won an early haiku contest. Anne asked me if I was a writer, and when I responded that I was a software engineer, she expressed shock and told me I needed to change careers immediately. She was so kind to me.

Overwhelmed with inspiration, I began my own site that November. I asked Anne what she thought of it, and she admitted that she didn't care too much for college basketball. So I tried to make this the kind of place that fans and non-fans would enjoy. Then, Anne was the first person I told when I was invited to join ESPN.com five months after I had started from scratch, and she happily responded in all caps.

Anne and I fell out of touch, because that's what happens with invisible friends, but I work every day to try to make this site something more than a pale imitation of what she created. I loved Batgirl the way that some of you love this site. Most of the time, I fail to meet the impossible standard she set... but every so often, I know that the work here strikes the perfect balance of passion, gentleness and edge. It's a feeling as if the site is floating, transcending its digital prison. I felt that way every day for three years reading Batgirl.

It's crucial that all writers show the proper respect and homage towards their forbears, and exhibit humility befitting an art that requires teaching and inspiration to evolve and continue forward. Without Batgirl, I'd still be writing software, not columns and essays. That's really all there is to it.

THE WAITING ROOM FOR THE EXIT INTERVIEW

MAR 23, 2009

MADISON, WISC.—I've long felt that the word "heartbreak" doesn't do a proper job as a member of the English language. It implies shatter or malfunction, and sounds so dry. The true feeling is more of a burst—so closely related to the challenge of capacity that joy brings, but with a method of fluid release that's painfully different. A heart can fill up with desire, then suffer from complete structural failure.

But you don't need poetry to illustrate this. For instance, put two basketball teams on a court in an elimination game, one side with eight or ten times the available resources than the other. One measures itself against perfection, while the other has to fight for the opportunity to even show up on the same court. If the score is close near the end of the game, and the fight falls away, that's a graphical depiction of the border between hope and heart-collapse that any spectator can understand.

Now repeat this 20 times, until the heart can't fill up and collapse any more, and that's what these past four days have been like.

In the remaining pool of 16 aspirants to the National Championship, there are two programs that come from schools that should be too small to compete with the power-conference Goliaths and their unlimited funds. Of all the teams that we've talked about this year, only one remains. Among the institutions that don't refuse to be labelled as "mid-majors," none remain at all.

Much of the history of the site has been tied up with arguments about definitions; I've spent more time trying to reinvent and defend descriptors than I would have preferred. Within these digital walls, "mid-major" doesn't mean underdog. It doesn't mean cute, cuddly, irrelevant, or "sucks." For our purposes, the hyphenated term was co-opted because all sports fans know it, and nobody has the time or patience to learn new vocabulary words. Here, it's intended to be more closely related to "middle class," the generally accepted term for those without large inheritances or key connections, those of us who have to rely on our own skills, determination and ingenuity to get ahead.

We've talked about Xavier from Day One, included it in our computer index every week, previewed and reviewed the Musketeers' games, and have been correct on most counts due to laser-focused observation and statistical analysis. There's nothing special about the latter part, because observation and statistical analysis are not the private domains of experts—the internet has given you so many "experts" that the noun fails its original purpose of exclusion.

Our original plan was to spend this week exploring the differences between Gonzaga and Xavier. It's a discussion that should happen: why one has captured the nation's imagination, and why the other is barely cared for outside its own metropolitan area and alumni base... despite very similar circumstances and accomplishments. We hoped to talk about why Xavier has few consistent defenders in the national media ("but you forgot to mention Xavier, Digger!"), and why few media members can even name three players on this year's team (an informal study this weekend in Minneapolis proved this to be a problem).

All of this would have been followed with an exploration into why winning with a certain kind of style points is more important than winning-period in the ESPN Age, and a look at the public relations consequences of defiance against labels and absolute insistence on respect. In the past decade, Xavier seems to have become the Pete Sampras, Tim Duncan and Fredo Corleone of college basketball.

But to approach the week like this, with this particular focus, would turn this site into a touchstone for the same old debate about labels, which we've spent five years trying to transcend. It distracts from the true struggle that binds all these programs together. The mailbag volume over the past 12 hours, however, would seem to indicate that plenty of people want to argue about what's this and what's that, and that some want to do it in all-caps. Bully for them. We don't want to go out like a radio call-in show or a "sports blog," and it's an indication that perhaps we haven't altered the conversation as much as we wanted to. Which brings its own small version of heart-collapse.

In the meantime, we implore Hoops Nation to throw its collective weight behind Xavier this week. Root on the Musketeers to victory against Pitt on Thursday. Look past the arrogance of a certain small subset of school representatives, recognize Xavier's struggle as similar to your own team's. Appreciate the Musketeers' selflessness and star-free roster—you probably won't see any of these guys in the NBA with James Posey and David West. In the words of their local columnist, this team gives "scholarships to humility."

Look at each one of those successful NCAA appearances and know that this program had to fight for every last one of them—without the advantages other schools had, financial or otherwise. Learn something about the players, even though it might be hard to find feature stories about them. Appreciate their defense, which makes things so ugly for opponents that it generally defies appreciation.

Bally and I will be in Boston rooting for Xavier, hoping that the Musketeers once again keep carrying the flag of a league I've closely followed for over a decade. We wish Messrs. Raymond and Anderson future success (and seven-figure pro contracts somewhere) as their college careers wind down. But as far as Season 5 goes, this is the end of the end. The epilogue is coming; in the meantime, we have a long drive back to Columbus to drop this car off, and some hard decisions to make about the future.

PART V

EPILOGUE

WHO CARES LEAST

MAR 25, 2009

I. INTO THE WILD

INDIANAPOLIS, Crowne Plaza Indianapolis Airport, March 25—One of my favorite books of the past 15 years is Into The Wild. It was a national New York Times bestseller that was made into a major motion picture (Emile Hirsch was great in it). It's the non-fictional story of a young student-athlete named Chris McCandless whom, after graduation from college in 1990, renamed himself Alexander Supertramp, gave his savings to charity and hitchhiked around North America. He ended up dead in a remote region of Alaska, where his decomposed body was discovered by hunters.

The book is so powerful, and contains such immediate language, that it's pretty much made Catcher in the Rye obsolete as a meditation on young American male restlessness and wanderlust. And it hits quite close to home, too: that was same era during which I was thumbing my way around the United States, separated from my family with a new name, aloof to the dangers of the road. In the summer of 1989, between my junior and senior years of prep school, I hitchhiked from New Hampshire to California and back, looking for something pure that I never found. In Indiana, on my way west, the driver of an El Dorado stabbed me with a hunting knife while trying to take my backpack. I still have the scar, a two-inch permanent sunburn above my right hip.

But perceived simpatico is not why I love Into The Wild. Two-thirds of the way through the book, author Jon Krakauer slides into the narrative all Kilgore Trout-like, and tells his own adventure story in two cutaway chapters. In 1979, a young Krakauer made a solo 20-day expedition to Alaska and successfully reached the summit of the Devils Thumb—a 9,000-foot unclimbable peak in the state's Boundary Range. It was a difficult ascent up a diorite wall covered in feathery ice, a climb that repeatedly came close to costing him his life.

Upon his return to civilization, however, Krakauer learned a sobering lesson: it didn't matter.

The euphoria, the overwhelming sense of relief, that had initially accompanied my return to Petersburg faded, and an unexpected melancholy took its place. The people I chatted with in Kito's didn't seem to doubt that I'd been to the top of the Thumb; they just didn't much care.

> ...Less than a month after sitting on the summit of the Thumb, I was back in Boulder, nailing up siding on the Spruce Street Townhouses, the same condos I'd been framing when I left for Alaska. I got a raise, to four bucks an hour, and at the end of the summer moved out of the job-site trailer to a cheap studio apartment west of the downtown mall.
>
> It is easy, when you are young, to believe that what you desire is no less than what you deserve, to assume that if you want something badly enough, it is your God-given right to have it. When I decided to go to Alaska that April, like Chris McCandless, I was a raw youth who mistook passion for insight and acted according to a obscure, gap-ridden logic. I thought climbing the Devils Thumb would fix all that was wrong with my life. In the end, it changed almost nothing. But I came to appreciate that mountains make poor receptacles for dreams.

This was not a popular section of the book with most readers, and I've heard it described as grandstanding, unnecessary filler, narcissistic even. Hollywood had little use for Krakauer's tale—the film version edited him out altogether, and opted to make Chris' sister the primary narrator instead. But for me, this threw the entire book into a five-dimensional perspective, give the work ballast and true weight. Without the inclusion of the two chapters on the Stikine Ice Cap, Into The Wild is a third-hand, third-rate version of Catcher—a point proven, perhaps, by the massive story exaggerations contained in the movie script.

The author never had to announce it in so many words, but he was detailing exactly why he felt so compelled to give this particular ghost a new life and a new voice, why he cared enough to spend three years and hundreds of pages writing this biography. Without a chronicler, nobody would give a crap about Chris McCandless. Without Jon Krakauer to tell the story, this great adventure of Alexander Supertramp is worthless—like so many million other great adventures. Without Jon Krakauer, Chris McCandless is a human dead end, an uncelebrated thrill-seeker who brought back no lessons for anyone else.

A dead end, just like I would have been if I hadn't twisted out of the way awkwardly that day on the flat blue leather seat, if that knife had found its intended mark. My life might have ended meaninglessly, with no curious biographer to document it. Roads, after all, make poor receptacles for dreams too.

II. THE CARE DEFICIT

There is no vacuum as powerful as the absence of attention. Attendance and popularity and audience size are often described by cumulative numbers, but can be more truly measured by those with something better to do. The size and scope of just about everything, the only metric that really matters, is the overwhelming majority of the population that doesn't care.

In any relationship—business, personal or otherwise—the rules are set by the entity that cares less. The most beautiful words in the language may be "I love you," but there are none quite as powerful as "I don't care." "Who cares?" brings down the weight of the entire uncaring world, and it forces defense. The lack of caring surrounds and engulfs, isolates absolutely. Loneliness is a country of caring, population one. There are far too many of those in the world, and life's absurdity is best illustrated by the idea that one other person, one among billions, can validate one's existence.

Fifteen years after I hitchhiked across the country and back, I went to 83 college basketball games in a single winter. It's the lost season of The Mid-Majority, the one that may have well never happened at all. I told people that summer what I'd done, and I would always tell the story about how I drove overnight from Richmond to Dayton, through a snowstorm in the West Virginia mountains, so I could see both the CAA title game and the A-10 first round. Out of context, this made no sense. They cared as much as the bar patrons in Kito's did about Jon Krakauer's Devils Thumb climb.

With an idea I'd hatched in the stands of the Palestra, spurred on by inspiration from a wonderful author, I tried to make the next journey mean something. I chronicled my quest to attend 100 games, and wove in stories of my struggle as well as those of the teams, players and coaches I was observing. I had the power to tell the story of my own adventure, in real time, and that approach made all the difference. The success of the 100 Games

Project is the foundation of all that's happened since; The Mid-Majority has changed my life, and I've made great friends that I would never have met if I'd kept this all to myself.

But sitting on press row nowadays, I still encounter the care deficit in a very real way. At nearly every game I go to, in places like Ogden and Baton Rouge and San Luis Obispo, the absence of fans and TV cameras and reporters is palpable—I can feel the outer borders of Unfriend and Unfollow pushing inwards, oozing past the gymnasium walls and across sections of empty plastic seats. When I'm there alone, the only credentialed journalist at the game, I often wonder why I'm making the effort at all.

Then I remember those who do care, the people who want to push back against those encroaching walls too. This season, my friends stepped up and helped me out of an incredibly difficult dilemma. When I lost my big-media meal ticket, many of you paid my way for the rest of the season, and helped underwrite the thousands of miles of travel it's taken to get from January 20 to this moment—all in the name of keeping this voice intact. I want to take a moment now and thank them all specifically, and in one place.

The last two months of Season 5 would not have been possible or plausible without the generosity of Max Kosub, Neal Walther, Katie Bickford, Rick Kulacki Jr, Michael Miller, Darin Martinez, Brendon Mulvihill, Justin Kundrat, Ethan Erickson, Ben Case, Michael Kremer, Bradley Swanson, Christopher Dobbertean, J.W. Scott, Thomas McCoy, Daniel H Fuertges, Matthew Mauro, Jason Planck, Joshua Weinhold, Hillel Soifer, Shawn Connolly, Matthew Hamparian, Andrew Stem, Pierce Greenberg, Scott Halnon, John Berlyn, David Elliott, Garrett Wheeler, Elizabeth Gallagher, Robert Hoy, David Bykowski, Eric Vilhelmsen, Richard Brunet, Robert Simkins, Robert Canedo, David Brown, Jarrett Carter, Joe DeBord, Ben Schneider, Colin FitzGerald, Josh Greenbaum, Charles Cochrum, Sarah Tipka, Greg Gardella, Timothy Bieniosek, Matt Konrad, Zach Brown, Anthony Montana, Kenneth Bethune, Mike Etheridge, Kevin Prigge, Vinny Polito, Kyle Jen, Jeff Phillips, Darren Hein, Erik Nell, Paymon Hashemi, Robert Bower, Robert Frueh, Alexander M Chaiken, Jeff Pojanowski, Jeremy Velasco, Ty Patton, Steve Timble, Mark Hanoian, Michael Litos, Christian Hoffman, Shane Smith, David Beaudoin, Lawrence Powers, Eric Angevine, Matt Anderson, James Richards, Michael Brodsky, Kevin Kremer, Frank Vitale, Dan Bowman, Jon Ralston, James Hosier, Alex Keil, Jacob Nix, Raymond Truesdell, Ronald DiPaola, Steven Stroud, Alex White, Todd Jensen, Jeffrey Fitzwater, Stephen Gentle, Christopher Sammon, Louis Izzo, Matt Sonnenberg,

Mark Riley, David Newcome, Jeffrey Valler, Daniel Bradley, Katharine Gold, Thomas Feely, Kirk Becker, Patricia Dubyoski, DeMont McNeil, Devin Moeller, Jennifer Ahearn, Rhett Butler, Jeff Grubb, Gregory Layton, Kraig Williams, Miles Janssen, Keith Powers, Bruce Sparks and Jonathan Tannenwald.

(This is an incomplete list; it does not include PayPal business accounts, anonymous donations and those for whom an appearance on this list would cause known workplace issues.)

I also get a lot of letters through this website—they come every day, and there have been thousands of them. I don't have time to answer many, and I always regret that. But I read and appreciate each one, and each has a profound effect. If you've sent in an encouraging note or expression of gratitude, or offered a long and detailed description of what this site has meant to you, thank you. Many have come at times when I thought about giving up, and they've helped me through many a dark night.

I've said this several times throughout Season 5, but I've relied on the kindness of my audience more so than at any point in this site's history. You have no idea how much, but you soon will.

III. FULL DISCLOSURE

This season began with a declaration of the challenges that the college basketball teams in Division I's middle class would face in 2008-09, and the past five months were dedicated to finding the common elements among those that rose to those challenges. The few that were able to excel beyond expectations usually did so because of full adherence to selfless systems upon which they could rely when adversity inevitably came.

Back in November when I wrote that and hit the road, heading south for North Carolina, I was full of hope that for the following five months, adversity would be kept at an absolute minimum. This was supposed to be the year that made sense, when the finances and logistics and planning all came together to create the perfect season.

It didn't turn out that way, not at all. Here is what happened instead.

In late January, I was relieved of my duties as a weekly columnist at a major sports website for writing this essay called "The Sports Bubble" on this site. It detailed budget cuts at a subsidiary of one of the largest publicly-traded companies in America, one with millions of shareholders, and was based on information sent to me in a series of e-mails, which I have kept.

Had I been an employee and not a private contractor, a cat with a single life among many with nine, I would have been within my rights to pursue a case for wrongful termination. As it was, the man who made the final decision was perfectly within his power to do so, and I accepted that.

Two weeks after I was fired, my wife of four years and I made an amicable decision to seek a divorce. She has made many appearances on this site in the past as The Official Wife of the Mid-Majority™, and is currently serving in Iraq as a Navy Seabee. She's been deployed since last May and spent the entire summer of 2007 in training out in Illinois and California. When I get home this weekend, one of my first tasks is the sad duty of packing up all her belongings and moving them into a mini-storage unit.

Because I haven't mentioned her in quite some time, I've fielded plenty of speculation about this. This had nothing to do with basketball, or too much time on the road, or ESPN's decision, or the military-industrial complex. After two years of separation, people simply don't know each other any more, and sometimes the attempt to reconnect just doesn't seem worth it. There is a comforting homily crafted to fit this particular circumstance, but it's nothing more than a convenient greeting-card lie for incurable romantics. Absence makes the heart grow colder.

The true signal that the marriage was over came over Christmas, a time when I was dealing with other news that was crushing my spirit. Thomas Rubick, one of my true heroes, my primary graphic design professor out in Oregon a decade ago and a man I call "Sensei," returned my holiday card with the news that he had been diagnosed with grade 4 brain cancer. He had taken a year of medical leave after a tumor appeared over the summer, one which he had beaten with blasts of chemo and radiation... a clean MRI in October had put everyone's dears to rest.

But as of December 17, it was back, and many times nastier. There is, of course, no grade 5.

Thomas Rubick is a brilliant painter and illustrator, an artist who plies his craft for love and for whomever around him cares enough to appreciate his work. He taught me to always make the effort to see myself through the eyes of others, to be careful not to be a narcissistic jerk. Each day now, every time I open my e-mail inbox, I'm afraid that there will be the message from a stranger that says he's gone. Whatever happens, I will honor my Sensei by never referring to him in the past tense, the basic academic respect afforded for departed creators whose work transcends the mundane. "What is Rubick trying to say with this work?"

I offered to scrap my scheduled New Year's trip to Utah and be by his side out in Oregon, but he wasn't in a position to take visitors—and most likely never will be again. I spent most of my time in Logan locked in my hotel room, crying until all I could manage was screaming dry heaves into a pillow. When the first warning about the ESPN budget cuts came, I drafted a resignation letter I never sent. I bought a plane ticket home that I never used. I didn't want to travel around the country and write about basketball anymore.

I was also fighting my own health problems, though considerably less terminal. Last April, I woke up from an afternoon nap and noticed that my hearing was different. Music sounded strange, all the notes were distorted, flat and muddy. In the weeks that followed, I kept hearing a sound of an oncoming tractor-trailer, but there was none around. The whooshing noise would last for hours and sometimes days, and I couldn't hear what people were saying over the din. I couldn't talk on the phone.

I tried to treat this—which I learned was the mystery disease tinnitus— with internet information and a series of homeopathic remedies. That seemed to keep it at bay over the summer. But in November, after I left for the season, the Mack trucks were back and would not be silenced. There were screaming headaches and vertigo, and sometimes colors of things would change and separate. Worse still, the onset of these episodes came without warning and was accompanied by panic attacks and heart palpitations, as my entire system struggled to catch up with a suddenly shifting reality.

A doctor later told me I should probably not travel, and I brushed off the advice as the lazy mumbles of an uncaring HMO-quality hack who had diagnosed me based on nothing more than a conversation. The imbalances and the hearing problems continued, but I ignored any danger. I'd pull over to the side of the road when I felt things "get weird." I'd always allow extra time to write a story, I'd postpone or cancel a chat if I had to, and alter the timestamp of a post if "Good Morning Hoops Nation" turned out to be mid-afternoon. If I couldn't hear an interview subject, I'd smile and nod and then listen to the tape later when my head was back in order. I'd find out later that some people had asked me questions more complicated than those that required yes or no answers, and I'd feel really embarrassed. You know what they always say, nobody likes an occasionally deaf sportswriter.

But basketball taught me the key lesson that was necessary to overcome all of this. When life has you down 30 points with 18 minutes remaining, you keep playing as hard as you can. The most dishonorable thing of all is to quit, to slump your shoulders and give up trying. There is always something to play for, even if it's just the pride of making it to the end of the game with your head up.

And here we are, :00.00 on the clock, the last echos of the final buzzer still faintly audible, that eerie red glow illuminating the backboards. And it feels good to have made it to the end.

I've spilled too many words this season not to provide the full picture of what happened—and as many of you are invested personally (and financially) in this, you deserve the truth. I also tell you this now, and not back then, because it would have distracted from the running narrative. I wanted you to care about this for the right reasons, not sympathetic ones.

IV. OWNERSHIP

I want to interrupt for a minute and talk to you about ownership.

I live in a rented house, drive rented cars, reserve seats on airplanes for short times, rent hotel rooms for single nights. The tools and implements and clothes I carry are temporary, I'll only have use of them until they wear out and become useless (or somebody steals them). My job had an expiration date, which I had no control over, and yours does too if you have a boss. The brain and heart and body that are bringing you this long essay are on loan from God.

Take a moment, look around you, think about what is really yours. Chances are that the house you "own" doesn't really belong to you—too many people have found that out the hard way over the past year, and I hope you're not one of the unfortunate foreclosed-upon. Even if you hold the deed, property can always be snatched away by way of eminent domain. Those items that you surround yourself with, make your time on Earth more tolerable, are yours only for a short time.

You own your feelings, but they're not worth very much on their own. As Chris McCandless wrote in his journal before he died, "Happiness is nothing unless shared." Love is worth precious little if it's not received, and families can be sadly impermanent. You own your faith, but it's worthless in a vacuum, without the similar and shared faith of others to illuminate it. The value of care is increased exponentially when others around you care about the same thing.

When I was hired at ESPN in the summer of 2005, I was asked if I would be willing to make "The Mid-Majority" the title of my column, perhaps even close this site down? I refused. Throughout my nearly four years there, I kept posting on this site every day. Having a place where I was free to create and draw and sing kept me from grousing about the constantly looming censorship, or the cut paragraphs, or editing that more often than not drummed the passion and life out of my writing. I always had TMM, and as a result I always kept my sanity.

Whenever I get an e-mail from somebody who wants me to join their "blog network," or paste the site over with gambling or ticket ads, I become angry and territorial. I tell them in no uncertain terms to fuck off. The Mid-Majority belongs to me, I own it. It is my intellectual property, and nobody is going to take a piece of it for their own selfish uses. If you own something, truly own something, you know this feeling well. You are just as possessive as I am.

Ask anyone who creates and does, especially those who use their talents for commercial purposes, and they'll probably use the same types of terms: freedom, ownership, sanity, territory. Thomas Rubick is a painter who gets paid for teaching. Jon Krakauer is a mountain climber who gets paid for writing magazine columns. I was a blogger and cartoonist and web developer who was paid for writing basketball feature stories.

I've spent many unpaid hours each day making sure there was quality work presented in this space, simply because The Mid-Majority is the only thing I truly own. Since I've started, I've lost just about everything else. I haven't cleared a penny from my work here, and the audience isn't nearly as big as it was at the other place—but I've poured five years of my life into this, and it's become my true home. Describing something ethereal and non-geographical in those terms may sound odd, but this really is where I live five months out of the year. And there's no mortgage on it, so it's all mine.

And right now, at this moment, I own something that a lot of people care deeply about. That's why I can't leave, not just yet.

V. SEASON 6

Last spring, when Davidson head coach Bob McKillop was charming the corduroy pants off the American sportswriting establishment on his team's path to the Elite Eight, he spoke often about striving for the perfect moment, the beautiful game, the quest for capacity's limit. Even if that pinnacle isn't reached, he said, the struggle to reach that peak is clearly superior to settling for mediocrity. For his team, this year ended up far from the summit—as has been painfully documented in excruciating detail here, Davidson just didn't have the horses this time.

Every year at the end, there are always regrets here, we always fall short of our own lofty expectations. The writing, though, especially over the past two months, is the most passionate and focused and alive that I've done here—of that I'm very proud. But, as always, there can always be more cartoons. It was the most difficult season yet, and too many things kept it from being a quest for perfection.

But the biggest folly was to expect a perfect season, and more folly still to rely on it. My idea for a book completely collapsed because I chose to follow three star-crossed teams that would have ended up producing the most depressing sports book ever. I want to apologize once again to the players, coaches, staff and fans of Southern Illinois, Miami (Oh.) and Northwestern State. I have hours of interviews that I don't have a ready use for, and there are a few angry people because of expectations I'd fostered. Unfortunately, none of those three squads made it past the quarterfinals in their respective conference tourneys.

That, however, is the past. How does one go about creating a perfect season?

One way is to go forward into the past. This is my original book concept, the one from back in May that came before things got complicated, the recipe was handled by too many cooks, and my publisher went out of business. It went something like this:

> *There are 343 universities and colleges that compete for the NCAA Division I men's basketball championship every year, but nearly two-thirds of those schools languish in the shadows of the well-moneyed and constantly televised power conferences. For the past five years, I've travelled from coast to coast covering "mid-major" conferences like the Big South, Big Sky and Big West, leagues that are only as "big time" as their exceedingly hopeful titles.*
>
> *I plan to chronicle my 2009-10 season on the road, as I travel to and between over 100 Division I games. Along the way, we'll stop by hallowed halls like Butler's Hinkle Fieldhouse and Penn's Palestra. We'll meet head coaches on the rise, as well as on career declines and rebounds. We'll visit with student section superfans and explore their odd rituals, and reveal heated local rivalries often overlooked by the national media. Invariably, a previously unknown school will*

*leap into the limelight as a surprise nationally-ranked instant pow-
erhouse. We'll discover players who go from unknowns to legends in
a single episode of March Madness. And as winter turns to spring,
small towns across America will become transformed, as tiny local
colleges achieve berths in America's ultimate college sports showcase, the NCAA Tournament.*

*The real texture to this story of mid-major basketball, however,
is provided by its inherent struggle. There will also be trips to run-
down, dimly-lit 1,000-seat gymnasiums with empty seats, failed
recruiting trips. There will be November "guarantee games," in
which power-conference teams exchange five-figure checks for certain beatings, and long 700-mile team bus rides through the night.
Players who excel in smaller leagues often have their weaknesses
cruelly exposed against higher competition. All of these programs
are defined by their relative lack of finances, and struggle to achieve
or maintain excellence at the highest level. It's a world where big
success becomes bittersweet --larger programs routinely lure away
winning coaches with multi-million dollar contracts, reducing the
role of mid-major schools to simple stepping stones.*

*The chronicle will be narrated in an even-handed, philosophical
style that's been honed and perfected over three years as a national
college basketball reporter. Travelogue-style elements will be woven
into the story as I criss-cross the country for five months, driving
tens of thousands of miles in pursuit of small college basketball's
pulse. In book form, the 2009-10 mid-major college basketball season promises to be a patchwork of hope, faith, expectation, disap-
pointment, pride and heartbreak—it may end for each team with
inevitable elimination, but it's always an interesting journey.*

That's what this book should have been, and what this site should be: a
100 Games Project with insider access. I'm going to take this chance to do
it right. If I stopped now, I'd always regret quitting without achieving that
perfect season.

But here's the twist: it will be a work in progress as Season 6 goes on,
unspooled chapter by chapter as I travel the country, and it will be posted
right here on this very site. You all will be my proofreaders: if there are any
mistakes, you'll be able to correct me in real-time. At the end of the season,
when this is finished, it will be professionally edited, reordered for narra-

tive flow, and all the locker-room secrets that couldn't be leaked during the season (due to competition reasons and such) will be added. Then it will be published. The book is the blog, and the blog is the book.

I will be a character in this, but not the stifling narrator who seeks to make appearances on every page. Like Krakauer, I'll mostly stay in the background, illuminating the proceedings with personal experience. There will be long roads and bad food and truck stops.

But I'll need some help with this. For the first time in site history, there will be a third Conchord, a third member of our Royal We, the Nate Silver to my Sean Quinn and RonDavis to my Batgirl. His name is Damon Lewis, he's very passionate about mid-major basketball, and you will grow to like him very much if you don't already. He's a big hitter with the Horizon League Network (this will be completely separate from his TV-star work there) and someone who will be learning a lot of new territory. I trust you will be as patient with him as you were with me in 2004, back when I was branching out from the CAA and Big West.

One thing I know you will find refreshing is Damon's innate and natural wide-eyed Midwestern-ness, which stands in stark contrast to my crusty-punk East Coast cynicism (the result of having all the Minnesota Nice beaten and mugged out of me). Damon also uses blue cussy-words less than I do, which I understand irks certain folks.

Starting in November, Damon will take over the daily posts, the MMBOW and G!O!T!N! selections, all the tempo-free stat stuff and the State ratings. He's also got some ideas of his own, which will be certified fresh. Analysis is an important part of this, but I'll be happy to pass that part of the site into very capable hands. This move will free me up to write about the road, which I'm sure makes a lot of the old fans from the 100 Games Project days very happy indeed, the ones who always tell me there aren't nearly enough travelogues.

And because of all this, we are also moving the capital of Hoops Nation to Indianapolis. It's been a great five-year run, Dayton, and we still think you have the best fans in college basketball. This has nothing to do with what happened Sunday, I promise. But Indianapolis is home of Damon, location of the Official Hotel and Western HQ (where this and this were written and this was drawn), and of course, Sports Bubble Stadium. Not to mention the defending No. 1 team in our TS-22 ratings. It's a rotating capital, other places will get their chance.

All virtual fun aside, the question remains: how are we going to pay for all of this?

VI. THE WHOLE TO-DO OF WHAT TO DO FOR MONEY

I want to share a letter I received after shortly the donation drive. It's from someone who felt slighted because I didn't have time to send a personal note in return, a feeling that was exacerbated when I posted a scathing critique of the play of his alma mater's basketball team. He took all of this very personally.

> *I send you some money because I actually felt*
> *bad for you and your situation.*
> *You slag [school redacted], you don't return*
> *an email nor say thanks for a donation.*
> *I think you suck and I want my money back.*
> *Thanks!*

That I couldn't personally thank everyone who donated and wrote in was regrettable. So, too, was the play of this gentleman's favorite team at the end of the season—its destiny was to lose in the biggest seed-upset in that conference's tourney history. But far more regrettable was the open nature of my request for funds, though at the time and under the circumstances this was the only course of action. The ESPN situation forced my hand.

Trust me, begging is not my preferred way of doing things. It goes against the spirit of the teams that are covered here, the ones that fight for every inch and yard. And, as illustrated above, asking for money over the internet provides no way to filter out those folks who think they're buying positive coverage of their teams, or to stop people from giving for the wrong reasons. Sympathy is a wrong reason. Sympathy is no substitute for real caring.

Most of the $15,000 required to make Season 6 happen will come from partnerships with conferences and their related entities, those with whom The Mid-Majority shares a mutual benefit. It will not be funded by the Sports Bubble or large corporations or mega-things that want my "numbers." The primary goal is to ensure that Season 6 will have as few mid-season surprises as possible.

And some of this operating budget, hopefully up to 25 percent, will be funded by readers. Not by donation drive or bailout or panhandling, but by a method with which there is a clear and present reward. Each contribution will be a real transaction, a purchase, not grants for which return expectations are fluid and gaseous. You have something that I need, and I have something that you want... so let's do business.

If you'd like to be a part of making Season 6 happen, please click on the button below this paragraph or click this link. All I ask is that you include a short reason why you're doing this in the "Special Instructions" box (just so I know you've thought this through). If you give $100, you will get a Bally.

You heard right, no typos there. There are only 28 in existence now, and has been the most ferociously fought-over item since Tickle Me Elmo v1.0, but it's time to flood the market. Do it however you need to do it, pool your money in the dorm, break your piggy bank and your brother's too.

The rules are simple: No limit, first-come first-serve, allow one to 10 weeks for delivery (there's hand-sewing involved), and PayPal only (sorry... paper checks are messy). Furthermore, for every $100 you contribute, you will receive one Bally. That means you can fill your kid's room with them if you're rich enough. You hear me, Kyle Korver? Jason Thompson? George Hill?

We fully understand that not everybody has that kind of cash, we're just trying to raise the barrier to entry a little and maintain Bally's rarity, specialness and awesomeness. Some already have an eternally smiling orange friend, and some are just tapped out from the last time we threw PayPal links around.

So there's another option. Thanks to a fantastic idea from No. 1 Bally fan Rod in Asheville, I'm going to compile all the essays from Season 5 (and anything that wasn't time-sensitive yesterday's-news) into a self-published book, which will have a nice cover and nice clean pages thanks to advances in DIY internet publishing

Look at me, I'm a published author! Okay, it's not going to have an ISBN or be in the Library of Congress or anything, but I'll sign it if you think that's important. All this is not to say that anything I wrote this year was special enough to read a second time or pay actual money for, or that it is anywhere near as good as next year's chronicle is going to be—but you might like this stuff better if it's on paper and in chronological order. With bonus material. And edited, with all the mad-dash bloggy typos corrected.

I know there won't be a reason to come back here until November 1, and that's why I'm mentioning this now. You'll forget, I will too, because that's what happens with college basketball when April comes. The summer is on its way now, can you feel it? It's the end, for real this time.

VII. IT ALWAYS ENDS IN A LOSS

It always ends in a loss. The only unanswered question at the beginning is where and when it will come. It might arrive with squeaky shoes against silence, in front of thousands of empty seats at a neutral-site league quarter-final that few care enough to attend. It could happen at the brink of glory in a packed and hot arena, as a conference championship slips through the fingers of a team destined to play out its string as phantoms in an ghosts' exhibition tournament. It can come at the NCAA Tournament, before CBS cameras and a million strangers. The loss will come, you can always count on that.

What I've asked you to do in the last five years has required a leap of faith on your part, and it likely hasn't been an easy one. I've asked you to find meaning in college basketball beyond what you can readily see, beyond brand names and hyphenated labels, the tedious "carousel" and imagined soap-opera personality conflicts between coaches. I've invited you to forsake polls, "bracketology" and disposable underdogs. I've put forward the idea that small-college teams should be judged less on their wins and losses, and more on the valiance of their struggle. In short, I've implored you to care about inevitable failures; most sportswriting celebrates perfect champions, and harshly judges those who fall short. I do not fit in with that world, and never really did.

There will always be more of them than there are of us. The size of our relatively tiny Hoops Nation will always be defined by borders drawn around us by those who don't care, and we will always be surrounded by sheer apathy. But if you've read this far, I've somehow convinced you that you should care, and I don't take the trust between us lightly.

For the time being, though, I have some personal matters to take care of, and I have to find some good medicine to make my head work right again. I have a wonderful African adventure that will change my worldview, and a book to write about a great and wonderful man. In seven months, when these new green leaves outside your window have aged and fallen, when the wind blows cold and the dry trees creak, I will be back with you again.

It always ends with a loss. But there's a caveat, an exception, an asterisk with some fine print so small you need a microscope to read it. College basketball is not like life, thankfully so, because that loss is never terminal. Though it's ruled by the greedy and corrupt, Our Game is not like many other sports, there is no strike or lockout or disruption to fear. There is always another season, just as beautiful as the last, and it's waiting for us on the other side of summer. It seems so far away now, with all these recent losses so fresh and painful, but it will come in time. Our Game always offers another chance... if you dare to take it.

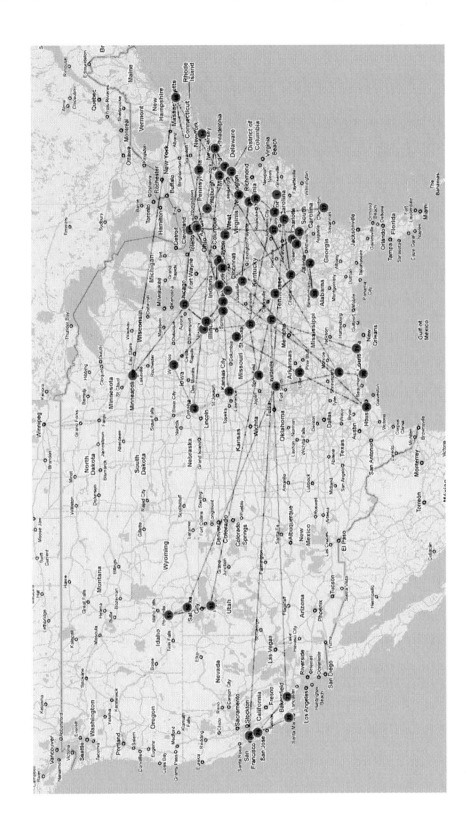

APPENDIX

APPENDIX
109 GAME TWITTERCASTS

GAME NO. 1 — Georgia Southern against Houston, Coaches vs. Cancer. The first game of the season!

Game on! Season on! Everything on!

GS, hanging tough against HOU. Decent inside game!

I have a Cameron Crazie for a backpack.

Georgia Southern, the first 1-0 team.

GAME NO. 2 — Presbyterian at Duke... Remember, we're on ESPNU this time!

Thanks for the notes... Yeah, that's me, no beard anymore.

A Presby cheerleader in the stands brought a sign that says HOSE, the Crazies are all over that.

Bring back goofy head Devil.

I don't know if this is new, but the Blue Devil acts as a policeman. Just gestured down a "Dirty! Hose!" chant.

Lots more miles today.

First awesome truck stop merch find of season in western NC — Charlotte zipup sweatshirt that says "UNC Charlotte"

500 miles, 9 hrs to tip... Will be close. Might have to post at the game.

Over the E. Continental Divide and into TN. Many of the D2 schools the SoCon will beat on are around here.

Cleared Nashville and EST too.

In Illinois. Need a shower.

GAME NO. 3 — UMass versus Arkansas-Monticello, Coaches vs. Cancer.

Made it! SIU Arena is empty.

Ark Mont just turned a 23-12 deficit to 32-31 lead

D2 name watch — opponents tonight are the Boll Weevils and Vulcans.

GAME NO. 4 — California of Pennsylvania at Southern Illinois.

Cali PA and SIU tied at the half @ 25...

The kids are wearing T-shirts that say "So Ill Hoops"

Great to be in one place for one day. Shootarounds in an hour, SIU-MASS at 7.
   Unfortunately, the D2 vs D2 game at 5 can't count in my tally.

Still trying to figure out how to sneak away for lunch, though.

Accomplishment this afternoon: shoehorning another game into my schedule. (W&M; at Ohio on Sunday.) The MAC folks are so persuasive.

Holy crap, I've been invited to the Mock Selection in Feb.

GAME NO. 5 — UMass at Southern Illinois.

UMass blowing SIU out early.

So here's the deal on the D2's: Ark-Monticello and Calif. (PA) played a closed-door scrimmage at 10 this morning. No doubleheader tonight.

SIU just scored 7 quick points to cut down an 11-point halftime deficit.

SIU freshman Kevin Dillard: Good At Basketball. Three 3's in 3 minutes, SIU up 53-51...

Huge win for SIU.

GAME NO. 6 — Illinois-Chicago at Bradley.

Josh Mayo: good at basketball! (7 points early on)

New Bradley players have passed it to non-existent recipients thrice so far... UIC 12, BRAD 12 7:47 1H

UIC opens up a 28-16 lead. Kreps has 11!

The Flames' rotation of Eurobigs are moiderizing Bradley inside. Kids in the stands are terrified.

I just saw an old dude wearing a Space Jam tie. WANT.

Bradley shot 17 pct in the 1st half.

A little distracted by the Slingbox right now... VMI beating Kentucky...

Bradley surging, up 44-41 with eight to go.

All you upset clubbers just got your memos: VMI 111, UK 103!!

Just put in my congratu-call to Coach Baucom.

Bradley's got this... up by 9 with two to go. Dodie Dunson has a future in this league.

Meeeeenwhile... Southeastern Lousiana leading Arkansas, Cal Davis with an edge on Iowa State late...

Who's scoring a crapload of points? Tenn-Martin: 121, Chicago State: 112, against non-D1's though...

Bradley broke this open with a 12-3 run halfway through the 2nd... Gotta run, I've got a date with the next chapter of Indiana basketball...

Postgame pizza with some great Bradley folks last night. Totally forgot that I lose an hour today.

Got about 100 miles in last night, crashed 4 hrs in a rest area, should get to Bloomie by noon.

Gotta remember to get a case of Ski before I leave IN.

GAME NO. 7 — Northwestern State at Indiana.

I'm the only national here, if you can believe that.

Demons open an 8-2 lead...

Five in, five out... NWSU 12, IND 5

2nd team gave up most of the lead, 18-16 and the starters are back out

The championship banners here are as tall as four or five dudes.

Indiana up by 9, foul diff 20-9 NWSU. Draw your own conclusions.

Officially incorporating the "dude" as a system of measurement.

The Assembly Hall scoreboard is 3.2 dudes tall.

NWSU is 3 dudes short of the lead in this game.

Just said "I'm a big hit at truck stops" on a halftime interview. That could probably be misconstrued.

Teetering on the edge of a blowout — 58-42, 10 left.

GAME NO. 8 — William & Mary at Ohio.

Snowing in Indiana this morning. Headed for Ohio U.

The wire service BBState uses is still missing 28 of the 112 boxscores from Friday. This happened on the first weekend last year too.

Truck stop bathroom walls have URL's scrawled on them now. Wow, this really is the 21st Century.

Mid-major blues: when local gas station signs support the power school an hour away. "Go Buckeyes"? Come ahn.

Convo is evacuated, fire alarm. 30 degrees out. The refs are staying warm in an Impala.

OK, all in. Half hour delay, 2:30 start.

The Bobcats are not fooled by your paint-by-numbers halfcourt offense. OHIO 8, CWM 0 at first media.

CWM closes to 15-11 with transition and increased HC motion, but Tillman is drawing a foul on just about every Ohio possession.

17-16 Ohio, but Schneider (Litos' favorite Triber) has 3 fouls already. Bad weekend for him (3/13 in loss vs Penn State Friday)

Halftime, 30-28 CWM. Ohio brickfest in progress, please stand by.

Ohio's outscored CWM 21-8 out of the break. 49-38 with 11 to go.

Ohio 37% 1st half, 61% 2nd half.

Jerome Tillman (19 pts) inside, Tommy Freeman (18 pts) outside... Ohio up by 18 at the final media TO.

GAME NO. 9 — Miami Ohio at Pitt.

Pittsburgh has too many cars and not enough highway.

Pitt out 9-0, nothing's working for the RedHawx.

16-7 Pitt at 2nd media... Coach Coles is smiling though.

8-0 Miami run, down 21-17 now.

35-30 at the half. Miami hanging in, mainly thanks to Kenny Hayes.

I'll bet you didn't know that the Pitt media room is named after Carroll H. Cook, better known by his nickname. We're cookin' with Beano!

Monster Pitt run out of halftime, a five-point lead is now 17 after seven minutes.

Charlie Coles, as usual, looking as if someone replaced his gum with Sour Patch Kids.

This was ugly at one point, now it's something else. 77-49, just about finished.

No! Sleep! Til Breezewooooood!

Loyola! Listened to the game on XM, the Georgia announcers were quite respectful.

GAME NO. 10 — Penn at Drexel. It's 10 am.

Drexel fans, you're totally doing the rollouts wrong. They *descend*.

Really, stop it. You're embarrassing the city.

I just saw someone roll one back up instead of tear it up. I am seriously going to cry on national TV.

Dragons up 19-15. That part's going well.

DU pouring it on, 32-18, and what they're pouring is hot, yummy maple syrup.

The new Quaker looks like Jay Leno in 15 years. Has anyone made note of that yet? If not, (tm).

GAME NO. 11 — Florida State at LaSalle.

Florida State has big feathers down the sides of its uniforms.

LaSalle's band has moved from the baseline to the far reaches of the stands since I was here last.

The drummer in LaSalle's band has a serious rock drum cage. I want a five-minute Neil Peart solo by the end of the night.

FSU is up 7-3 after 8 minutes.

Huge Goodridge dunk, LAS up 10-7.

I've wriiten "3" then crossed it out and put "long 2" many times so far this season.

LAS up 21-13. Explorer fans should be excited about Vernon Goodridge. Brooklynnnn!

28 all with 16 to go.

LaSalle's poise and confidence have really improved. Tied at 59, a minute left.

Buuuut they threw it away at the end. FSU 65, LAS 61. Day off tomorrow.

GAME NO. 12 — Southern Illinois and Duke in the CvC semis.

About my 200th time at the Garden, but first in the press box.

SIU leads 7-3 at the first media.

Wishing they put the dumb Elton John and Billy Joel banners on the Knicks side.

Duke up 27-23 19 min in. Not a lot of Duke fans here, they usually draw well at MSG.

Most of it is held together by spackle and gum, but MSG is a great building.

SIU hanging in, down by 7 with 10 to go.

The corner press box at MSG is called "The Ramp," and it shakes like a mofo. There is a Jerry Lee Lewis song about it.

Seriously considering walking out before UCLA-Michigan.

Not sure if Boyle would have been given the X if Coach Amex hadn't gone apeshit. But that's the way things are. Game slipping away, 63-49.

16-2 run for Duke, but I'm sure there are other ways you could frame it.

Gerald Henderson just made a two point dunk shot, and Duke is up by 24.

Originally scheduled game for tonight ended in an 85-62 win for Rhode Island over Monmouth, but this wasn't that bad. We got free T-shirts.

GAME NO. 13 — Michigan vs UCLA. Just scouting.

Since I'm off duty, I get to drink. And start "Let's Go Rangers" chants.

Standing ovation for the UCLA cheerleaders. Only in New York, kids, only in New York.

My stars, power conference basketball is boring.

GAME NO. 14 — UCLA vs. Southern Illinois.

SIU-UCLA should be good.

Testing, testing, mic checka 1 2...

Game No. 14, SIU and UCLA.

24-18 UCLA 10 minutes in.

Pretty empty here... More room for Bob Knight.

SIU is down by four and missing foul shots.

Halftime, UCLA 35-33. Dillard hit a sweet NBA 3 a minute ago.

New York City <3 synchronized hair flips.

Tony Boyle just tipped in a Man Layup, but Dragovic answered with a 3. UCLA 48, SIU 43,
    12:03.

Arena playlist selectors of America: Less remakes of 80's cheez-hits, more "Shake It."

Dude just won a free RT airline ticket for hitting a layup, free throw and 3. This is MSG. At
    a mid-major arena, that'll get you a sandwich.

Put a body on Dragovic, dammit.

This UCLA run is all Fay's fault. Lowery's not going to play him much again if that's what
    he calls D.

Just noticed there's a mascot out there too.

Forget what the patterns look like, SIU's issue is depth. That will fix itself over the next few
    months.

Not staying for Duke-Michigan. Yawn.

GAME NO. 15 — Old Dominion at Bucknell.

It took some 85 mph driving, but I made it.

Bucknell up 14-10 eleven minutes in.

Bucknell 37-28 near the half. ODU's shooters are having problems with the "sightlines."

Overtime!

Double overtime!

83-82 Bucknell in 2OT, what a game!

GAME NO. 16 — Mercer vs. Texas Southern at the Chicago Invitational Challenge in
    LOVEly Hoffman Estates, Ill.

This will probably be a 90-possession game. Both teams are quicker than quick.

TXSO first four possessions: 2 offensive fouls, a five-second call and a 35-second violation.
    Easily the most inept team I've seen all year.

It's a shame, meanwhile, that Mercer is in the "loser" daytime bracket in this 8-team thing...
    they could play with any of the PM teams.

MERC up 12-4 eight minutes in.

20-11. Sling-timeshifting Siena blowing a lead against Wichita State from earlier. Saints have run out of gas late in both games...

Speaking of depth issues, Mercer's lead is now 2.

TXSO does one thing well: press.

This Chicago Challenge is a good event, I'm pretty sure it's the first eight-team, four-game, multi-site double-bracket MTE.

I went to the first one two years ago, I didn't think it would survive.

Plug: if you like basketball scores, follow bbstate. Finally got that working.

Mercer by 11, 12:38 left. Still figuring this team out.

Hoffman Estates is the Glendale, AZ of Chicagoland; it doesn't get many events. Scoreboard REALLY pushing a monster truck show on March 14.

Mercer has a lot of talent in their starting 5, but if you throw a press or some intensity at them, they fold up. 53 all, 6 to go.

Mercer escapes, 71-68. Hmmmm.

GAME NO. 17 — Chicago State (indep.) vs. Bethune-Cookman (MEAC) at the Chicago Challenge. Plenty of great seats still available.

The Sears Centre is no sixth-rate suburban arena. Cirque du frickin' Soleil coming for a 10-show run in late January.

Guy in front of me with a thick binder of press info he printed out this morning. Brought his son. They're staying for all 4 games. Awesome.

This is the first time I've seen David Holston (CST) play live. I can see why he scores so much. The man has elastic forearms.

We're in Chicago this year, but part of me wishes I was in the Palestra watching NJIT shoot 25 percent. Much love for y'all.

I like watching David Holston play basketball.

Chicago State 40, Bethune-Cookman 21 at the half.

One constant truth in the A-14: Dayton travels well.

CST 79, BETH 64. Two down, two to go! No break, no evening session. Dayton-Auburn in 25 minutes!

GAME NO. 18 — Dayton vs. Auburn.

No UD band, though. Shucks.

Dayton and Auburn tied at 9, and six of AUB's points are from two-point dunk shots.

Dayton 26, Auburn 21 at the half.

I have intercepted a secret internal memo from catering that pizza will be served at 6:30 PM CST SHARP.

Here's a show of respect for Dayton: Buzz Williams is out here scouting the Flyers himself, instead of leaving it to his assistants.

This, BTW, is not a "championship"... tomorrow's matchups (UD-MARQ, UNI-AUB) are preassigned instead of dependent on today's results.

Overtime!

Dayton wins!

Man... one joke about the "Marquette Gold" and the drunk MU fans are on me all night. Unbelievable.

GAME NO. 19 — Marquette and Northern Iowa. What? Only one more game? I could go for at least four more! Oh, that's right, tomorrow.

No idea where these Marquette fans are getting all these drinks from. Seriously suspect fat guy over there is really carrying a BellyKeg.

28-8 with seven to go in the first half. Really, the only uninteresting/lopsided game of the day.

Storming The Court needs to add Jordan Eglseder to its Big Ant club.

45-20 Marquette, quickly moving towards recycling time.

Drunk Marquette fans are harassing the two female student paper reporters, which qualifies them as "assclowns."

That's not a misprint, BTW. Dayton really did go 0-for-24 from 3 in the last game. (And still won.)

Drunk Marquette fan just challenged me to a fight, so I told him to try outdrinking a UNI fan instead.

I've been to Cedar Falls, and that ain't happening.

GAME NO. 20 — Texas Southern vs. Bethune-Cookman at the Chi-Chall. MEAC-SWAC explosion.

It's a Paul Lukas special, with both teams wearing their home jerseys. (BETH yellow, TXSO light gray)

I also wanted to mention that Sparkle Motion was staying at my hotel last night.

BETH 19, TXSO 14, 5:26 1H. I have a quick-notation system that puts a black dot next to the away team. I'm not sure which is which.

Playing the All American Rejects over the P.A. at a MEAC-SWAC game is so, so wrong.

Tony Harvey (TXSO head coach) has said "goddamnit" at least 20 times in this game. 67-61 BETH, about to go final.

69-61 BETH. Texas Southern is now 0-6.

GAME NO. 21 — Mercer vs. Chicago State. Chicago Challenge. It's on.

P.A. is the XM channel from hell: Yeah Yeah Yeahs -> Kool & the Gang -> Usher -> Gerry Rafferty. That's right, fucking "Baker S

Mercer up 38-27 over Chicago State, late in first half.

I don't know how I missed this yesterday... Chicago State has a guy whose last name is Kielbasa.

You write the jokes, I'm on duty today.

Kielbasa didn't play yesterday, and he's out of the game already. I guess he just slips in and out. (oh!)

Mercer 44-34 at the half, but Chi-State's David Holston has 17.

Mercer wins by 11. Two more games to go.

GAME NO. 22 — Auburn, Northern Iowa. In Chicago. Of all places.

Auburn 30, Northern Iowa 28 early in the second half. My BlackBerry crashed earlier.

NEWS FLASH: Auburn is not very good at basketball right now.

Or American-style football.

Northern Iowa looked like crap last night, is grinding down Auburn today. Up by five with less than a minute to go.

Auburn now 3-3 against its all-mid schedule, and the last coach that took them to the NCAA's is at Coastal Carolina. How does it feeeeel...

GAME NO. 23 — Marquette vs. Dayton, Chicago Cha-Ching Kick-Push-Coast Challenge. The whole press row is calling the upset on this one.

Wow, this is an atmosphere. Half the arena red, the other half yellow.

Dear Wesley Matthews: Wearing No. 23 does not give you license to do the LeBron chalk thing. Besides, you're too messy with it. Thanks, TMM

Dayton up by eight halfway through the first.

The drunk Marquette fans from last night have been replaced by sober Dayton fans who are going to scream their lungs out by halftime.

Nobody in here gave a F about the Chicago Shamrox lacrosse team until the Shamrox dance team came out. Now they're screaming for t-shirts.

UD leading Marquette 33-32 at the half.

A large number of the Dayton players are good at basketball. UD opens up an eight-point lead in first four minutes of second half.

UD's Chris Wright just threw down a HUGE dunk. The video board rewinded it, stopped, then cut to live. The fans chanted "Re-play, Re-play!!"

UD is getting a lot of easy layups in halfcourt sets. 63-48, 10:44 2H.

This Dayton team is MUCH better than the one that beat Pitt and UL last year. These guys are much more physical and aren't afraid to drive.

UD 71, Marquette 61. Dominic James gets 4 steps (because he's a STAR) and every call is going against UD, but sheer skill is prevailing.

Lots of "everybody on their feet" possessions in this game... real fieldhouse flavor (despite the minor league hockey arena). I love it.

UD 75, MARQ 65 4:04 2H.

P.A. (D-minus performance all weekend) just played the non-radio version of that Maroon 5 song where the singer says "fuck." EDGY

Dear Marquette, the point of pressure defense is not to commit a halfcourt foul every def. possession. Two Gold players have fouled out.

Dayton's Rasta Twins (Lowery and Warren) are good at basketball.

Sealed up. UD 83, MARQ 71, 1:25. "Overrated" chant begins.

Three upsets in eight games. Not a bad two-day tournament. Now it's on to Ill. State for a pair tomorrow afternoon.

89-75 is the final. Good night Hoops Nation!

GAME NO. 24 — Winston-Salem State vs Nicholls State at Illinois State.

It's the World Vision Classic in Normal IL.

There are exactly 23 people in the stands.

Some more stats: inches of snow outside — 3, WSSU record — 0-5, media members present — 1

Winston-Salem State by 7 at halftime.

The charities that sponsor these preseason events should get more than vague timeout announcements. No idea what World Vision does or is.

One of the Australian dudes on Nicholls (So. Anatoly Bose) has 5 3's and has outdone his season ppg by a factor of 20.

Ingredients of a short game — wide margin and refs who are in a hurry. TOG is 1h30m with a minute to go.

We slid under 1:45, and Nicholls won 67-61. WSSU is 0-6.

GAME NO. 25 — UC Santa Barbara (Big West) at Illinois State (MVC). Either or both could make the national postseason.

Redbird Arena's court is named for Doug Collins, who made a lot of jump shots in very short shorts.

From the Thunderdome page in UCSB's media guide: "You can't tell, but just about everyone's dressed in yellow."

I wonder if anyone's ever hurt their hand on the Battle Bird. That beak is sharp.

ILST lost three starters, but the defensive intensity's up a few notches. Redbirds by 5 early.

UCSB liked playing defense once, recently, but now they like shooting 3's and making turnovers more.

ILST is 6-12 from 3, 14 minutes in.

Osiris Eldridge still has the fro-hawk going, but he isn't carving patterns anymore.

ILST is blowing UCSB off the floor, 36-20.

Not sure the "show your bank card" promotion will survive 20 megapixel cameras.

ILST 42-26 at the half.

Cheer Time USA is kicking the audience's collective ass right now with its high-energy age 8-10 freakshow!!!

Someone please explain to me the incessant "laser" and "photon" sound effects in every pre-teen cheer megamix.

ILST is shooting 65%. Won't likely be tested until MVC season, could be 11-0 going in.

ILST will have zero non-conf strength of sched, but looks good enough to be 2nd or 3rd behind CREI, maybe ahead of SIU...

ILST 67-39 with 10 minutes left.

ILST is the Redbirds because the school didn't want to be confused with the nearby St Louis Cardinals. But what about Fredbird?

82-57 at 2:11 2H, a situation only a walk-on could love.

87-59 final. Sham trophy presentation on deck!

Dunkin Donuts coffee outside of New England tastes like camel urine. Why is this so?

GAME NO. 26 — Arkansas State at Indiana State. This is my first visit to the House That Bird Built, my collection of MVC arenas is complete.

The weather is ridiculous here in western Indiana, I saw three upside-down SUV's on my way in. What I do for the cause.

Indiana State up early 7-0. Arkansas State is now the RED WOLVES, but their uniforms still seem somewhat... I dunno, tribal.

ARST's defense is hardcore. Won't be much of a factor this year in the Sun Belt, but will give the contenders some bruising losses.

ARST is the first team I've seen in a while that loves to take charges. In a "sir, may I have another" kind of way.

INST is figuring it out, though — just shoot over them. Four 3's, up 20-7 at 7:43 1H.

Dance teams in Santa hats. Everyone thought of that one.

INST 25-23 at the half. Gave up a 16-5 run. Their football was winless and MBB is 0-4, not good times here.

ARST became a lot more potent offensively once Donald Boone (jr-TR guard) checked in. Remember that name, Belt fans.

The Trees are getting smoked... on the boards. ARST 28-21 margin, lead now 31-29.

If INST wants to get good again, they have to change the I on the unis back to the state outline. LIKE BIRD, BABY

Arkansas State's play can be summed up thus: a pain in the ass.

ARST wins 56-54. For the Sycamores, the futility continues.

Band is good though.

GAME NO. 27 — St. Louis at Southern Illinois. Light tweeting tonight, no wifi in here and the batteries are all dying.

Like Saint Louis' offense. 13 points in 19 minutes.

SIU leads 24-16 at halftime.

I don't know how to describe that halftime show in 140 characters, but it involved life-sized Village People puppets.

SIU fans gave it a standing ovation.

Only 40 shots have been taken in this game; SLU is 5 for 22. Most of the game has been played on the floor, in the neutral zone.

26-20 at 15:57 2H. This game could end up in the 30's.

SIU 32-22 at 13:04 2H. I think the Saluki freshmen are starting to "get" the defense thing.

Seven minutes left. OK, if you remember last year's SIU-SLU game, this is where the Saluki offense blew a gasket. So. Ill up 43-33.

Lisch (SLU) just walked into an offensive foul, and Majerus got T'ed up for saying "fuck." You've used up your one tech a year, Coach....

SIU second-half offense: 5 field goals, 16 free throws.

Dillard just flashed through the lane like the kid from "The Incredibles" for a layup. And one. 52-39 Salukis, four minutes left.

Fay with the dagger three. 57-39, time out, fight song.

Hunan Restaurant ball toss. Lunardi was right, it's the best restaurant in Carbondale.

The I.V. comes in a close second. Oh, the game's going on. Liddell said "fuck," got a T,
   Salukis running up the score now.
64-48 is the final. Good night!

GAME NO. 28 — Arkansas-Little Rock at Missouri State.
Very nice new building. The Bears get a big light show during intros now.
Not full tonight, but it is a little echoey. High aluminum panel ceiling.
Don't know if this happened in the wash, but UALR's uniforms are black & maroon with
   barf green trim. I think that's supposed to be silver.
Mo St. has not sold much ad space in the JQH. One car dealership and something called
   Prime Overtime, which I think was a Diana Ross song.
All-Beer Belly Team nomination: Mike Smith (UALR)
MOST 14, UALR 11 at second media.
Fun fact: both UALR and Ark State have better records than Arkansas.
Here at courtside, you can't hear the band. Just noticed them tucked in the corner. It's
   cavernous.
Boomer Bear rules.
STF needs to get on this Mike Smith thing. A dude with a gut starting for a 6-0 team.
   That's the American dream right there.
Just as I said that, he airballed a free throw.
Then travelled trying to do the Dream Shake.
MOST 33-19, 2:13 1H.
Missouri State 33, UALR 23 at the half.
The Missouri State dance team never has a bad recruting class.
MOST 45-29 with 10 to go.
UALR will have beaten Creighton and lost to Mo-State.
UIC about to beat Vanderbilt.
That's a better game than this — MOST leads 57-33.
UALR has 2 assists in this game.
Annnnd the final is 59-37, Missouri State over UALR. Drive home (or to Kansas City)
   safely!

GAME NO. 29 — Oakland at UMKC. My first conference game of the year.
Oakland's uniforms are FRICKIN SWEET
Black numbers on light gold, numbers over names on back. Oakland is Nike's second
   favorite evil lab experiment, behind Oregon.
I am on some major OTC cold medicine, so I may not make a lot of sense this evening
10-9 OAK six minutes in. The 3 point shooting jamboree has yet to materialize.
UMKC has changed its logo again. Boxing Roo is gone, Disney Roo is long gone. Now it's
   SexyRoo.
There have been some two-point dunk shots in this game. Throwin' dowwwwn in the
   Badlands Conference!!!
Good memories of KC. 2004 first/2nd rounds, Pacific making the R32. There's a great,

famous pizza place up in Liberty I forget the name of.

If my karma is good, there's a KC resident out there who knows of this Liberty, Mo. pizza place of which I speak and can help me out.

3-a-thon... It's AHN. Brumagin 2, Kangas 1. OAK up 23-21 at 6:58 1H.

Sleater-Kinney > McKinney-Jones

Brumagin is hot like heat. 4 of 6 from 3.

Oakland is — how do I put this — not a sum of its parts.

OAK 41-39 at the break. Nineties, here we come.

The Citadel beat UNC Greensboro, first time in seven years. Mindblowing.

Saint Mary's won the G!O!T!N!, and state No. 9 Buffalo came within four of UConn. So there's that.

Here, it's Oakland 53, UMKC 49 at 15:55 2H.

On the Slingbox, my Rangers are getting killed by the Canadiens 5-2. That's your score update, brought to you by the BellyKegTM.

They take the Chicken Dance pretty f-ing seriously here in Kansas City.

Oakland and UMKC going down to the wire. 79-77 OAK, :52 2H.

"The Final Countdown" should always be played with Sketches Of Spain-style horn flourishes.

UMKC folded like laundry. Oakland wins 84-78. Happy travel day!

Final note: it's Greg Kampe's 400th coaching win.

GAME NO. 30 — Northwestern State at Miami (Oh.).

GAME NO. 31 — Ohio vs Indiana State at the Marques Maybin Classic.

Freedom Hall should be put on the Historical Register of gyms that can't be replaced.

It's pretty much the Boston Garden of college basketball.

There has been no effort whatsoever to make Freedom Hall modern, and that's what's great about it.

It's part of the Kentucky Expo, so there are horse barns literally 500 feet from the court.

Ohio 27, Ind State 25 at the half.

The luxury boxes at Freedom Hall look like the offices at Sterling Cooper.

Ohio has opened up an 8 point lead.

There is a Kentucky Colonels banner scrunched up in a far rafter. All those ABA games that were played at this place...

Artis Gilmore, Dan Issel, that logo with the runnin' redneck and his dog...

Louisville used to be in the Missouri Valley, people forget. Left for the Metro in the 70's.

Early-era ESPN was all about the Metro. All those Memphis State-Louisville games from Freedom Hall. Nothing mid-major about the Metro.

And that LED hustle stat board on the mezzanine that you could read on a little black and white TV... Still there. Damn.

Never thought I'd end up sitting front row timeline at Freedom Hall. Every day is an honor and a priviledge.

Anyhow, Ohio is up by 10. with three to go. They've been a strong 2nd half team all year.

Ind State's 6-8 dude Tunnell has 20, and has owned the paint. File this: Ohio has a world of trouble shutting down mobile bigs.

Over. Ohio, 62-50. Ind State has finals this week and will be busing back to Terre Haute immediately.

Keeping with the V Week theme, former St Francis NY head coach Bob Valvano is calling tonight's second game.

GAME NO. 32 — Lamar at Louisville. My first double-nickname game. The Cardinals will win tonight.

My next project is designing a line of brown sweaters for basketball writers.

Hoping this is still close at halftime.

This game pre-empted "Charlie Brown Christmas" locally. Sorry, Linus — in Louisville, Rick Pitino is what Christmas is all about.

Louisville up 21-23 at 9:14 1H.

Louisville by 11 at the half.

Cameo's "Word Up" still resonates at a bone marrow level in Louisville, KY.

Quickly getting away from Lamar... 40-25 at 18:42 2H.

Down by 16 with 6 to go, Lamar HC Roccaforte got T'ed up... that'll do it.

Lamar has some decent shooters, but don't all Southland teams?

Not that I care about such things, but I wonder if Terrence Jennings is on any of those power-league frosh-to-wotsh lists. He's really good.

78-56 is the final, good night from Freedom Hall. We're heading east.

GAME NO. 33 — Campbell at VMI. Making the opponent team run out on the floor for warmups to Coldplay... harsh, dude.

VMI 39-38 at the half.

I can't believe "pants-dissolving" got through the Desk.

GAME NO. 34 — Coppin State at Loyola (Md.). I'm on duty tonight.

I KNOW Campbell is a University. Find a "Campbell College" reference on TMM, I dare you.

Coppin up 34-23 at halftime.

NJIT is playing St. Peter's tonight... this might be the one for them.

Here, Loyola has come back from 20 down to lead by five. 67-62, 2:18 2H.

We are on MASN tonight if you are endowed with the Sports Pak.

Done. Loyola 73-70. And the Marching Flock leaves the hall, thumping the drums.

GAME NO. 35 — Chattanooga at Davidson. SoCon game!

Chat was up 9-2 but Davidson has slowly come back and is up 26-25 at 6:16 1h.

Curry has 9, including the 3 that put them ahead.

Stephen Curry is Batman, Captain America and Dr. Dooooom all in one man.

Chatty is shooting the 3 well — up 44-39 late in half.

Curry has 15 and Davidson is up by 4.

The Wave is still cool in Davidson, NC.

Key differences between Red Sox and Davidson Sweet Carolines: DC uses the techno version; fans scream out 1-2-3-4, and are not drunk.

Curry will someday (soon?) be a player whom nobody has to make excuses for.

Davidson is up by 10 with four to go. All but a few BCS teams would have a tough time winning in this building. Not like they'd try.

Curry made a two-point dunk shot and the crowd went wild! DAV 96, CHAT 89, #30 has 37 and is going to the line.

Done! Davidson wins 100-95 in a 40-minute defensive showcase. Mr. Curry had 41 points, which is a lot.

GAME NO. 36 — Wright State at Wake Forest. GUARANTEED to be a good time.

The Raiders' game plan in one UTF-8 character: 3

Wake is up 24-12.

Oh crap, we're on regional teevee! I'm seated near Erin Andrews Jr.

I should have worn my good suit.

Wright is on a mini run of 8-0... A little early to start thinking win + check, but the shots are falling.

Is a Holiday Inn Select better than a regular HI, or is that what they call the old ones that are in danger of caving in?

A Wake dude just dunked it and flexed his pecs, but went too hard and the ball popped up out of the rim. I want a poster of THAT.

35-25 WF at the half.

They have something called "Deacon McNugget Trivia" on the video board.

They call Georgia Tech the Ramblin' Wreck... Call me Deacon McNugget.

50-29 Wake. Wonder how deep in the notes the Fox broadcasters have gone. Are they talking about airplanes yet?

A Demon Raider would be scarier than a Demon Deacon.

I'm not one of those conspiracy people, but there is a guy who looks EXACTLY like Robert Goulet in the courtside VIP seats.

Ball boy is sweeping the three square feet behind the live sideline reporter really good. Get your shine, kid!

The WF fans are calling Scott Grote "Stephen" because he wears No. 30.

Done! Wake 66, Wright 53.

GAME NO. 37 — UC Davis at the Citadel.

We will be playing an intertronic Twit-game. I will count the actual attendance, and you guess the diff between that and the announced.

When I get the announced attendance at the end of the game, the closest guess to the diff will win. Not a Bally, something else.

I think someone should do an in-depth report about white guys who mouth rap lyrics during warmups. That hasn't been done yet.

Reggie Theus was fired at Sacramento. NMSU won't take him back.

UC Davis is No. 1 in the RPI — the Rad Perm Index. Some serious hairdos on this squad.

El Cit, unlike many schools, still has only one 3-point line painted on the floor. Can you guess why?

UC Davis scored 10 points in the first 3 minutes. 10-2.

If you're driving a grey Hyundai, your lights are on.

We are gathered here today because Ted Valentine needed a game to call.

20-8 UC Davis at 9:21 1H. Valentine was just over at the scorer's table telling those moron timekeepers how the big boys do it.

Here's what you need to know about The Citadel. Big senior dude named Demetrius Nelson, everyone else a sophomore. Get the ball to Big D.

Nelson has 8 points, the rest of the team 9. UCD is leading 30-17 and is shooting 69%.

Cleveland State is leading at Syracuse. They have Stony Brook-UConn on the scorer's screen (?) and it's saying "two-point dunk shot" a lot.

Stony Brook is not the team making the two-point dunk shots.

My favorite Citadeler is Jon Brick. He's a hard-nosed defender and decent shooter, and I like him even though he looks like Dave Matthews.

I've been thinking about the difference between VMI and the Citadel (who hate each other). VMI is good now. Does Citadel need a gimmick?

Here's my idea: the "Press of Tides" defense where they line up on the timeline and dare the other team to break the chain.

While we're on Pat Conroy books, I once had an idea for a basketball horror movie called "My Oozing Season."

UC Davis leads The Citadel 43-28 at the half. Yes, I tweet more when it's a blowout.

The tip-off attendance was 238. They haven't called the official yet. There's still time to enter our contest.

Guess the diff between the actual and the (inflated) official attendance at The Citadel. Closest gets a TBA prize, which is not a Bally.

The Citadel has two live bulldog mascots, General and Boo. Here is General's house. http://tinyurl.com/6pzzm6

In the media room, there are pictures of General chasing other team's mascots (like the Furman Paladin) and peeing on campuses he visits.

Teddy Valentine just called an offensive foul with "Ileeegal, Illeeegal"... Dude. I thought an episode of Cop Rock was about to break out.

By the end of the week, I will have spent more consecutive time in South Carolina than at any point in my life.

Elsewhere on the TMM scoreboard, brought to you by Gay Chubby Dating... Cleveland State is tied with Syracuse at the half.

Here's a name for you: The Citadel freshman Cosmo Morabbi. He's from Beverly Hills. I bet Hell Week was real fun for him.

Score checka 1, 2: UC Davis 60, Citadel 41. Did I mention I drove 260 miles for this, and will drive 260 miles back north after the game?

There's a redshirting freshman on UC Davis named Jake Ranger. STF needs to do an All-Bad Ass Names Team.

Slingboxing CLST-SYR. Vikings have opened up a 5-pt. lead with 2.5 minutes left.

Final score here is 79-61 UC Davis.

I still don't know what the prize is.

GAME NO. 38 — North Florida at Clemson. A historic moment. No game in DI history has ever has a bigger RPI gap.

Clemson is No. 1 in the RPI, UNF is No. 343.

UNF up 13-12 on Clemson. OOoooOOOOOooo

Orange. Purple. Yeah, that makes sense.

Clemson's hype man is J Dew. He and the mascot have zero chemistry.

Clemson is up by 8 now. Crowd is silent, hoping some football will break out.

Here are 5 things I'll never understand about South Carolina.

1 — Guys with a first letter, then a nickname that totally undercuts its seriousness (T. Ed Smith, R. "Snuffy" Brown)

2 — Truck Nutz on midsize cars

3 — Fatz Cafe

4 — Why the moon over the Palmetto tree has to be a crescent tipped to the side like that

5 — All the off-brand gas stations with names like "Mack n' Jack" and "Destiny Petroleum"

Clemson 39-23 out of the half.

North Florida hasn't scored in the first 5 minutes of the second half. Clemson by 25.

I just saw a stack of Gator Bowl tix. What do you think the street value of those is?

Tree Rollins went to Clemson, his No. 30 jersey is retired here.

Clemson has outscored UNF 29-7 in the second half.

Final score — Clemson 76-36.

I sat in a scouting seat, a dude asked me who I scouted for. I said the Flint Tropics. Kids like Will Ferrell-related jokes.

GAME NO. 39 — UC Davis at Presbyterian.

Tonight I've got Blue Hose fever.

Presby is playing UCD much tighter than The Citadel did. 12-8 Hose at 11:59 1H.

There was no room for me at the three-seat media table, so I'm sitting next to the official scorer. Awkward!

I have a front row seat to a major scoreboard malfunction. They had to manually reset everything.

Shooting the 3 well and actually playing physical down low is a really good combination with the new arc. Both UCD and Presby do this.

Some band members are wearing kilts, which is awesome.

Some band members have Blue Hose body paint, which is also awesome.

El Hose are shooting badly from outside tonight, UC Davis has opened up a 29-21 lead. I forgot about Joe Harden, the ND transfer. Big, good.

For many years, the Blue Hose were Champions of the SAC. Wasn't that a Ween album?

Hose run! 7-0, it's 31-29 Presby at the half.

Chase Holmes has hit 3 3's for Presby. UC Davis can't Superman these Hose. (Outdated, I know.)

Phantom tech on UC Davis HC Gary Stewart. There's nothing worse than grandstanding refs when the attendance is under 500.

Reminded of the Duke-Pres game, when Duke fans behind the PC bench collected $1 bills to throw at the PC cheerleaders. My joke was better.

Worth noting that there are some very pretty girls at Presby.

Blue Hose are now up 54-45. Al'Lonzo Coleman has 20, mostly layups.

The Blue Hose just got caught with a name that became an unfortunate slur. This nevereverever happens if your team is, say, the Cougars.

UC Davis coming back… Within 6 at 64-58. Both teams love the floorburns.

The Lady Blue Hose are playing Stetson at 11:30 am tomorrow. You're all invited!

Fans just like yelling out "Blue Hose." Presby winning going away.

Presby simply unbeatable at the Hose House. 82-69 is the final. See you from Furman tomorrow!

GAME NO. 40 — North Florida at Furman. Four-oh, baby.

Thin crowd at Timmons Arena.

And by that I mean remarkably sexy.

Furman's PA is playing some serious classic rock. Springsteen, 38 Special, Georgia Satellites, 10cc. Is that Furman Rock? Turn it UP!!!

North Florida up 7-6 early. Is this the night the Ospreys break the 53-game road L streak?

The special guest tonight is "Fro Bro", who brought in the most obvious fake ref I've ever seen.

No wifi tonight, someone check out frobro.com and let me know how to book him for my next party.

If you're going to do a fake ref gag, make sure he doesn't look 18 and have his "whistle" on a giant hobbit rope.

Furman has not beaten a DI opponent yet. They lost to Dartmouth. Not a misprint.

He's being followed around by a cameraman, so I'm sure this footage will make it out somewhere.

Small children are being scared by Fro Bro. This footage will be edited out.

I beg your patience, gentle twitterers, but I'm going to spend a good portion of the evening speaking directly to Fro Bro.

UNF 23, Furman 18 at 3:07 1H. The classic rock PA should play Neil Young's "Tonight's The Night."

UNF is up 30-23 before the second half. Which can't begin soon enough.

@frobro I know this is your first show, but we've seen you before. You're a stock character. The kids are laughing AT you, not with you.

@frobro The old white ladies, who make up most of the crowd, are scared and confused.

@frobro You're talented. You have dance moves. Why waste your gifts like this? You could be so much more.

@frobro The Stayin' Alive halftime dance is tanking. Two people are clapping along. The general reaction is "stunned."

@frobro The girl you picked out of the crowd is an obvious plant. The "broken jukebox" bit was stolen from J.J. Jumper.

@frobro You're in the way of warmups now. You need to plan that in.

@frobro It's over. Now go to the woodshed and work on a new character. I have faith in you.

I'm openly rooting for North Florida now. They know it's in their grasp, they want this so bad...

UNF 36, Furman 25 at 15:37 2H. History in the maaaaaking...

The SoCon in one tweet — Davidson is really good. Furman is a soccer team in basketball uniforms.

Just a reminder: UNF has not won a D-I road game (0-45) and has lost their last 53 roadies. Up 42-25 with 12 to go.

Furman claws back to within 10. Who wants it less?

In the next 7:23, there will either be Osprey magic, or a collapse to tell your kids about. North Florida by 9.

If UNF wins, the school is going to pay Fro Bro to travel with them.

Furman's press defense can be best described as similar to putting a flower in a thick book.

Furman is down by 13 with 3:30 left, fouling on every possession. Not nice.

Which is worse: a four-minute foulathon, or "Caught Up In You" three times in a game?

One minute left, or 10 if Furman doesn't back off. UNF by 11.

Coach Kilcullen is subbing like a maniac. I'm right next to the UNF bench. He's shaking. This is huge.

Furman just got X'ed on a UNF breakaway. Let's end this.

NORTH FLORIDA WINS A ROAD GAME

GO APESHIT, JACKSONVILLE!

OSPREYS OSPREYS OSPREYS

Final is 77-66. Good night and good riddance.

Final note: it's Coach Kilcullen's birthday today. Sweet. 1-45, baby!

GAME NO. 41 — Purdue vs. Davidson in Indianapolis.

Even the Purdue fans are snapping cellphone pics of Curry.

The game program has profiles of one player per team. For Davidson, it's... Lovedale?

Forgot what a TV delay felt like.

Curry's shot is wayyyy off. Here we go again...

But not as bad as Allison's! Yuck!

This isn't going well. 7-0 Purdue.

This might be the bloodbath we hinted at this week. Curry will need to be five superheroes at once today.

17-0 Purdue.

I'm sitting two seats away from the Davidson bench. It's already in hangdog mode. This is the quickest I've ever seen a game end. 21-0.

After Chattanooga, I thought their structural flaws would come out, but not all at once! 25-2.

Maybe that Barr 3 will trigger something. Oh! A Curry 3!

There are two Davidsons — one that stands around waiting for what 30 does, and the actual team.

After a few minutes of the latter, we"re back to the former.

Forde's here fretting about what to write if Curry can't bail out the Wildcats.

On the good side, Ben-Eze had a few good minutes, 3 boards and a nice assist.

Curry is 3 for 15 and the first half isn't done. What is this, the SWAC?

Curry might need IV fluids during the half. He looks like he's been pulling an ox cart for an hour.

Back to the, um, action. Purdue 58, Davidson 29.

Curry looks more tired now than before halftime. Did he run a 5000 meter race in there or something?

Curry just put up a no-look pass that hit the rim. We're nearing Greek tragedy territory now.

Archambault deserves a Tommy Point for playing hard.

Davidson is not compensating for its weaknesses. It's expecting Curry to fix everything. Not a good plan.

Look at Butler 2007. They had no size, but took such good care of the ball that they made the Sweet 16.

Southern Illinois the same year. They couldn't hit the side of a barn but played such good defense they made the S16.

Davidson 2009 has bad D, no size but their answer to those problems is... Stephen Curry. This has. To. Change.

Curry's 20th missed shot of the game.

Rossiter exits with five fouls in 10 minutes. Way to rep, buddy.

This game was over at 16:13 1H, which may be a new NCAA record.

I'll say it again: Archambault deserves a lot of credit for showing up. Can't say the same for most of the rest of the team.

There's nothing left to say about this one. See you at Game 2.

Drake big over Iowa, for you non-Upset Clubbaz.

GAME NO. 42 — Southern Illinois vs St Mary's at the Wooden Tradition in Indy.

Not surprisingly, half the crowd is gone. Too bad this will be a much better game than the last.

I may have 10 times more Twitter followers than SMC has fans here.

Sitting near the SMC bench. There are a lot of people talking in Aussie accents.

I used to think Australians were great, until Flight of the Conchords convinced me that they were the enemy.

Nick Evans is back for SIU with his wrist taped.

6-6 about nine minutes in. Definitely SIU's kind of game.

Patty Mills is 1 for 4 and has dribbled off his foot twice.

SIU shooting 28 pct, SMC 26. Add those up and you get a pretty good shooting night.

I've got to say, Mills looks a whole lot more comfortable playing the 2 than the 1, but

Mickey McConnell (Fr) is still a general liability.

SIU up 25-18 with 4 to go in the firs.

The Drum Cam is new. Put 3 drums on the screen and have people "play" them. So new that everyone looks like uncoordinated idiots doing it.

In other news, "Rock Band" and "Guitar Hero" have guaranteed that America will never have good music again.

SMC is shooting 20 percent but is only down by four. Salukiball is back, baby!

Saint Mary's may test the limit of our low-shooting/winning stat from last week. 24.2% from the floor, score tied at 33.

Bad day for Ohio teams, but Cle State will look pretty good if Syracuse beats Memphis.

Never mind — SMC outscoring SIU 17-5 in the half.

SIU getting killed on the glass and losing every 50-50 ball.

Salukis unravelling again. 55-41 with eight left.

Omar Samhan is having a monster game for SMC. 17 points, 15 boards.

Gawd, I haven't heard Mix-a-Lot's "Jump On It" in years.

Would have rather seen Saint Mary's against Davidson.

PA announcer just called an "over the back error". Sounds like something out of Windows.

Finito. SMC wins 65-52, but it wasn't as close as all that.

GAME NO. 43 — Southern-N.O. at Northwestern State. A non-D1 game before the holiday break.

Light tweeting tonight, because I've been granted a special opportunity.

SUNO is an NAIA team.

I now have one game of asst coaching experience.

NWSU up 41-29 at the half.

NWSU won 92-64. A few upsets coming up tonight — Corpus, James Madison, Oral Bob...

GAME NO. 44 — NW St. At Arkansas. We are on le Dooce.

It's what we like to call a change of plans.

NWSU out to a 5-2 lead. They're loose as can be.

There is a big, quiet crowd here today. I can hear Mark Adams calling the game for 2 from across the floor.

A little-known fact is that ESPN.com is internally considered "ESPN3" in Bristol.

Arkansas is pressing pretty much all the time and forced their first 10 second call. 23-12.

Kinda getting away from NWSU — 39-18 at 7:46 1H. Sometimes calm means confident, other times it means docile.

Anybody out there not switching over to a bowl game gets a Tommy Point.

54-23 Arkansas just before the half.

The only thing I can stand about this level of basketball is that the bands are really good.

A game like this gives the impression that Arkansas is awesome, but NWSU would be down by 30 even if the Razorbacks weren't on the court.

Arkansas is up by 41 and we're in deep garbage now.

95-56 is the final. See you Monday.

Game No. 45 — Wyoming vs Houston Baptist at the Duel in the "Desert", Logan UT.

Late arrival, will have the parking figured out by tomorrow. There's a blue section and a BLUE section, knamean.

Already got a shoutout from The Refraction! They brought.a sign too!

Sean Ogirri (Wichita 06) is on Wyoming now. He wears No. 0, fro tied back, and just bounced the ball off his own elbow bringing it up.

Wyoming is trapped in a deathmatch with Houston Baptist. 28-28 at 5:30 1H.

This is a three day event with predetermined matchups. Howard plays host Utah State later.

I just witnessed the most awesome souvenir giveaway ever. 15 people with two giant barrels of t-shirts and miniballs. Total f-ing bedlam.

Little girls in tiaras throwing stuff from the court. "Back in Black" on the PA. I got hit in the head by a miniball.

It's 41-39 Wyo at the half.

Just bricked a FT and was photographed doing it. Totally on purpose.

Off-topic: At a Colorado truck stop yesterday, I saw three people wearing Hollister t-shirts.

HBU hanging in, down 48-47 at 14:24 2H.

I can't imagine there are many 9-2 teams out there as bad as Wyoming. Recall that Houston Baptist is 0-12.

Bad idea: velcro-enclosure headbands. A Wyo. dude has one, and it's popped off twice in the middle of plays.

Houston Baptist has nine seniors.

Wyo on a run, up 69-60 with five left.

OMG it's another barrel of miniballs!!!!!!! DUCK AND COVER

I love it when a fouled-out player has fun with the "left, right" chant.

Djibril Thiam (Wyo) danced a little jig on the sidelines and dared the USU student section to keep up. They did, he gave up.

HBU loses again, 84-74, still winless at 0-13. They'll win one in the next few days.

GAME NO. 46 — Howard at Utah State at the Gossner Foods Holiday Classic, or whatever they're calling it now.

Out of the corner of my eye, those barrels. Will this mini-ball nightmare EVER END?!?!?

Nothing like a lost contact mystery. Everybody on the floor trying to get a good angle to see it. USU up 14-8 early.

If you're near a TV and are one of the 186 households with ESPNU, the Davidson-CofC G!O!T!N! is really good. 52-50 Wildcats 1t 14:15 2H.

I got hit by another mini-ball. Nightmares for life.

Slingbox G!O!T!N! update: Curry has 22, tied at 61 halfway through the 2nd half.

Here, it's 33-18 Utah State late in the 1st half. The second string has played most of the first half for the Aggies.

Davidson on a run, up 72-64 now. Curry made a two-point dunk shot!

I don't usually do this type of observation, but Bobby Cremins looks like he just slept in a car. I can say that, I recently slept in a car.

From what I've seen, McKillop is running more point and Curry is playing off the ball. Davidson's pretty much put them away, up by 10 late.

But no! Charleston comes back and cuts it to two with less than 30 seconds remaining.

Curry made 1 of 2 FT's, Charleston missed a 3, fouled, Davidson is on the line up three with :05.7 left.

Curry hit one FT, missed the second to force Charleston to run the length of the floor... Davidson escapes!

Here in beautiful Logan, UT, it's Utah State 45, Howard 24.

There are going to be people who leave here with 20 miniballs. Seriously.

Utah State is up 40 on Howard, 78-38. Onnnnly 2:42 to go.

GAME NO. 47 — Howard and Wyoming at the Intermountain Roundup brought to you by the good folks at Gossner Foods.

Gossner could have sponsored a bowl game like San Diego County Credit Union did, but this event is a better deal.

Sean Ogirri is braided up tonight. Better look. Once again, Wyoming flirting with a RLU, only up 13-11.

I'm really thrilled because I'm sitting next to mid-major legend Joe Cravens.

No offense, but I'm glad to hear stories about the 03 Weber State team that almost beat Wisconsin than watch this game.

Miniball hell is back. The Cache County dairy ambassadors are cute, but they can't throw anything but line drives.

Wyoming is up 48-41 early in the second half. Elsewhere, Vermont beat Colorado at the Rainbow Classic. Woot!

Wyoming 58, Howard 47 at 11:42 2H. Wright up on Cleveland State by 10 in the second in the G!O!T!N!.

Wyoming has taken three techs on three consecutive possessions. Howard is getting a lot of time alone on the free throw line.

I don't think Uni Watch has done anything with the fact that Howard's logo is an exact replica of the Buffalo Bills'.

Butler in a battle with UAB, Wright extending the lead over Cle State, and Mason and Dayton are tied up late. Another interesting night.

Butler escapes, Dayton beats Mason by four, doesn't look like Cleveland State is going to mount a full comeback.

@therefraction put up a "Kyle - Duck and Cover" sign when the miniballs came out again. Classic.

Here in Logan, UT, Wyoming beats Howard 84-75. Which means that Utah State will likely beat Wyoming by 30 tomorrow.

OK, I've got to tell you about this. Gossner Foods, which sponsors this event, makes cheese products. They also produce curds.

I just had curds for the first time ever. Wow, man... it's not quite cheese, not nearly a Cheeto, and it squeaks in your mouth.

We don't have curds back east.

GAME NO. 48 — Houston Baptist at Utah State in the fourth game of the SnowSlam
   Shootout in Logan, Utah (brought to you by Gossner Foods).

T.I. had my respect until the Numa Numa rap song.

Houston Baptist is matching Utah State 3 for 3 so far. 14-12 HBU seven minutes in.

Houston Baptist still leading with 6 to go in the first half... remember, this is 0-13 HBU vs.
   10-1 Utah State.

I can tell @therefraction is one nervous student section right now... I can smell the fear
   from across the court...

Was this supposed to be "Duel in the Dessert?" The ice cream stand is doing some good
   business.

HBU is really overclocked, they're playing way faster than they know how to. I like to call
   this style of basketball "bunnyhumpin'."

HBU up 42-34 at the half. Utah State definitely thought it was in for a day off.

USU has cut it to six. Meanwhile, I'll have miniball nightmares for life after these three
   days.

RLU: San Diego over Mississippi State. Good for them, it's been a tough year for the
   Toreros.

Utah State pulling away now, up by seven after catching HBU at the 13:30 mark.

USU on an 11-2 run, up 77-65. In the paper tomorrow, it'll look like a regular ol' blowout.

They've upgraded from miniballs to frisbees. Good God.

94-77 the final. Good night from the Beehive State!

GAME NO. 49 — Houston Baptist vs Howard at the Northern Utah Curd Challenge
   sponsored by Gossner Foods. .

I'm guessing everyone back east is pretty much drunk already.

HBU is rocking some sweet orange alternate unis tonight.

Score checka 1, 2: Howard up 51-49 over HBU with seven to go. Only one win between
   these teams (Howard).

3:27 to go and HBU is up 57-55. Like I always say, a close game is a close game, even if it's
   between two teams with a combined 1-24 record.

Never mind. HBU is up by seven with a minute to go. Huskies on the way to first win as an
   RPI counter since coming back to D1!

Just wanted to mention that Drexel beat Saint Joe's today. No particular reason.

Houston Baptist is really happy about this. Jumping around, man-hugs, the whole nine.
   1-14!

GAME NO. 50 — Wyoming at Utah State at the Aggie Ice Cream Classic.

Sitting in with @therefraction for the game.

QOTD: "Kyle doesn't give a shit about Wyoming."

USU up at the half 36-31.

Overtime! Arrrrrgh

Happy New Year, east coast!

GAME NO. 51 — Northern Colorado at Idaho State. Pocatello? I hardly know her.

Holt Arena is freaking huge. If there was a 100-yard version of hoops, something I fully endorse, you could play it here.

Stacy Draghila honed her high jump skillz in this building.

There are some arenas that have the Lite FM as warmup music. This is one of them.

NoCo up 17-13 in this Big Sky bash.

Idaho State's SOS is four. Its strength of basketball ability is somewhat lower.

We got two decent pop songs out of 2008: "Shake It" and "Let It Rock". And my God, the crap.

I really hope this is the last time I EVER hear Kenny G at a basketball game.

NoCo is pulling away, Idaho State isn't a very good halfcourt team. 47-40, eight to go.

A lot of people have problems with refs, but I believe that this corner of the country is the only place those gripes are valid.

55-55, down to the last possession...

Overtime!

They told him don't you ever come around here. Don't wanna see your face, you better disappear. Hardest song they've played yet over the PA.

Idaho State last-second tip-in winner! 62-61 the final. Tweets will resume Saturday from Orem, Utah, home of Utah Valley U.

GAME NO. 52 — UT Arlington at Utah Valley. Late because they forgot to credential me.

3 year old gymnasts for the halftime show. Easily the creepiest thing I've seen so far in 2009.

Utah Valley is NOT Utah Valley State, or Utah Valley State College. It's a new thing for them this year.

UT Arlington is up 36-27 at the half.

There are about 750 people here. I'm the best-dressed ticketholder by far!

UVU's nickname is the Wolverines. The mascot is a dead ringer for Teen Wolf when he's "on."

I've thought of publishing a list of schools that promised to cred me but forgot. Not griping, it's just hard to do the job without tools.

They have the Great West logos on the floor already.

Utah Valley on a 8-2 run, only down 46-42 now.

Perhaps the most thrilling moment in UVU history is the 81-80 win over Florida Gulf Coast in the 2004 DI provisional tournament.

They have a banner up for that.

UTA's Dwight Gentry has "Gentry II" on the back fof his shirt. What's wrong with "Jr"? Too diminutive?

The collapsible bleachers here are incredible, 10 walls of them. Looks like thousands of yellow duck lips.

Ryan Toolson (UVU) is really good at free throws. He's made around 95 pct for his career.

UTA has this one, up by 10 with two left. Very tough and athletic. They also have Marquez Haynes, the BC transfer.

UT Arlington wins 75-64! Loooong drive ahead.

That was pretty much a disappointing, negative experience all around.

Finally getting out of Dallas, going to make tip tonight.

As per the weather map, we're flying into a pool of Pepto-Bismol.

Hello, commenters: I'm headed for BELMONT tonight, not Lipscomb. No voting this time.

GAME NO. 53 — Florida Gulf Coast at Belmont. Thought I was late, but saved by the WBB-MBB doubleheader.

Thanks, progressive Atlantic Sun scheduling!

For the record, drove 1450 miles from Orem to Dallas, then flew to Nashvegas via Birmingham. Lots of freezing rain all around.

Belmont slow start against Fug-Q... Up only 13-10.

FGCU's Derrick O'Neill is playing with a cast on his hand, which may explain why he's 0 for 4 shooting.

Belmont 39-25 at the half.

Members of the Nashville Predators took part in the halftime shooting contest. They shoot worse than I do.

Belmont was the site of the second pres. debate. You know, "that one."

Speaking of hockey, the Rangers beat Pittsburgh 4-0.

OK, more non-hoops (this is a blowout)... But Google Belmont's Greer Stadium. Weirdest baseball scoreboard ever.

It's shaped like a guitar. Info screens and ads on the body, The innings are on the neck, balls and strikes up on the knobs.

Somewhere in this building is the stack of audience and internet questions Tom Brokaw ignored.

Here, it's 71-56 Belmont with eight long minutes to go.

I went to a Predators game here that first year. They had "Hockey 101" museum earpiece rentals for $5 so people could figure things out.

Sweden, down 3-1, has an empty net with 3 min to go.

Er, 4-1. O Canada!

If this game gets any more lethargic, I'm busting out the World Cup skiing chattr. How bout that Snow Queen race? The Italian Tour de Ski?

Looks like Belmont sleepwalked and garbage-timed its way to a 10 point win. Time to go earn my meal money.

GAME NO. 54 — Northeastern at Georgia State. Get your CAA on! They can use that slogan for free if they want.

I gotta say... It feels good to be back in the Eastern time zone! For a day, at least.

This Boston-Atlanta matchup will have people recalling Bird-Nique clashes of old. Okay, maybe not.

But I do have lots of 1996 Olympics stories if the game gets out of hand.

GSU plays Space Jam clips before tip to get fans fired up. Officially on my good side.

GSU has two shots at the 35 buzzer, that's it. NU up 11-5 at the first media.

The Georgia State campus has undergone major upgrades since 96. I got lost in this area a couple of times.

The campus is IN Atlanta. Between the Varsity and Turnerlympic Stadium Field.

NU up 18-8, so here we go. My memorabilia buddies were always at pin shows at the Varsity, so I did that walk a lot.

I was in Centennial Park the night of the "bombing," two hours before, walking back from a field hockey session. .

My gf at the time and I were staying two hours away in Alabama, and the guy we were staying with opened the door thanking God we were alive.

Nobody had cell phones then. In retrospect, they would have really helped defuse all the bad info coming out of the park that night.

Janning reverse layup, NU up 28-10. Don't worry, I've got material.

And whatever happened to Jack Mack and the Heart Attack, anyway? And how did they get that plum gig that night? Mysteries.

Atlanta 96 was the last Games that the corporate stuff was out of control. They reined that in by Sydney.

The Bud/Coke stuff went on for blocks around the park. I remember that after the "bombing" most of them had BS "tributes" to the "victims."

Then, a week after the Closing, everyone packed up so fast that you'd have never guessed the Olympics were there at all.

I've always called them the "Disposable Olympics." That's what they were.

We were staying 100 miles out, got up every morning at 5 to drive to the MARTA station to make a morning session. Hardly ever made it.

The trains were as bad as everyone said they were. AC kept going out, trains would stop, and the employees were overworked and rude.

NU 31-16. The legacy of that was that Olympic bid cities had to put in multiple-contingency plans for transport.

Pounce the Panther just shook my hand.

Another legacy was the organized fan experience. Wasn't there in Barca, but it was one of the (few) annoying things about Sydney.

At every 96 event: "Hey USA, let's show our visitors how we do the YMCA!" Hoops, handball, weightlifting, didn't matter.

It infected beach volleyball, that's for sure. I'll never get why classic rock and hype men make that fun. The bikinis are enough.

Northeastern up 31-18 at the half.

You know what I miss? The Omni. Built like a brick shithouse — literally. They had volleyball there in 96.

Sat in with the Dutch fans. They took us drinking and gave me an orange hat.

Basketball story. Saw a lot of women's hoops at the split Georgia Dome, which was really two arenas because of a giant black baggie.

Looked a lot better on TV. Gymnastics was on the other side.

Matt Janning has 10 boards already. Anyway, went to some US women's BB games in 96...

I'm pretty sure one was US against Australia. Was sitting way back in the corner near the edge of the baggie. It was a great game.

But the people in the section noticed that Dream Team II was sitting behind one basket. The girls started squealing and taking pics.

Pretty soon, nobody cared about the game. It was all "Ooh, marry me, Sir Charles!" Stuff like that. And these were the women.

I'd like to believe that's why the WNBA Atlanta Dream will always suck. It's payback for the city treating women's hoops like shit in 1996.

In case you're just "joining us," I'm stuck at a Northeastern-Georgia State blowout in Atlanta, so I'm blabbing on about the 1996 Olympics.

NU is up 57-44 with six minutes left, it's a garbage-time thing in the ATL.

Atlanta is also where the Swimming Pool Q's are/were from. Whatever happened to Anne Richmond Boston? She had an amazing voice.

OK, we're final. 68-54 Huskies... on to Birmingham!

GAME NO. 55 — Furman at Samford. It's the SoCon!

This is Samford's first-ever SoCon home game. They were in the OVC before.

It's 5 PM CST, there are about 200 fans here. Can you guess why we're doing this so early?

Because this is Alabama, and basketball means nothing here. The game was moved up so people could get home and watch the BCS final.

Despite the fact that Oklahoma and Florida are hundreds of miles away, this game was moved up two hours for the BCS turd toss. Unbelievable.

8-7 Furman at the first media.

The refs are in a hurry to go watch some football too. The first 16 minutes took 20 actual minutes to play. 27-26 SAMF, five total fouls.

Moving a basketball game for the BCS is just another step towards making this a national holiday like the Super Bowl. We must hold the line.

If you can't guess, I'm pretty upset about this.

Samford 31-28 at the half. I have that clocked at 28 minutes. We may have a NCAA record for shortest game ever.

We are 70 minutes into this game and there's 6:05 left in the second half. 54-50 Furman.

If I were allowed to give myself a nickname, it would be "The Baby-Faced Curmudgeon."

@HuhWhatOhOk Don't let me ruin it for you... football is one of the most important and powerful social lubricants America has.

Over! Quickly. 71-60 Samford.

GAME NO. 56 — Winthrop at Presbyterian. Hose!

Good crowd in Hose Hall tonight. Had trouble finding parking! Presby is 3-1 in the Big South.

This is so weird — seeing a Winthrop team with zero swagger.

It's all frosh and sophs. They're playing like wobbly hatchlings. Presby up 10-8.

Presby has collected over $1 million in guarantee money in their first two D-I seasons.

Last time I was here, Coach Nibert showed me what they did with some of it.

Presby's locker room has a biometric fingerprint reader on the lock, and inside there's a giant mural.

The lockers all have frosted-glass nameplates like in the NBA. They even light up, but they're not hardwired yet.

When recruits come, they put those infomercial battery-op closet lights behind the namplates and bring them in with the main lights off.

Presby is not eligible for the NCAA's until 2012.

Winthrop's bench looks better than the starting 5. Raymond Davis just flashed a couple hot moves. Eagles up 18-14 now.

Presby shooting 27% but is tied up at 19. Driving, getting to the line.

Presby's band has the balls to do Carmina Burana, and does a pretty decent job.

Winthrop up 21-19 at the half.

Awesome jump rope show for halftime. They all have day-glo shoelaces.

The Simpsonville Elementary Skippers are here to kick YOUR ass. It's on.

In the four minutes of the second half, only 3 total points have been scored.

Presby's band has a cowbell player. Relatedly, saying "more cowbell" in 2009 should result in fines and jail time.

Presby's band has THREE cowbell players. They take turns.

Great Big South pickup lines, Vol 31: "I play cowbell in the Presbyterian band."

One minute left, Winthrop up 45-44. Who wants this?

Tied at 47, 10 seconds left, Winthrop ball, inbound at halfcourt after the timeout.

Airball! Overtime!

I thought I was going to get to see the end of the Ranger game.

Oh, wifi works. Tied at 51 with one minute left in OT here, Blueshirts up 2-0 on Ottawa.

54-53 Winthrop with 3.7 to go, Presby ball at halfcourt. Inept refs can't read the monitor to set the clock. OK, 2.0 to go.

Done! Winthrop wins 54-53 and dances on the floor. DUDE you're the champs and you just beat a transitional.

GAME NO. 57 — Davidson at Appalachian State.

I know it's not "cool" to talk about scouts, but I didn't get that memo. We have one from Dallas and two from Oklahoma City.

Just take a moment and imagine Stephen Curry in an OKC Thunder uniform. I'll give you a few minutes to stop shuddering.

Just like last year, Curry hits a 3 to start things out.

Had a vurrry interesting pregame discussion with the Dallas guy about No. 30's pro prospects.

Dallas took a chance on multiple-MMBOW Jose Juan Barea. That sure worked out for the best.

Curry on the bench (for McKillop) at 15:00 (one foul) and Davidson up 9-4.

I've never noticed this before, but Brendan McKillop looks like noted Philadelphia blogger Daniel McQuade.

Curry's 3-minute break is over. It's interesting to get a whole different perspective on him...
I'll be encoding that in future TMM posts.

Curry has two fouls. Ruh-roh!

P-Goss and McK are on a 3-point rampage while Curry sits with fouls. Davidson up 19-7.
App State is shooting FOURTEEN percent.

In other news, Ben-Eze means "tentative" in 10 different languages.

The App State student section behind me is trying to figure out who the White Lobster is.
That's funny on a lot of levels.

Best sign: "Stephen's Mom Has Got It Going On"

Well, this was inevitable. App is on a 9-0 run and has cut the deficit to 19-16, 5:35 1H.

Curry back, shooting 2-for-6, Davidson up 33-26 with a minute to go in the half.

Weird sequences here at the end of the half. 33-30 Davidson at the break. Can't believe it
took 57 games to see a redhead dance team member.

Dance team is doing a routine to America's No. 1 song, according to Billboard. In the spirit
of today's TMM post... CONTEST CONTEST CONTEST

First person to tweet back a line from the No. 1 song in the nation (according to Billboard)
gets a one-year BBState subscription. Go!

Awesome dog frisbee halftime show.

I want a Jack Russell Terrier who catches frisbees. Little guy had miniature sneakers so he
wouldn't slip on the floor. Adorable.

Curry third foul, stays in. Davidson out to a 39-30 lead.

15:11 2H, Curry's fourth foul! Davidson up 42-33.

Some teams could take advantage of Curry playing only 15-16 minutes. App State isn't one
of them. 8:22 to go, Davidson up 52-39.

Will Archambault is hitting some crazy 3's, putting this away. 60-44 Wildcats with six to
go.

Curry's back in, so the scouts have put down their BlackBerries.

And he's giving us stuff to look at. He just his a fallaway 3 five feet away from my seat.
FLASH! Ah, ahhhhh!

App State's jersey numbers are screened on to their Nike unis, Davidson's are tackle twill.
That's the Paul Lukas difference in this game.

Done! Davidson wins 70-52.

GAME NO. 58 — Buffalo at Akron. I hate snow.

One of these teams might win the MAC. Pretty odd. Akron now has an indoor fireworks
display before the starting lineups.

I'll bet LeBron paid for that!

The L-23 logo is everywhere now. There's an ad board, it's all over the glass separators
between the chairbacks and the bleachers...

LeBron also outfitted the team. They look a lot sharper than in previous years.

Akron is up 10-8 after seven minutes.

Both teams have already gone deep into their benches. Lots of youngness on both sides.

Actual Akron fight song lyrics: "Ziii-ip! Zip go the Zips!"

Akron and Buffalo lobbing 3's at each other. Tied at 33 just before halftime.

Cell coverage here sucks and the wifi is locked, but it's 55-48 Buffalo with eight to go.

Just noticed that there's a banner for Zippy, 2007 Capital One mascot of the year. It's bigger than the NCAA banners.

Akron was national College Division runnerup in 64 and 72, but did they beat Big Red from WKU at mini-golf? NOOOO

The Bob Huggins banner is approx. 8x the size of Zippy's.

The retired number banners are 1.5x the size of Zippy's. This should give you a basic overview of the priority scale here. 58-57 Buffalo.

I just high-fived Zippy.

Buffalo and Akron tied at 61 with a minute left in reg.

Calvin Betts (BUFF) with a runner at :42, Bulls up 2.

Three Akron misses, abd Buffalo escapes! 63-61.

GAME NO. 59 — Oral Roberts at IUPUI. Or, as it might go down in history, the Frostbite Game. It's minus something ridiculous out there.

Fun facts: This place is referred to in all official literature as "The Jungle," not IUPUI Gym.

Or, rather, The Jungle! The exclamation point is actually painted on the floor.

And this is, of course, the Badlands Conference. Special Twit-xclusive: there's a rumor that the BLC is talking to North and South Dakota.

They's totally have to change the name if those two join up. This league would be Bad Ass with four Dakota teams.

Ooee Pooee up 12-8 early. Marcus Lewis has 6 for Oral Bob.

IUPUI has ˜ 35 cheerleaders, and one's a redhead. This is well above the natl average, and a shame. I advocate a NCAA bylaw. Title R.

Title R: Every Division I school must have at least one redhead cheerleader, or face immediate decertification and cash penalties.

ORU is hitting the boards, up 26-21 now.

Make that a 10-0 run for ORU, up by 9. This is my 59th game of the year, I've seen 3 redheaded cheerleaders. Yeah, I count.

Next, we'll explore the phenomenon of professors playing in mid-major bands. There are some gleaming domes up in there.

The Doobie Brothers-heavy playlist is also a dead giveaway.

YOU (dun na na) tellin' me the things you gonna do-for-me.... ORU up 34-25 right before the half.

I see a George Hill Spurs jersey. Awesome.

Across the hall from The Jungle is IU's natatorium, with banners of basically every great US swimmer of the past 20 years. Incredible place.

IUPUI has cut the lead to four with layups and two-point dunk shots.

I was offered the chance to pick a PA song. I requested "Baker Street," but they only have a playist of 20.

IUPUI has outscored Oral Bob 14-0 in the half, up 39-37.

Robert Glenn, a juco transfer for IUPUI, is having a massive game. 20 points on 9-for-15.

Jags up five, there was a near-fight just now.

It occurred to me that IUPUI is more PU than IU. Black and gold are in its color scheme, and the other color is a deeper red than crimson.

You're going to have to Google it for yourself, but IUPUI has the goofiest fight song ever. Especially the "power of two" part.

ORU has retaken the lead, 59-56 with two to go.

Kyron Stokes of ORU with the dagger! 3 with 1:26 left makes it 62-58.

Andre Hardy (ORU) has a TWISM tat! I would have noted that earlier if the game wasn't so good.

Free throw padding underway, ORU has pushed it to 67-58. And that's your final.

GAME NO. 60 — Miami at Kent State. Late arrival, screwed by bad GPS directions.

Kent has erased a six-point lead since I came in. 21-20 Flashes.

I always get lost when I come here. This time, the GPS sent me to MAC Road in Stow. That's 9 miles away.

Miami could really use a point guard. Watching Michael Bramos having to dribble is painful.

They miss Kenny Hayes big time. Miami clinging to a 26-25 lead.

Tyree Evans (KENT) living up to his number. Zero points on four really bad shots.

Kent's just jacking 3's. Where's Q wheb you need him? 32-29 Miami right before halftime.

If I'm making a lot of typos, it's because I can't feel my thubs.

Al Fisher's spin move is hott. Miami 38, Kent 34 four minutes into the second.

Bad idea: KSU combining the kids' put-on-the-uniform contest with tricycles. The fabric got caught in the wheels and the thing took forever.

Kent has banners for all its sports' championships and NCAA's, but has a football one that's blank. Why put one up at all?

Miami has a five-point lead, which translates into 12 in any other league.

Jordan Mincy is seriously grooving out to the Kent band during a timeout. Miami 44, KSU 39.

Miami gets a lead, Kent erases it... Rinse and repeat. Just another great MAC game. MIO 56-55 with four to go.

Bramos + 1, 61-55 Miami with a minute left. Ice, ice baby... to gooo...

Miami pulling away at the line. And it's final! RedHawks win 66-55.

GAME NO. 61 — SC State at Howard. MLK Day. Inauguration Eve. ESPNU. Let's go!

There is an Obama merch table inside the arena.

Now, usually when I walk across a campus in a suit ans silver Nikes, I get a lot of weird looks. Lots of hoots and compliments at Howard.

Specially from the llllaaaaayyydayyyyys...

Sparse crows, but big time Greek atmosphere. Handmade banners on the walls.

Eugene Myatt's (HOW) name is being called a lot. Howard is up 23-19.

Howard up 35-28 if you're not watching along on the U. And why aren't you?

HBCU halftimes are usually pretty crazy, but once the band started up this place exploded into a glowing ball of joy.

"Please do not sit or stand in front of the scoreboard." Don't hear that one too often.

The hype man just asked the crowd to stand up and make some noise for Obama. BIG MISTAKE. Place almost caved in.

Howard's women have the men beat in banners (22-10) and honored numbers (12-10).

In the MEAC, a lot of literature puts the team nickname in quotes... Like this: Howard "Bison". I love that so much, I can't explain why.

Fun fact: Howard's swim teams, who compete in the natatorium next door, are the Sharks and not the Bison.

Howard's got this one, up 70-53 with three to go. Pretty good for a 2-14 team.

The SWAC game is next on the U, I can hear them teasing it.

Final. 74-65 Howard. Happy Bison!

GAME NO. 62 — Delaware at Drexel. C! A! A!

The crowd is about three times what it was for Delaware-Drexel matchups back in my day.

Drexel up 21-17 13 minutes in.

More on this later on the site, but ESPN just let me go.

Sorry, a little distracted tonight! Drexel up 50-46 with 10 to go.

Ex-SPN — http://tinyurl.com/7tjnjn

Hey, it was my 1000th Twitter update AND it happened at my alma mater. The chances of that!

50-49 Dragons, awaiting the breakout of the big-time Delaware Sucks chants.

Ooooh, rollout! "Joe Biden had to become VP just to get out of Delaware." Good one, B+.

Still doing it backwards though.

I'm serious, tweeples. There will be no bridge-burning.

Totally removed from context, but true still: "People will judge you on what you can build, not what you destroy."

Drexel 78, Delaware 68 is the final. The Dragons' free-taco threshold is 68 points... that seem a little low to you?

GAME NO. 63 — Central Connecticut State at Mount Saint Mary's. Thursday night NEC, baby!

MSM's Jean Cajou's got some hops! Tight game, 19-18 CCSU with 4 left in the first half.

This is the House Jim Phelan Built. The court is named after him, with two giant blue bowties painted in the far corners.

The Fresh Prince theme is a really good arena song. Everyone my age knows it, and all the kids know it because of Nick at Nite.

Both teams, Central Conn. and Mt. St. Mary's are 4-3 in the NEC. It's a down league this year, which is down from the down of last year.

Robert Morris is really breaking the conference open, they're 7-1, scoring 80 PA, and just beat Wagner 104-56. Long Island is second at 5-2.

Lots of really, really bad teams in the NEC this year. Five with 10+ overall losses. Fairleigh Dickinson is allowing almost 80 pts a game.

It's halftime, and Central Connecticut is leading 29-22. Ken Horton (CCSU), who I was excited to see play, is 0-for-5.

Just struck me. I've been to 63 games, and no arena I've been to has had the gumption to play "Paper Planes."

Shemik Thompson (CCSU) in his prehistoric face mask has been all over the floor. 5-for-7, 11 points.

MSM had an 8-2 run out of the break, but Ken Horton shut the crowd up with a 3. 34-32, MSM.

UWGB up by 3 on Butler at halftime in the G!O!T!N!... OoooOOOOoooo

11:45 left, CCSU is up 43-42. Back and forth they go...

16 fouls in 30 minutes. There must be a really good restaurant in Emmitsburg that the refs want to hit...

Bernard Clinton's the lead guy, he's been coast to coast this season:

Mount is building a little lead late... up 57-49, just made a steal/layup-in-transition statement that forced a Central timeout...

I know I've said this, but a player in a conference with an RPI in the 20's shouldn't be able to leap like Jean Cajou (MSM). Pogo-man!

David Simmons (CCSU) has the weirdest free-throw shooting hitch I've seen all year. The ball pops off his fingers.

Oh, he's shooting 48% from the line. Don't try that at home, kids.

CCSU trying to come back in the final minutes, just cut it to 2 with a Ken Horton +1. 62-60, 1:28 left.

Both teams just traded empty clock-killing possessions. MSM with the ball, 20 seconds left, up two.

Cajou hits two FT's for Mount, up 64-60 with 12.5 seconds to go. NEC Thrillllzzzz

Central misses, fouls, Shawn Atupem misses the FT to make CCSU run the length of the floor, buzzer, Mount wins! 64-60 is the final.

BREAKING NEWS Zooperstars at Liberty Sat.

GAME NO. 64 — Indiana State at Creighton. I made it inside this time.

Sitting next to the Commish, so I'm on my best behavior.

I have the best namecard ever tonight. I'm posting a pic of it in tomorrow's GMHN.

INST head coach Kevin McKenna's sweater vest brings new meaning to the term "directing traffic."

Creighton is going 5 in, 5 out. Easier when your starters get 2 pts in four minutes. Jays up 4-3.

If any of my SIU peeps are out there: how bad are the roads in C'dale?

This isn't exactly the prettiest game ever played. 19-16 Creighton at 7:45 1H.

Not many people on the row like my Butler-SMC Buster idea. Logic, man!

Don't understand the "wave your debit card in the air" contest, especially in an age of HD cameras.

29-26 Creighton at the start of the second.

30-29 INST. Reminder that this is a 4-win team leading the preseason league consensus pick. Bizarro Valley!

Creighton's rebounding issues are painful for fan and impartial observer alike.

Creighton finally pulling away with a P'Allen takeover. 53-46.

Northeastern is up early in that CAA title fight.

Northeastern is puttin' the Thwack down.

People leaving here. 68-60 Bluejays with a minute left.

Stinnett with a rim-hanging T that I'm sure was worth it. Most of those are.

Over! Creighton 73, Indiana State 62. Off to watch VCU and NU.

Um, a little too prescient with all the boxing analogies...

GAME NO. 65 — Illinois State at Northern Iowa. We are frozen at the top of the Valley instead of snowbound in its midsection.

Did not make the trip to Carbondale, and good thing: that game is postponed.

Three games postponed tonight due to the storm: Evansville-Drake, Ohio-Central Michigan, Mo-State-Southern Illinois.

Northern Iowa has no redheaded cheerleaders. My theory about a correlation between that and good basketball is really not doing too well.

McLeod Center is great, btw; first game here, I've been to the UNI-Dome a few times. No central scoreboard, which makes the place look huge.

I'll say this: UNI guard Ali Farokhmanesh is no Chief Kickingstallionsims.

UNI is old school if there were 3's back then. Very deliberate on offense, and each play seems to result in an open outside look. 11-9 ILST.

There are "Beat the Redbirds" shirts in the student section, and a few leftover "Beat the Bison" and "Beat State" shirts too.

UNI might earn the historical title of "team with most wins without bending its knees." 16-13 Illinois State for now.

Quickly devolving into a 3-off. UNI dropped two quick ones, Phillips (ILST) quieted the crowd with a response. 25-23 Redbirds, 4:31 1H.

UNI holding for the last shot of the half annnnnd... misses it. Tied at 32 at the break.

For Illinois State, Oguchi has four points and Osiris two. And somehow they're still up by one. Tenuous lead at best.

Just occurred to me: am I breaking the NCAA's blogging policy by live-Twittering games every night? That would be so punk rock.

The Redbirds' big two have 8 combined points, and the team offense is predicated on stealing inbounds passes. I think a UNI run's coming.

Little kid with a whiteboard behind the Illinois State bench, I think it says "Redbirds stink." The next Pavarotti in training.

Mini-run, anyway... 6-2; UNI up 49-46 with a Travis Brown 3 (and one).

Eldridge has head in the clouds and Oguchi has four fouls. UNI up 49-46 with five minutes left.

This place gets LOUD. One seating level, no hanging scoreboard, low ceiling.

@dannyhamer I feel like Christian Slater in "Pump Up The Volume."

TALK HARD

Panthers are clinging to a three-point lead with a minute and a half left. They've had opportunities to put the game away, that's for sure.

Ahelegbe layup for UNI at :31, then Champ Oguchi leaps (leaps!) off the bench to sink a 3 at :20. Northern Iowa up 56-55 with the ball.

Ahelegbe (UNI) makes both FT's after a hard foul, Philips missed 3 on the other end, Ahelegbe can ice it at the line with :02.9 left.

One of two. UNI is up 59-55, Illinois State calls timeout so that the fans have time to gather their coats.

Won't say that this lived up to billing, but UNI is a flawed team that knows how to survive. The final is 59-55, and the Panthers are 9-1.

GAME NO. 66 — Tennessee Tech at Eastern Illinois. Late start due to doubleheader.

The "Welcome to Illinois" signs still have Blago's name on them, as of this afternoon.

EIU has a winning OVC record for the first time I can remember. And one redheaded cheerleader.

On a related note, "Cinnamon Girl" is not about redheads, it's about being high on dope.

On another related note, my awesome new fedora was catcalled by a dude in the student section wearing a blue cheerleader outfit.

EIU actually looks like a basketball team. Up 17-10 12 minutes in.

The late Kevin Duckworth went to Eastern Illinois. I missed his tribute night by two days. He died of congestive heart failure last August.

EIU has a 6-7 dude named Suljic who just dropped three sweet layups in a row. They also have Tyler Laser. Totally not his real name.

"Tyler LAYYYYYYYser... For 3!" Hmmmm. 28-17 Eastern Illinois.

Tenn Tech is probably best known for HC Mike Sutton's battle with Guillain-Barre Syndrome, which nearly killed him a few years back.

He's out of the wheelchair, he coaches using a walker. There's a TMM interview with him in the archives. Incredible man.

You know, this Mattoon-Charleston area seems so familiar to me somehow. It's just like walking into Will Leitch's landmark novel, "Catch."

My Slingbox has locked me out, so I can't watch the Utah State-Nevada game. Bollocks.

Eastern Illinois is pouring it on in slo-motion. 44-28 at 16:00 2H... Been a while since I've seen a blowout.

I think they're piping the scent of warm, soft buckwheat pancakes into this arena.

Eastern Illinois up 57-40 with six left. The closest BWW is 40 miles away. Do the math.

The student section chants "E-I, E-I, E-I-U!" When the win's in the bag. It is. 73-53, minute or so left.

75-58 Eastern Illinois the final. Butler on the morrow.

GAME NO. 67 — Butler vs. Valpo. We meet again, Butler vs. Valpo.

It's the lighting in here. Everything is very 16mm Panavision, if you get my drift.

Butler out early 10-0.

If you haven't seen them, Butler's zone is so precise and well-principled, they could stop anyone.

With the Mills injury at SMC, you have to believe Butler will get Davidson in the Busters. That leaves Utah State with Saint Mary's.

I could watch Matt Howard on the fast break all night. Coach Stevens would probably have a heart attack though.

Butler... This team is just so cohesive, it logically shouldn't have happened this quickly. Just dropped a couple 3's, up 18-8.

Valpo's tied it up at 19 with a 11-1 run. Most of the Butler starters are back in.

24-22 nearing the half. Off to do radio... Butler is one of the few I'll break that rule for, on account of longtime friendship.

Annnd we're back. Butler fans are so nice.

Butler had 12 turnovers in the first half, their season per-game avg.

Gordon Hayward is getting all freaky. Four quick points, Valpo forced into a timeout. 28-22.

I honestly never understood the piggyback Gary Glitter thing the cheerleaders do here.

If Valpo pulls this out, it would be Homer Drew's 600th win.

Butler would not face sanctions under Title R.

Matt Howard is one of the few players who can get a rebound with his crotch. Butler up 8.

Valpo: Tha Fightback. Tied at 37 with eight left.

Butler seven straight points to end the suspense. Up 50-43 with 2:48 left.

But no! Valpo won't go away, cuts it to two, free throw and time out city from here on out. 52-50 with a minute left in reg.

Butler is going to gut this out — up 57-51...

59-51, it's over. Butler fever, catch it!

GAME NO. 68 — Albany at Boston University. Took a while for my BlackBerry to charge up.

Been a while, eh? BU is up 39-25 at halftime.

John Holland has 20. We are at the Agannis Arena, not The Roof. Unfortunate, we have a longtime affection for the place.

Eek, Twitter slowness. 64-58, it's devolving into a 3-off.

It's odd seeing a BU team with a huge 1-2 scoring punch like Corey Lowe and John Holland. Should be winning games 35-32, right?

Lowe + Holland = 45 points tonight. And BU's defense is still the best in the AE! No wonder they're 7-2 and in first. 67-60, three to go.

Holland just slammed a two-point dunk shot to hurt UA's dreams right in the pants. BU up 72-65, 1:39 2H.

The Scoobs are doing their best to keep this interesting: 61-54 at six left.

GAME NO. 69 (tee hee!) — Texas-Arlington at Northwestern State.

Just wanted to note that cell coverage is better in rural Louisiana than it was in freaking Boston the other night.

Hot up n down action... Not many shots falling. 9-6 Arlington six minutes in.

Baton twirling is huge down here. Remind me to figure out why.

NWSU announcer Patrick Netherton is reading this tweet.

At quite a few Louisiana schools, a baton twirler will come out to center court and perform at time outs.

"Steel Magnolias" was filmed in Natchitoches. It's NWSU announcer Patrick Netherton's favorite movie.

I'm just saying that because he's sitting next to me. It's really "Beaches."

NWSU is sliding back whenever the second unit comes in. 39-26 Arlington.

Halftime at Prather! 43-34 UT Arlington.

Natchitoches is home to the XMas Festival of Lights, the Meat Pie, and a Sonic that has never got my order right in over 10 tries.

The town name is pronounced Nack-a-Dish. As it's 54-37 and getting worse, I have one more local story.

I was stuck here on XMas day last year, and the only places that were open were a Chinese restaurant and Walgreen's.

Nobody showed up to run the one run-down movie theater in town, and there was a line of people at the door at 12:00. They were angry.

Most of them were teenage girls, who were screaming mad because they couldn't get in. I will always refer to this as "The Marley & Me Riot."

NWSU announcer Patrick Netherton would riot if Netflix ever ran out of copies of "Moonstruck."

It's 63-44 UT Arlington and everybody in the building thinks the officials are awful.

Arlington, up 16, is dribbling out 30 seconds of clock every time down, and NWSU is too gassed to chase them.

BREAKING NEWS — This game just tested positive... for boredom.

This isn't because Will Leitch showed up today, but next week is TMM's No Press Pass Week. I haven't sat in the stands for years.

Maybe that will clear out most or all the recent lethargy.

There have been a lot of bad games for NWSU this year, but there's press row consensus that this is a real low point.

Losing at LSU, Oklahoma State, getting swept by Nicholls... They haven't been beat this bad at home in years. 83-56 Arlington, almost done.

I've said it a lot, but with nearly 150 D-1 games going today, a Southland Conference game isn't going to get very good refs. Simple logic.

"One minute left in the game" gets an ovation.

The shot clock going off gets an ovation. Okay, that was just me.

85-66 Arlington is the final. See you from Lake Charles tomorrow.

GAME NO. 70 — Texas State at McNeese State.

I'm here in Lake Charles LA with Northwestern State's legendary Coach Black. NWSU head coach Mike McConathy drove down with us.

McConathy is in the car because of an NCAA rule prohibiting coaches from attending other teams' games. There's an exception for Black.

McNeese State head coach Dave Simmons was an assistant at NWSU in 2006 when they beat Iowa.

We are in the Lake Charles Civic Center on a Sunday evening for a couple reasons. There's a rodeo going on at McNeese's regular gym.

There was a Mardi Gras ball here at the Civic Center this afternoon, so the basketball game was played here and delayed.

Because it's easier to clean up crepe paper than horseshit.

Texas State is the fastest team in the nation, averaging 82 or so possessions a game. McNeese is not slowing them down..

Texas State scored nine points in the first three minutes.

Primary tenants of the Lake Charles Civic Center are the Louisiana Swashbucklers, two-time defending champs of the Indoor Football League.

20-19 Texas State after 10 minutes. Nineties, here we come!

Texas State 41, McNeese State 39 at the half.

I'm convinced now that half of all preteen cheerleading squads are National Champions.

I've asked this before, but WHY WHY WHY do all preteen cheer megamixes have "laser" and "photon" sound effects?!?

55-55 with 11 minutes left. Both teams in twin shooting slumps all half.

Tight game, 71-68 McNeese with four left.

Texas State is getting off. rebounds because they snap into position well offensively. A lot different than the complete mess I'm used to.

Buuuut a few bad turnovers, and McNeese is quickly up seven with a minute left. That was fast.

Texas State just burns itself out and doesn't have enough at the end. Foul, lousy 3 attempt, foul, bad 3... McNeese up five, almost over.

85-79 McNeese is the final. Til tomorrow!

GAME NO. 71 — Jackson State at Southern. SWAC! Late start due to late-starting women's game. We're 20 minutes away.

Jackson State has hoods on its shooting shirts, which is awesome.

Jackson out to a 9-2 lead quickly. They are as good as I thought they were.

Southern was the last SWAC team to win an NCAA game, back in 1993. Ben Jobe would sit you if you didn't shoot within 7 seconds.

The Southern mascot has been given a stern talking-to by the ref for being too nutty.

Southern making a comeback against JSU's bench, which may be what does them in. 21-19 Jackson with 6 to go in the first half.

Jackson State 32-28 at the half.

You know the contest where kids put on a jersey and shoes and try to make a layup? Here, they have dance team members do it. WAY better.

SWAC dance teams generally have a lot of costume changes. We're up to three now.

Southern's Chris Davis dropped a flying teabag dunk on JSU two minutes ago, and the crowd is still buzzing about it.

Jackson State still up by nine though.

Jackson State up by six with seven left. I wish I could mention Southern's dance team again without sounding overly creepy.

Just want to do something special... for all the ladies of the SWAC...

The refs are totally in control of this game — calling lots of charges, bossing the cheerleaders and the mascot around, etc.

The ref just kicked out all the cheerleaders!!!!!!!!!

They were standing too close to the endline. I've never seen that before.

Jackson State up by 12 with three left. Pretty much over.

No matter the final score, this will always be The Game When The Cheerleaders Were Kicked Out.

65-53 Jackson. I think. (They switched off the scoreboard 30 seconds after the buzzer)

Watching Xavier-Dayton at a BWW in Indy while, umm, studying.

Too bad this is on Classic... More people need to see how good Dayton is

There are apparently 60 mph winds out there...

Had trouble getting the BWW to turn on UD-X with all the Purdue fans there; hotel bar is full of Dayton fans in town for a motorcycle expo.

No court-storm. Good fans.

We can't use ouer own computers in here — I'll try to Twitter until they stop me

Everybody gets access to a Dell Latitude that looks about five years old

We do all get one of those basketball grain binders, something I've always wanted

There's a giant projection screen up front playing the Big Ten Network.

Oops, Blackberries off.

I survived. Not sure I can look at another bracket for a while though.

GAME NO. 72 — Tennessee Tech at UT Martin. There's a guy here wearing #5 who's pretty good.

Decent crowd, but it's a cold Saturday night out and it's warm in Skyhawk Arena.

I'm looking for changes or upgrades since I was here. Nope, can't find any.

I'm looking for changes or upgrades since I was here last. Nope, can't find any.

Lester Hudson just jumped over the press table next to me to try to save a ball from going out of bounds.

Ben from Cincinnati is a legend down here now. People are coming up to me and asking about him.

35-33 UTM at halftime. Every NBA team has been here to see Lester... Except the Lakers.

Another day, another creepy mid-South halftime gymnastics show.

Lester Hudson has 18 points and 6 boards at halftime.

They've added greeters at the door and improved the concessions in the past couple weeks... It's the BFC Effect.

They don't care about me anymore, it's all about Ben. Get this: there's Courtside Dining, and a guy in a chef hat who takes your ticket.

The students still aren't showing up — the season ticket side is full, and the student bleachers are just about empty.

TTech leading by 3 at the 15:37 mark. Hudson is hitting, Weddle notsomuch. They need both to win.

Some of the things Hudson's done in past five minutes: dunk, floater, two steals and a block.

Hudson just leapt four feet in the air to deflect a crosscourt pass. I'm not making any of this up.

Hudson 26 points, nine boards — Skyhawks up 51-45 with seven minutes left.

Hudson just teabagged a dude on a flying layup and got an and-one. OUCH

Because it's V-Day, I'm happy to report that UT Martin has fulfilled its Title R requirements and must be given the OVC title immediately.

Has any guy ever used "Hey baby, I wanna know if you'll be my girl" as a successful pickup line?

UT Martin's got this. 62-54 with a minute and a half left.

71-62 UTM winner. Morehead State won, Austin Peay lost, Martin is alone in second. 10 game win streak!

GAME NO. 73 — Seattle at Cal State Bakersfield. Anyone awake out there?

This game is at the Rabobank Arena in Bakersfield, a newish 10K seater. They serve beer here!!

CSUB is in its second year at Division I. Seattle is doing its exploratory year and will be included on BBState next season.

Seattle was up before, of course. They had Elgin Baylor and stuff The team is called the Redhawks now .

Seattle is up 17-8. A great deal more athletic than the Roadrunners.

A Seattle Redhawk familiar to Big West fans is Austen Powers, who played for CS Northridge. He's 6-8 and has four points already. SU 23-10.

Bakersfield starts baseball this year. They seem very excited about it. First game is Thursday against Saint Louis.

I hope the baseball team is better than this. Kinda the five random guys in basketball uniforms approach to the game.

But seriously, I'm glad I drove 280 miles for this. They get a decent crowd here, but it's laid back to the point of laid down.

This is a really weird halftime show. Kids came out with giant colored french fries, then went to a mat and started doing pushups.

All this with the Darth Vader music playing over the PA. This is creepier than any little-girl gymnastic show in the South.

West Coast gymnastics megamixes don't have laser/photon sound fx. That must be a southern thing, like crunk.

However, 8 year old girls dancing to a sped up "Shorty got low, low, low" is exactly why God hates America.

The Mexican restaurant I went to today up in Oakland didn't have horchata. All the ones in Utah do.

Bakersfield is an indy, but has beaten two Big West teams, a WAC team and a WCC team. They're losing by 16 to a D-II at home.

This arena floor has the men's 3-arc, the women's AND the NBA line. I have a headache.

If your school has a cheerleader who obviously dyed her hair red, you're not in compliance with Title R. Just so that's clear going forward.

I don't know who won Pitt-UConn, but I will tell you this: Seattle U 53, Cal State Bakersfield 34 at 10:19 2H. That's real time.

Cal State Bakersfield has eight juco transfers. Yeah, that's probably a few too many.

CSUB is being blown out by 26 on its own court but nobody's really leaving. Just a pleasant night out on the I-5 corridor.

And just like that, it's over. 78-54 Seattle. Happy Tuesday, east coast!

GAME NO. 74 — Utah Valley at San Jose State. Whatcha gonna do when you get out of jail? I'm gonna have some fun!

Thanks for all the beer-enabled NCAA venue tips. Somebody's got to put together a definitive and comprehensive list, might as well be us.

Utah Valley has Ryan Toolson, who might go all craz-ay and drop 63 points or something, like he did at Chi-State last month.

SJSU has been bad since Adrian Oliver was injured two weeks ago. He came in as a transfer from Washington, and was scoring a lot of points.

Hardly any crowd tonight, it's not a conference game. I might have mentioned this last time I was here, but the band is really good.

SJSU up 9-2. If this game gets to be enough of a blowout, I'll tell you all about today's horchata adventure.

14-5 SJSU. Okay. So it was pregame and I had to have some horchata. I went to a Chipotle here in SJ, asked if they had it. They didn't.

Mexican dude behind the counter had a sad ashamed expression, like he was embarrassed to work at a place that didn't sell horchata.

So he whispered to me that there was a place a few blocks over that had it. He drew me really intricate directions how to get there.

So it's down some alley, this dark restaurant where NObody spoke English. There was a 10-year old girl working the cash register.

I asked the girl, "Horchata?" and tried to signal "large." She held up two fingers: "dos." It took me a while, but I finally realized $2.

It came from a churning machine like the kind that makes slushies. Cold and milky, whipped and bubbly. So delicious. Horchata. The end.

In the meantime, Utah Valley has dropped an 11-4 run and is down by only four.

Justin Graham (SJSU) is a really good player with some intense surfer-dude hair. He took a fall and his jersey is spattered in blood.

They're letting Graham play though, so much for that whole blood rule. Tied at 23 at halftime.

I've found that Californians, more than folks in other places, don't think the whole silver shoes thing is too far out there.

Utah Valley turned it over three straight possessions, SJSU now up 36-29. Ryan Toolson (UVU) having a bad night, shooting 2-for-8, 6 points.

Alright WHY WHY WHY didn't anyone tell me about Lance Olivier!?!?!?!?

The man is EVERY inch of 5-2. Got a standing ovation when he came in. Took one shot, then back to the bench.

Lance Olivier has not scored a point in D-I basketball.

Lance Olivier was in and out of the game so fast, I couldn't grab my camera. SJSU up 43-35 with 7:30 to go.

Utah Valley is playing San Jose tough, just killing the Spartans on the boards. SJSU is up by only two with 3:45 left.

SJSU up 50-47 with 1:19 left, threw the ball away. Then UVU threw the ball away. This win is currently available on eBay via "Buy it Now."

Toolson three missed 3's, Tim Pierce (SJSU) blew an exclamation point dunk, San Jose wins 52-47 anyway. SLO jamz tomorrow!

GAME NO. 75 — UC Davis at Cal Poly. Big West NERD ALERT!

Cal Poly made the BWC final two years ago. Now the team's in last place. It's very fluourescent in here.

UC Davis is out to a 12-9 lead. They have big guards.

There aren't many gyms where you can see the court from the street. You could watch the game from outside here, for free.

South Dakota State is coming here Saturday in the worst travel BracketBuster game there is this year.

For those who don't know, Curry didn't play and Davidson got blown out. Ominous.

It's 34-28 Poly here with four left in half one. An impressive display of pylonic defense.

Cal Poly 42, UC Davis 36 at halftime. Big West, Big Fun.

The Cal Poly media room has Hi-C Orange Lavaburst, so that's pretty awesome.

Here's a hint about how academic it is in this game: CP's band is doing a Latin-infused version of "She Blinded Me With Science."

UC Davis can be a little, um, undisciplined. Poly is running away with this, 56-42. Mott Mania is in full effect!

The CP cheerleaders are chanting "Poly," but it sounds a whole lot like "Bally, Bally."

UC Davis just tied it on a Kyle Brucculeri 3. 69 all with 2:33 to go.

If it's this exciting all the way down the stretch, I may not be able to share the special horchata song I wrote for you.

Vince Oliver (UCD) just missed two FT's with 30 seconds left, down 73-72.

But Oliver redeems himself with a 3 to give UC Davis a 75-73 with 10 seconds left! Foul on the crosscourt drive... foul shots for Poly!

Chaz Thomas at line for Poly... MISSES the first one! .9 seconds left, UC Davis tries to ice Thomas with a time out! Deliberate miss OTW!

Out of bounds, didn't hit the rim! Davis inbounding... annnnnnd... UC Davis throws it the length of the court and nobody gets it! Poly ball!

Poly inbounds w/ .9 secs left... 3 attempt no good! UCD 75-73! Big West basketball's got me acting like an animal, now here's my scandal!

Good night! Moraga! Tomorrow!

GAME NO. 76 — San Diego at Saint Mary's. If you're small and on a search, I've got a feeder for you to perch on.

I ilike how the new Gael mascot looks vaguely Australian.

SMC 7-4 early. The bigs are having their way.

13-9 SMC at 11:37, Samhan has drawn three fouls. This is on the U is you have it, and you're awake.

USD finished the half strong with an 11-3 run, but Simpson nailed a 3 as time expired. Tied at 32.

Patty Mills update — he's out of the riht hand cast and is wearing a splint.

This is a really good game. My special horchata song may have to wait another night.

SMC up 42-41 at 14:45. Bill Grier just got T'd up.

USD note: Trumane Johnson is DNP because of another team rules violation.

Carlin Hughes hits a breakaway layup, and the Aussie/Oi chant starts up. 11:34 to go Gaels by seven.

I did have some horchata, my last day in Cali. After the chat, Bally and I went to a taqueria in Danville. The horchata was smooth and sweet

There was a huge poster of Zapata in the dining room. I got a picture of the poster, Bally and the horchata.

USD hanging tuff, down 55-50. Toreros have lost seven straight and are down a key player due to suspension.

Samhan fallaway and one, Gaels 58-54 with 2:44 left.

And now, the ritual playing of "Down Under." You better run, you better take cover.

61-58 SMC with 33 seconds left, USD hoping Samhan misses some FT's.

2 FT's good, San Diego gets a 3 and is down 63-61 with 23 seconds left. Getting three good down-to_the-wire games this week.

McConnell 2 FT's good, USD busted possession, it's over! SMC wins 65-61.

GAME NO. 77 — Butler at Davidson. KEEP BUSTIN', AMERICA!

Curry has one of those cyborg-braces on his ankle, but he appeared to be running well in warmups. It's a blizzard of white t-shirts in here.

The place almost collapsed when Curry was announced. Big, white towel-waving madness.

Butler, as usual, starting three frosh. This will be a good national introduction to this team. OK, we're live!

Wanted to thanks to donors once again for sending me here.

Butler up 7-5, would be more if they could convert some steals into transition points. Curry's taken two bad 3's that weren't close.

Curry took a minute on the bench, huge collective inhale, he's back out. The ESPN ScoreThingTM is blocking Bally, but he might show up in HD

Getting a little physical, which may favor Butler. It's been 7-4 for the last three minutes.

The only Wildcat standing up to Butler is Ben-Eze, and he was just planted back on the bench. The Bulldogs are just pushing them around.

Butler 15-7 at 10:55 1H. Can I say this again? The previous few Butler teams couldn't muscle opponents around like this. They're less Euro.

Matt Howard is… THE MONSTERIZER

Big cheer for Ben-Eze's return. The only Davidson player who will go near the paint. Barr hit a 3 to draw within four… Butler 17-13.

Gordon Hayward, slight return. Curry finally gets a basket… 1-for-9, if my count is right.

Cheerleaders. Since I'm back in the south, there are laser and photon sound fx in the megamix. They don't do that jazz out west.

Big time national writers updating Facebook during big TV games: BUSTED

America, meet Gordon Hayward. Two contested 3's to put Butler back up by seven.

Gordon Hayward is a big tall Dennis the Menace-lookin' dude who kicks ass. 10 points now for him, Butler up 10.

Curry threw a pass at Will Archambault's back a minute or so ago.

Who does Davidson miss more: Jason Richards, or the Sander/Meno combination up front? I've come to firmly believe it's the latter.

Seth isn't having a good day either: ODU 80, Liberty 56. That's a final now.

Here comes the Davidson run… spearheaded by P-Goss… within four now late in the half. Curry missed another 3 to kill the momentum.

Curry hits a soft j at the buzzer. Will that make folks forget his 1-for-12 first half? Butler 34, Davidson 29.

Northeastern is fending off Wright's comeback attempt. I'm going to guess the Huskies shot really well today.

Correction: Curry's 2-for-12. Buffalo-Vermont is the next game up.

Someone asked me if Davidson was in danger of not making it in as an at-large. Um, yuhh.

"Kicks for Cats" raised 500+ shoes for Samaritan's Feet, which is awesome. We're back with the second half now.

Curry vs. Hayward…. BIRD-NIQUE 2K9, Y'ALL

What I find irksome about Davidson: Curry strokes a 3 to start the half, and everyone else relaxes. NO WRONG NO

Still trying to get Bally on TV. Hoping the announcers are recasting the game as Dennis the Menace (Hayward) vs. Mr. Wilson (McKillop).

Curry another 3, Hayward another 3. SERIOUSLY. Butler by 12… You finally get the horchata song if this gets worse.

Buffalo up 20-11 on the other channel.

Archambault wants this… anyone else? I've had two good side-angle looks at Curry's shot… his mechanics are crap right now. Ankle: fine.

Matt Howard's back from his foul trouble… and now Curry has three of those. 55-42 Butler at 11:04.

Takeaway from this game: not that Curry was bad, it's that Gordon Hayward CAN HAZ YR ASS on a platter if he wants it. Just drew Curry's 4th.

Stunned silence at Belk.

Most depressing version of "Sweet Caroline" I've heard.

OK, Curry comes back, and there's Allison and Ben-Eze as sophs capable of playing big minutes, pushing people around. Sweet 16 team, right?

Vermont's making this a real ballgame on the Slingbox.

Anyone who's watching the telecast: are they saying enough nice things about Hayward, or are they stuck on Curry's struggles? Wondering.

Well, it looks like we have a solid week of hot league showdowns this week on the TMM Twittercast. Check out this lineup:

Mon: Charleston @ Chatty; Tue: VMI @ Liberty; Wed: VCU @ JMU; Thu: Miami @ Ohio; Sat: Cle. St. @ Butler. Just like I planned it in November.

This is a week that needs an ESPN-style nickname.

I can't believe Bally hasn't been on TV yet. I'm practically holding him aloft. He needs his shine!

Butler's losses were indeed a focus thing, as suspected. This team will get up for big games. Now let's get this regular season over with.

I made a little sign for Bally. It's not working.

Nored with the !!!. People leaving, including the jackass in the 1st row who made me sit down before tip so he could see the empty floor.

75-63 final. Gordon Hayward is... THE SPANKMASTER

27 points for Mr. Hayward. MMBOW, anyone?

I love that while Siena is pounding UNI, there's a sign that says "NCAA Sweet 16 Tickets For Sale" on the sideline ad boards. I know, WBB.

Northern Iowa fought until the end with those 3's they like to shoot so much, but Siena is stupid good. Utah State-SMC just tipped off.

Holy crap this is a good game

That was the first "Coach's Chalkboard" I've seen where the CGI endline action was more exciting than the play being described.

Mickey McConnell comes alive! Patty can stay in the booth and do his Australian sexytalk as a commentator, and MM can run the team. OK, not.

Wouldn't it be nice to see Creighton fans at a late-nite BracketBuster _sober_ for a change? Nahhh...

GAME NO. 78 — Charleston at Chattanooga. Lookout Mountain, Lookout Sea.

This is where the SoCon tourney is this year, which gives the 11-6 NorDiv leading Mocs a nice advantage. Davidson still 2 up in the Souf.

Senior night here at Chatty, which also means there is a guaranteed winner in the Vault Dash for Cash. No carryover to the tourney on that.

Chat up 11-7 early. STEFF-in McDowell has a pair of 3's.

Chatty maintaining a 21-17 lead halfway through the first half. Did you know Dennis "Mr. Belding" Haskins is a regular at UTC games?

Charleston chucking some dumb 3's, Chat shooting 54 percent and leading 29-25.

McDowell sweet no-look kickout to Goffney for 3, Chatty up eight now.

Can't get through a Mocs game without hearing "I've Been Working on the Railroad" 20 times from the band. At least it's not "Rocky Top."

Charleston on a 10-2 run late in the half. Chat notsogood from the line.

Charleston's hit three 3's in the first two minutes of the second half. Up 47-41 now.

Annnd Chattanooga goes back up 56-55 with a Patterson 3. It's a game of runs.

OK, picture this: city rivals Citadel and Charleston in the SoCon final... up the road in Chattanooga! Could definitely happen.

North 1 and South 2 on one side of the bracket, South 1 and North 2 on the other. Right now, that would be Chat/Citadel and Davidson/WCU.

But N2 is lined up to face S3 in the quarters, and that looks like CofC. They could take Western Carolina and play Davidson in the semis.

Charleston has shown the ability to beat Davidson, so if they eliminate Curry & Co. in the semis, and if Citadel can avenge a Chat loss...

Reason for all this bracket-think is that Charleston ripped this game open: 81-68, CofC shooting 66% in second half with 8 TO's all game.

Western Carolina lost to Wofford 81-66, so that clinches North 1 for Chattanooga. Considering they'll lose this, that's a certified back-in.

Annnnnd it's over. Charleston wins 86-77 and remains a dangerous SoCon threat. Tomorrow, VMI-Liberty!

GAME NO. 79 — VMI at Liberty. Jerry Falwell has a retired jersey here.

VMI up early 5-2... they brought some Keydets with them to fill out the endline near their bench.

I don't think enough's been made about Seth Curry's bitchin' sideburns.

Two Big South teams just lobbing 3's at each other. VMI up 15-9 at 12:50 1H.

Seth Curry's hit a pair of 3's, but Liberty still down 21-17.

11 3's between the two teams... 37-31 VMI at 4:00 1H. Liberty may have the most curly-haired cheerleaders in Division I.

VMI's Holmes family is combining for 21 points, and the Keydets are blitzing Liberty 44-33. Flames fans are pretty quiet now.

Halftime, VMI up 49-35. A dude in the VMI section has a sign that says "#1 scoring offense in the nation." They're almost halfway to 100.

There's a little kid wearing #1 in a white headband who's schoolin' mofos in the halftime kids game... steals, layups, anklebreakers...

Last time I was here was 4 years ago when I sat in the front row with Jerry Falwell and watched Liberty play Marist. The man loved popcorn.

Back at the Big South #2-seed face-off, VMI has opened up a 20-point lead over Liberty. Chavis Holmes has 20.

VMI is now up 67-43. If you've been tweeting along for the past week, I think you know what's coming soon.

69-43. The countdown has begun. It's coming. You've waited for it, and you're about to receive it.

VMI up by 27 with 11 to go. They used to call what's coming up "garbage time," but it's got a new name now.

90-55. Liberty has laid down. The time is here. Time for the horchata song.

Your skin is so pale, like the milk that is in horchata

Your hair, so red, like the cinnamon in... horchata

Your legs are so nice, like long grains of rice, an ingredient in my favorite drink
My love for you, second only to... horchata
Thank you, you're beautiful. VMI now up 102-62, not taking out the starters. It's payback
for earlier transgressions, so I'm OK with this.
Foot's off the gas and the VMI third team's in, but Liberty doesn't want to play anymore.
105-66, three to go.
109-71 VMI with a minute left. Not the response to adversity I was talking about.
Annnnnd it's a final. VMI fans chant "this is our house," Keydets win 109-72. VCU-JMU on
the morrow.

GAME NO. 80 — VCU at James Madison. Eric Maynor is 20 points away from the all-time
school scoring record. Bet he'll get it!
Some scouts here on the row to see Maynor. For just half a fleeting second, though, I
thought "Oklahoma City Thunder" was a newspaper.
4-4 after four minutes, chippy play all around. Rowdy Rams in the house tonight. I don't
see my boy Pavarotti up there though.
Very physical down low. Juwann James has 8, JMU up 16-14 at the third media.
Still below the Mason-Dixon, so the cheerleading megamixes have "photon" and "lazer"
sounds. Looking forward to a few days off from that.
Elsewhere in the CAA, NU and GMU putting the hurt on early.
Good crowd tonight, much bigger than last time I was here at the Convo Center. Of course,
last time I was here they were playing Dartmouth.
24-18 Rams at 3:47 1H... VCU 10-2 run, everyone's getting involved. JMU settling for bad
outside stuff.
Actual PA announcement: "Would a representative from the JMU Pregnancy Center please
report to section 203."
JMU scores eight straight points to go ahead 26-24, less than a minute left in the half.
Halftime score is 28-26 in favor of VCU. Drexel's closed the gap on NU, UNCW...
notsomuch.
Average margin of the five CAA games currently at the half is two.
URI up by eight at the half on Dayton in the G!O!T!N!. I think they extended the break
here, there was a salute to the football team.
And the Twins are up 3-1 on the Red Sox in the bottom of the fourth.
VCU on a huge 11-3 run to start the half, getting out in transition a lot.
Would VCU cut down the nets for a regular-season championship again? I don't think so.
Inspired by Drexel's two comebacks tonight, James Madison chipping away at the lead
with free throws. VCU up 45-40.
Some serious elbow-swinging going on. An intentional on JMU, then a bench tech, Maynor
has four all-along free throws. VCU up by 14, 6 left.
JMU's been done snapped: VCU, 59-44. I've learned to appreciate Bradford Burgess a lot in
the past two hours. What a player.
JMU is missing two key players with temporary injuries and it shows, but Juwann James is
having a great senior night. 19 points so far.

Drexel lost by only one point to Northeastern despite shooting 29 percent. Amazing. Astounding. ODU won as well.

Maynor with one of the sickest no-look double-fake passes I've ever seen him do; Sanders couldn't finish. VCU up by 17, it's almost over.

OHHHH YEAH, you liked that, didn't you, Oklahoma City Thunder??

We're in the 21st Century of sports information, but I can't get real time internet scoring for the Twins game. Dub to the T to the F.

MIN 3, BOS 2, top 7. Don't these people know the Mayor's Cup is at stake?!?!?

Maynor leaves with 18 points (to a standing ovation from the JMU fans, BTW — classy). He'll break the school scoring record at home vs. GSU.

Scott Renkin scores his third basket of the year for JMU, a thrill for the JMU fans. 67-50 VCU, one minute to go.

And we're done. 71-52, VCU wins. With Northeastern's victory tonight, the regular-season title will be decided on Saturday.

GAME NO. 81 — Miami at Ohio. I love Athens, but I don't think the town has discovered wireless internet yet.

How much DayQuil can you take before it shows up on drug tests? The O-Zone is hoppin', Ohio up 8-6 early with a couple of Tillmanisms.

Programming note: Horizon League doubleheader to close the regular season Sat.: Cleveland State-Butler, then Green Bay-Wright State.

Tillman took a hard fall after running into the basket stanchion, air went out of the building. On the bench now.

Just a scratch, Tillman's back in. Ohio and Miami tied at 11 at 15:00 1H.

Michael Bramos with a 3 and one for Miami, RedHawks up 23-22.

I love when the O-Zone throws the big foam bricks in the air. Tied at 29, 4:40 left in half one.

Halftime, Ohio's been hitting 3's and is up 41-37.

Ohio's not that good this year, but it has a band with 15 giant tubas and a a Title R-compliant dance team. What's not to like?

HOLY FUCK Ohio got Quick Change for its halftime entertainment

As seen on America's Got Talent and in every NBA arena, their act hasn't been adjusted for years. Still, nobody knows how they do it.

Speaking of which, I haven't seen the Jabali Acrobats in at least four years. Whatever happened to them?

http://www.costumechange.com/

Ohio slowly beginning to impose its will on this game. 49-42, four minutes in to the second half.

Ohio is shooting 61 percent for the game, 8-for-11 from 3.

Charlie Coles' finger starts to wiggle, and landscapes emerge.

Ohio has a good timeout contest: roll a tire from one end of the floor, through sets of cones progressively spaced closer together.

$50 if you roll the tire through all three sets of cones. Ohio up by 11.

Bobcats lead by 15 with under 8:00 to go. Given that the O-Zone loves to rub it in, how
soon will they bring out the WT/LT chant?

Elsewhere in the MAC, Bowling Green just beat Kent State. BG is 9-4 and will move into a
tie for East-1 if Buffalo loses tonight vs. Akron.

Blowout time, Ohio up 71-52 with 1:41 to go. I wish I had another horchata song for you.

Winning team! Losing team! Winning team! Losing team! Winning team! Losing team!
Winning team! Losing team! 75-56 Ohio, almost done.

Done, and that's your final score. Don't forget to come by and chat tomorrow, 3 pm Eastern!

GAME NO. 82 — Cleveland State at Butler. THANK YOU SALLY

So begins our whirlwind Horizon League day, and our regular season finale on the TMM
Twittercast. It's a whiteout at Hinkle, looks amazing.

We're getting Postseason Butler this afternoon. Two Howard explosions to the rim, a 3
from Veasley, Bulldogs up 12-8 at the first media.

High-ranking Butler employee: "We don't have anyone in the NBA, but we have two in the
IRL." We're on the Deuce, if I didn't mention it.

Cle-State on a 9-0 run out of the timeout. This game should indeed be in HD.

MMBOW Gordon Hayward with a strip and a two-point dunk shot in transition. Butler
back up 21-20.

Officials only calling fouls on drives and decapitations.

Cle-State fighting hard with 3's, but Butler is grinding out points. Bulldogs up 29-25 at 5:13
1H.

So this is what I found at my press row station when I arrived: http://i.glerb.net/
ballycupcakes.jpg

This is what the Next Level looks like, tweeps. Once again, THANK YOU SALLY!

Butler 11-2 run, Cleveland State stuck in quicksand. 36-25 with a minute and a half before
the break.

I love that Butler's 6-3 guys love to camp out under the rim and scoop boards. Up 38-32 at
the half, 20 minutes from an outright title.

It's Un-Senior Day, but there are still band members and cheerleaders getting a send-off.
Not that many, though! Butler's very young.

Butler putting the hurt on, 6-0 run, up 48-38 at the 11:38 mark. Twins, 3-0 in the Grapefruit
League, have a run in the 1st at NYY.

Hayward MASSIVE block on a Cleveland State breakaway, they're telling me not to write
anything nice about him.

Cle-State two 3's in a row, the first by Cedric Jackson, the dude who beat Syracuse with the
70-footer. Butler's lead is four at 7:56 2H.

Vikings take the lead 51-50 at 5:15. Butler's missing a lot of FT's.

We've said it before, but Gordon Hayward is the SPANKMASTER... Oop-slam!

One minute to go... Nored just put Butler back up 57-56 with a running layup. There's an
on-off switch on this team.

Bullock missed jumper... Butler ball with 20 seconds to go! Foul! Nored to the line with two
shots, 16.7 to go!

Nored one of two... 58-56 Butler with 16.7 seconds to go and a dude who's hit a 70-foot winner on the floor for Cle-State. Dangerous.

Missed 3... tangle... jump ball! Butler possession on the alternate! 58-56, 1.2 seconds to go!

Mack bounces the second... desperation heave... NO! Butler wins the Horizon League! And there is NO COURT STORMING! Thank you, Butler!

GAME NO. 83 — Wisconsin-Green Bay at Wright State. The regular-season finale for us.

GB rushes out to a 7-2 lead, a Mid-Majority Moral Dilemma. You're in a Waffle House in the part of the country I like to call West Virhio.

On the counter in front of you, $3 golden dollars. It's there for your whole meal. Staff doesn't realize that it's a tip, not arcade tokens.

Do you alert the waitress to the tip? Do you slip the golden dollars into your pocket? What would you do? What do you think I did?

Phoenix up 11-9 at 11:41. They've worked hard to make it more intimate in here, with giant Soviet-size signage.

A: The food took 20 min., the cook was on the phone the whole time, so I paid with a card, left a $2 tip on a $7 check, and pocketed the $$.

Then, on the way out, I used the golden dollars to plug the jukebox with 25 straight plays of "There are Raisins in my Toast."

I lied about that last part. Wright State went on a 8-4 spurt to take the lead, but UWGB hit a couple of threes to stifle the run.

Every time I come to Dayton, I drive by the Needmore Rd. exit and smile.

Since I'm ending the regular season in the capital of Hoops Nation, time for a tribute to the city's rock legacy I've always wanted to do.

An annoying school paper writer at JMU asked me all these questions about what I was doing there. I asked him if he was in the Teenage FBI.

UWGB's Quality Of Armor has been very high in this game. Wright State's shooting just 35%, GB is up 22-18.

If you count the six on the "kidz squad," Wright State actually has an 18 Cheerleader Coldfront.

Ryan Tillema, 6-8 but a great outside shooter, has a pair of huge 3's for UWGB. Everyone Thinks He's a Raincloud (When He's Not Looking).

We haven't talked a lot about Tod Kowalczyk of UWGB, who's pretty intense on the sidelines while he's   (S)mothering and Coaching.

Burning Flag Birthday Suit Scoreboard: Creighton W's Valley, VCU takes CAA while NU just lost @ home to ODU in OT. A-Sun: Jax over Belmont.

Green Bay up 27-26 at the half, here in the city of Self-Inflicted Aerial Nostalgia.

Cal State Northridge cracks the tie at the top of the Big West vs. Long Beach, 95-74.

My Impression Now is that this game is going to end up in the low 50's. 41-40 Wright State at 10:50 2H, no scoring for two minutes.

In this crowded gymasium (no shortage of knockouts), GB and Wright State lobbing empty possessions at each other. 51-50 Green Bay at 5:28.

This Contest Featuring Human Beings is tied at 54 with 3:20 to go.

Final media, and the hype-man called for — I swear — the rally song. Not the Official Ironmen one, though.

Exciting finish here, 45 secs left with Wright up 61-59. Wright steals, Fletcher (UWGB) recovers... but they call him for an over and back!

UWGB fouls on the inbound... Scott Grote hits both FT's, Wright up 63-59, :26 left. GB has No. 2 seed, WSU trying to pull into tie for 3rd.

Tillema 2/2 FT for UWGB, inbound stolen! Cotton layin, fouled! With under 20 seconds to go, GB erased a 4-pt deficit in 2 seconds!

Cotton hits the extra, but Evans hits a runner for Wright State! Time expires, Raiders win! 65-64. And they STORM THE COURT>!>!>! W T F

About 50 people bum-rushed to celebrate Wright State's 12-6 season. I've seen it all.

Regular season wrap party at the South Park Tavern in Dayton. Official P.I.G. H.Q. 17 days hence. All ages show, and the band is no GBV.

Needmore Hoops.

Folks have asked if the horchata song has a tune. YES YES IT DOES. http://tinyurl.com/can7om

GAME NO. 84 — (3) Belmont vs. (6) Mercer. Not many Bruin fans made their way over today.

The A-Sun is consistently one of the best catered tourneys in Hoops Nation. All the great Nashville restaurants get involved.

Sort of a "Mercer's going to beat Belmont" vibe in the building. The women just destroyed Stetson in the first round and there's some buzz.

Belmont's band does this thing at tournaments where they play the song the other band just played, except 300 times better. Showoffs.

It's March, and the Basketball Guys are back. Their embroidered-logo sweatsuits are dazzling. Pondering a tribute.

Bruins not in a messin'-around mood. Jumped out to a 7-2 lead with a couple of Matthew Dotson layups.

Belmont up 17-10, Keaton Belcher came off the bench to hit a couple of 3's. He's 6-9! And he's a junior. Lot of roster turnover this summer.

Belmont doubling up Mercer 24-12 at 12:28 1H. Bears are being 3's to death.

James Florence 3 at the halftime buzzer for Mercer stops the bleeding a bit. Belmont up 41-33 at the break.

Big 8-2 Mercer run to start the half, Bears cut the Belmont lead to 43-41. Then Andy Wicke hit a 3, so Belmont's back up by 5.

Whenever Belmont needs it, it uses the power of 3. Wicke one and Belcher 3, suddenly Belmont's up 57-46 at 13:43 2H.

Florence hit a 3 for Mercer, it's tied at 60 with 5:10 left to go. If Belmont loses, this is definitely the upset of the week so far.

One minute to go, Mercer up one with the ball. And they get a :35 violation! :48.3, Belmont has it!

A-Sun POY Alex Renfroe with an athletic move to get a layup. Belmont up 63-62, 26 ticks left.

Florence a layup in response! 64-63 Mercer!

But NO! Little-used sub Mick Hedgepeth with a layup with less than a second left! Belmont escapes! Belmont escapes!

Andy Wicke's shot was blocked by Mark Hall with 1 second left, than Hedgepeth scooped the offensive rebound for a putback! Belmont, 65-64!

VMI on to the Big South final, another big win over Liberty.

Robert Morris, The Mount, Sacred Heart defend top seed and home court in the NEC. Quinnipiac and LIU just went into OT in the 4/5 game.

(8) Indiana State beats (9) Drake by seven in the first Valley game. Bulldogs will not repeat their championship: not a shock.

(5) Quinnipiac minor upset at (4) Long Island in the NEC middle game, 86-78 final in overtime.

GAME NO. 85 — (5) Campbell at (4) Lipscomb. They're not booing, they're saying "LU."

Lipscomb's won eight in a row and has the MMBOW in Adnan Hodzic. Campbell has the best cheerleaders in the A-Sun.

Lipscomb can dump it down low to Hodzic whenever they want. Up 20-16, Mr. MMBOW has eight.

Bisons have six 3's and a "crazee fan" section that tries way too hard to be clever. 34-25 Lipscomb, 1:07 1H.

Actual things said by the fans behind me. "He's African... he's definitely gay." "Hey cheerleaders, do it to me... after the game!"

Lipscomb three quick baskets after halftime — all within :31 thanks to steals and dunks — and the Bisons lead 41-28.

Radford beat UNC Asheville by eight, but it was much closer than that. Highlanders and Keydets in the final on Saturday afternoon.

Lipscomb running away with this one, leading 60-36 with 12 minutes left.

Mega-geek press row rumor: apparently the A-Sun tourney will be in Macon, GA next year.

GAME NO. 86 — Indiana State vs. Northern Iowa. Bizarch Madness!

Sycamores wearing baby blue 1979 Bird throwbacks. They definitely want this upset.

UNI up 16-14. The atmosphere here in STL is fantastic.

INST ties it at 22. Those throwback Bird uniforms are sooooo sweet. Even the mascot has one.

Northern Iowa is so solid fundamentally, but ISU is risk-loving and crafty... like that weird fox mascot they have. That's a fox, right?

Georgia State-Delaware is the other game going on now. Big Hoops Nation shoutz from STL to Richmond. #caa09

Rashad Reed is the 3 Machine. Indiana State leads 35-34 with less than a minute to go in the first half.

Reed another j for Indiana State, he has 15 in the first half. Tied at halftime, 37-37.

Still tight at the first media of the second half: No. 1 UNI is up 46-43 on No. 8 Ind St. Ask me how beer sales are here at Arch Madness.

Not your average No. 1 vs. No. 9 game. Indiana State up 52-48 with 11:13 remaining in regulation. Bizarchical!

RUH-ROH Aaron Carter (not to be confused with the washed-up pop hotboy) hit a 3 and Indiana State is up 58-52. Chat in 30 minutes!

UNI easing ahead, up 67-63 on Indiana State, under a minute to go. Sycamores fighting themselves, as well as the officials a little bit.

Still, noble effort from Indiana State, coming back on 18 hours rest to put up a good fight against the No. 1 seed. 70-65 UNI, :22 left.

Ballito's Powdered Horchata March Madness Scoreboard: GSU > DEL in the #caa09, HOFS/UNCW starting; APST leads GS in the SoCon at the half.

Late intrigue... Indiana State has cut it to two with 05.1 remaining, 71-69. Will get one more chance at a foul/miss/heave miracle.

Farokhmanesh fouled, going to the line. It took me a year to spell his name correctly.

1 of 2, heave misses. 73-69, Northern Iowa barely survives No. 9. Indiana State. Heading over to chat at midmajority.com... tweet to join!

GAME NO. 87 — Bradley versus Southern Illinois. Win or go home!

Back from the half, 34-25 Bradley. There are a lot of Basketball Guys milling around backstage in their full Adidas tracksuits.

Elsewise: App State > Georgia Southern in the SoCon, Hofstra just eliminated UNCW in the #caa09.

Bradley just destroying SIU in transition: 45-31 with 15 min left. In an alternate universe, this turn of events would kill my book advance.

Here comes the SIU run, Tony Boyle not in the mood to have his career end like this. Two layups, a pair of FT's, and Salukis are down by 7.

Fun while it lasted. Bradley up 56-48 at 1:44, SIU can't seem to pick the right shot. Through it all, Tony Boyle is a TRUE DAWG

A sidenote: I've seen more ref talkback to the head coaches than I've seen in a loooong time. Tom Eades is nobody's bitch.

SIU's season ends at the hands of Bradley, 67-55. 75 minute break, then we're back with the evening sesh. Where's that media buffet?

GAME NO. 88 — (2) Creighton vs. (7) Wichita State. The St. Louis bars are all using these two hours to restock.

Kenny Lawson (CREI) just blocked a shot, and he's PUMPED. 4-0 Bluejays early.

Day 2 of the Valley tournament, and the whole place smells like a stale beer. Creighton putting the hurt on, up 13-5.

Creighton has no size, they say. But they DO have a 6-9 soph named Kenny Lawson who's playing lights out right now. 8 pts, CU up 19-14.

Huge "Let's Go Jays" chant goes up, SpongeBob ShockerPants covers his ears. Creighton up 33-23 just before the break.

Creighton wants to end this right NOW. Lawton with a sickkkk two-point dunk shot out of the break and the Bluejays are up 41-24.

JMU destroyed W&M; in the #caa09, Wright State beats Milwaukee in the HL to face Butler, Charleston beat UNCG.

Pillowfight Friday update: Loyola 26, Canisius 23 1H (MAAC), Hartford 41, Maine 30 2H (A-East). #pillowfightfriday

Watching the Done Ruthless show on Slingbox. Hudson has 25 of UTM's 40!

Cornell is on the verge of winning the Ivy.

Creighton has let an 18-point lead go down to six. 1:56 remaining, 59-53.

Refs giving UT Martin every chance to win, but Skyhawks can't make free throws. Doesn't look like Done Ruthless will make the Dance.

UT Martin: NIT. Morehead State: first title shot since 1984. Belmont: OUT. This is where the emotions start getting weird.

Wichita State battling to the end. Down by four with the ball, 18 seconds left.

Wichita has the ball back after two made free throws... time out, :08 left, Creighton up by just two!

Wichita outrebing Creighton 47-25. Clock reset 12.2 seconds, CREI 61, WICH 59....

Murry a 3!!!!!!!! WICHITA WINS!!! BIZARRO VALLEY STRIKES AGAIN!

Hold everything! The officials are putting 1.9 back on the clock, Creighton has it under their own basket...

WOODFOX HITS A J! CREIGHTON WINS!!! BIZARRO VALLEY STRIKES AGAIN!

Every Creighton fan needs to put the following names on their Christmas card list: Mike Sanzere, David Hall and Ted Hillary. All I'm saying.

GAME NO. 89 — (3) Illinois State vs. (6) Evansville. Ref Madness.

The Wichita fans just had their hearts ripped out Temple of Doom-style, but their fan section is still 2/3 full. Can your tourney do that?

Somebody needs to tell the truth about Ace Purple and his true identity/occupation. If it were to be me, I wouldn't live very long.

Ill. State is soooo good... up 11-4 early. Put them in the 2008 Anaheim Classic or Old Spice Thing or whatever, and we're talking different.

Illinois State cakewalking 28-19. Least threatening mascot in the Valley. So cuuute!

Evansville's mascot, on the other hand, would use his cane to connect your eye socket to your parietal lobe. Don't touch his "girls"!!

Taking nominations for the All-Bad Sportswriting Team, players whose names = terrible lede puns. Shy Ely (EVAN) and Dionte Christmas (TU)...

Evansville's snuck out in front 40-39. Shy Ely has 20 points. He has NOT been bashful, ladies and germs.

YES we have a WCC tourney mobile! You know, for kids! http://twitpic.com/1w9ex

SoCon winners: App St., CofC, Elon, Samford. CAA: Ga St, Hofstra, JMU, Towson. OVC final: Morehead/Peay. A-Sun final: Jax/ETSU.

Redbirds floating along, up by 9 with 3:10 to go. Eldridge and Oguchi have combined for 31, and when that kind of thing happens they win.

Evansville's season is over, Ill State advances 78-68. All top seeds through in the Valley...

back tomorrow for more.

Dick Enberg just walked through a crowd of fans, completely unrecognized.

Taco B.. http://tinyurl.com/bnjas7

GAME NO. 90 — Northern Iowa vs. Bradley. BAD INTERNET.

Bradley out to an early lead, but Les got t'ed up and UNI chipped away with free throws. 19-18 Bradley at 8:15 1H.

(7) Albany dumped (2) Vermont in the A-East (on its home court), Davidson trying to break away from App State in the SoCon qtrs.

Bradley fans outnumber UNI fans about 10-1, but there are still lots of Wichita fans wearing their colors. That's why this league rules.

Heading towards halftime here, UNI and Bradley exchanging paint points. 31-30 UNI at :55.5.

Elsewhere: Hofstra leading ODU in the 4/5 Game of #caa09 Doom. Davidson by 10 at halftime over App in the SoCon quarters.

Bradley held the ball for 30 seconds but couldn't make a play. 32-32 at the half.

Sitting next to Andy Pawlowski, played for Drake, working on Nike youth initiatives now. Only person I've sat with who's heard of Twitter.

Forgot to mention that Lipscomb and Campbell's bands lobbed "Holiday" at each other all Thurs. UNI band playing the extended remix now.

When "American Idiot" came out, I had no idea that it would spawn the most overused "cool" college band song since "Crazy Train."

Arena just had a "who am I" contest where all the clues were for Ben Jacobson but the picture on the screen was of Jamal Tatum. Awkward!

Adam Koch (UNI) is playing out of his freaking mind in this tourney. Just hit a huge 3, UNI is up 43-40 at 14:21 2H.

Midwesterners and Kiss Cams... I will never understand.

UNI pulling away with — gasp — 3-pointers. 51-44 Panthers at 9:34 2H.

Davidson > App State in the SoCon qtrs; UMass beats URI in the A-14. This is good news... FOR SOUTHERN ILLINOIS!

Koch another 3... he's got 20 points! UNI up 13 on Bradley at 5:31... Braves are not what you'd call a "run response" team.

Slingboxing the HOFS-ODU game #caa09. The production values are so bad on the telecast, it looks like it's being played in someone's closet.

Bradley players seem to be more interested in making SportsCenter than winning this game. UNI 66-52 at 3:54 2H.

Weird game. Bradley had 24 minutes' worth of hustle, UNI was its solid, steady, boring self throughout. 2 mins left, UNI by 13.

I propose the #caa09 hashtag be changed to #caa85, because this looks like it's on Betamax. ODU/HOFS down to the wire.

10.4 left in the #caa09 game, ODU is staying just ahead during the foul-off... 52-51 with ODU inbounding.

ODU survived always-dangerous 4/5 #caa09 game. Last few seconds were Alvin Ailey performance art. We just went final here, 76-62 UNI.

GAME NO. 91 — (2) Creighton vs. (3) Illinois State. Big time.

Each of the 3 low seeds so far in the A-East won. VMI/Radford tied in the second half, Charleston big over W. Carolina in the SoCon early.

Illinois State got out to a huge lead here, 14-3... Creighton's picking away at it, down 17-9 at the second media.

Holey moley! Illinois State out to a 24-9 lead, doing whatever they want whenever.

Major blowout in progress here in St. Louis, Illinois State up 34-15.

Creighton went 7-for-32 for the first half. 39-20 Illinois State as the second half gets underway.

Congratulations Radford for making the NCAA Tournament for the first time since 1998. #bigdance

Appears to be the game that'll carve out a place for Osiris Eldridge in the all-time Valley pantheon. 21 pts including some ridiculous 3's.

Higher seeds are 0-6 in Albany (MAAC/A-East). Jacksonville trying to climb back into A-Sun title game with ETSU.

Looking at Zapruder snapshots of the Creighton-Wichita ending with the commish.

Bench-emptying time. 1:28 remaining, 69-46 Illinois State. The Valley will get one bid.

73-49 Ill State. YES they could have scheduled up and played top 50 teams, or played in a real MTE. BUT THEY DIDN'T. And they're real good.

Feel bad for Cliff Warren, but ETSU is the only team in the A-Sun that could pull an upset.

Median age of present ETSU fans too high for courtstorming. Congrats on first A-Sun title. #bigdance

GAME NO. 92 — (1) Northern Iowa vs. (3) Illinois State. TITLE GAME.

Trying to get Bally on CBS. Second row, just slightly left of halfcourt.

So far, a Bird-Nique thing between Emmanuel Holloway and Kwadzo Ahelegbe. UNI 10-6.

UNI so solid, Illinois State inherited everyone-for-themselves mode that Creighton fell into yesterday. 20-12 at 7:42 1H.

Halftime. UNI up 27-19 in a grit-fest.

Osiris has been held completely scoreless, and Oguchi has 5. Remember what happens when both don't score in double figs (hint: they lose)

Osiris with a runback and megaDUNK to draw Illinois State within six at 29-23.

Illinois State MASSIVE run just stopped by an Ahelegbe 3. 31-28 at 16:25.

Eldridge just unleashed a loooong 3 with an arc that looked just like his mohawk. 37-37 at 9:41 2H.

Eldridge with another 3... and a BLOCK on 7-1 Eglseder... AND ANOTHER 3!!!! ISU up 43-40, and this is Tha Takeover.

Osiris: UNFUCKINGCONSCIOUS

Three minutes to go, and I don't know which side of the floor to go towards.

:53 to go, and I don't know which side of the floor to go towards.

Overtime in St. Louis!

The big question: is CBS holding up Duke-Carolina for the end of this game?

Huge pileup, Eldridge limps off the court... Holloway at the line, sinks both. 55-51 ILST.

Farokhmania! Two 3's in OT, UNI hanging close.

Confirmed: CBS staying in the Valley. ENJOY SOME REAL BASKETBALL, YOU ACC FUCKTARDS

Eldridge hobbling, being attended to in the timeout huddle. 57-54 ILST at 1:46.

Another floor-storming injury. Slipped on a puddle on the breakout, and my left knee has a softball-size bruise. Fitting that it's PURPLE.

Injury update: 4-6 weeks. Kidding, knee is just ugly and sore. Will be ready for another floorstorm on Tuesday.

All mid-major conference seedings final: http://www.bbstate.com/stan...

Bally loves floor storming! http://twitpic.com/1y0vv

Winarzzzz: Bingo and UMBC go to the A-East title game; PL: American/Holy Cross; VCU through in CAA; Robert Morris to the NEC championship.

SoCon: Davidson out, as Charleston marches on. Siena wins easily in the MAAC, George Mason scrapes by in the CAA.

GAME NO. 93 — (1) Western Kentucky vs. (4) North Texas. We're in HOT (78 degrees) Springs, Arkansas! YEEEEEEEhooooooooooooooooooooo!

Still don't know why we're doing this in the middle of nowhere in a weird convention center. Even well-traveling WKU only sent about 2,500.

"OMV": It's either Orlando Mendez-Valdez or Orchestral Maneuvers in the Van.

Seriously, horrible venue. I can't hear anything the PA guy is saying, and the scoreboards only have score, time, period, fouls, timeouts.

First media, WKU up 11-9.

Sally a circus pass in the paint to Evans for a layup, WKU up 18-13 at 12:11 1H.

Western KY and North Texas trading 3's... 26-23 Toppers at the eight minute mark.

If you have a Ford garblerarble with Arkansas license plate pfftxxxxcchhh, your lights are on. #suckypasystems #fail

Someone needs to put a stopwatch on Josh White's (UNT) shot hangtime when he puts up threes. Dude fires bullets. Tied at 28, 5:31 1H.

UNT's backcourt shooters are on like Pong. 36-29 Verdant Viciousness at 3:46 1H.

Say, this Kerusch feller is quite a player. WKU is chipping away at the lead, 38-35 North Texas at the half.

Kerusch has 12 for WKU, Hilltoppers putting on some aggressiveness to start the half. 42-39 North Texas 16:36 2H.

North Texas' cheerleaders have a lot of — how shall I phrase this — frontonkadonk.

Elsewhere: Chatty leads CofC late, VCU about to go back to the Dance out the CAA, Bison Fever! closing out SUU in the Badlands semis.

Major open-court collision between Sally (WKU) and Dennis (UNT). Both are still down on the floor.

Both players going to the locker room. That was a crazy crash. WKU is up 51-48 at 9:00.

Congrats VCU and Chattanooga! Good night for teams that wear yellow.

Kerusch a tapback, that's 17 for him. Western Kentucky leading 56-53 at 6:03 2H.

Slaughter two HUGE 3's in a row... WKU building a lead here. 64-58 at 3:08 2H.

There's a Don Imus lookalike contest on press row, or Tracy Ringolsby is taking any gig he can find.

WKU has this salted away at 68-61, 1:21... now to figure out how to get a picture of Bally with Big Red.

"Kentucky Fried Eagle" chant starts in the WKU student section. 74-70 Hilltoppers with 14 seconds to go, please enjoy some foul shooting.

Ballgame. Western Kentucky on to the Sun Belt final, 77-70 over North Texas. Semifinal #2 coming up!

GAME NO. 94 — (6) South Alabama vs. (2) Arkansas-Little Rock. Sun Belt semi No. 2!

I'll have to get Big Red tomorrow before the game. He grabbed his duffel bag and was Audi 5000 as soon as it was over.

I've counted four big screen ads for Hot Springs' Gangster Museum. Tee hee! http://www. tgmoa.com/

Cheerleaders on CoolerScooters! Team USA up 10-3 at 15:45 1H.

Cheerleaders on CoolerScooters is definitely the 2009 version of the "Frankenchrist" album cover.

Updatez: Gonzaga 55, Saint Mary's 33 at 14:38 2H (WCC final); Oakland 38, S. Dakota St 18 at halftime (Badlands semis)

Slight spoiler: this week's Bally contest was a total 30-point blowout, and I think this is a milestone: the first female Bally winner.

No. 6 South Alabama up 17-5 on No. 2 UALR. The Trojans look pretty gassed.

Mike Smith with the momentum-breaker! Did you see him bounce that defender off his belly?!!?

The only drama in this game right now is whether or not Bally's going to get on TV. 27-17 South-In-Your-Mouth at 3:05 1H.

Annnd whether or not Mike Smith is going to eat Bally.

Halftime... 32-19 USA. Bryan Sherrer, a guy I haven't seen play before, is getting hot from 3.

Congrats to Gonzaga, which just completed a blowout of Saint Mary's. Mills held to 5. Gaels at mercy of the bubble, but probably safe.

SMC backcourt collapsed, basically: SEVEN field goals from guards. Simpson and Samhan did it all, outrebounded Zags too.

Saint Mary's guards: 7-for 33. That's 21 percent.

I stormed the court with Siena last year and twisted my ankle. Memories...

Mike Smith and his gut on a dude constitutes a double-team. Team USA up 36-26 at 12:32, it's turned into something of a slog.

In 15 minutes of second-half "action," UALR has outscored South Alabama 11-8. 40-30 Jaguars.

Zzzzz.. whut? Annnnd it's over, USA wins 54-44, moves on to play Western Kentucky tomorrow at 9 local time. The No. 6 seed is in the final!

Bally loves the excitement of March basketball as much as anyo.. http://tinyurl.com/cvp8sa

GAME NO. 95 — (6) South Alabama vs. (1) Western Kentucky. This is the night Bally
   becomes a big TV star F'REALZ
On the ESPN2 telecast tonight, look right above the "I" in "Championships."
Elsewise: NDSU 66, Oakland 64.... BISON FEVER! Butler leads Cle-State at halftime.
The refs are playing with Bally!
http://bisonfever.ytmnd.com/
Bally is at the scorer's table, over the "P" in Championships. WKU out to a HUGE 6-0 lead,
   Team USA seems quite overwhelmed.
I'm on press row in my Grey SuitTM, I bribed the official scorer to let Bally sit with him.
   OK, just being able to sit with Bally was enough.
Coleman just scored two buckets, first for USA. Steffphon Pettigrew has nine already for
   WKU. 11-4 Tops.
WKU fans used the day to make lots of signs! Not to get all Billy Packer on you, but S.
   Alabama might not have it in them. 19-6 at 11:57 1H.
WKU student has a sign that says, "USA, where are your fans?" Good ? — I see about 30. If
   Jags come back and win: weakest court storm ever?
Still don't know whether to hope for Butler (high seed) or Cleveland State (2-bid HL). Kind
   of a win-win from this perspective.
It's 35-25 WKU here in Hot Springs... Bally's moving back to my side of the floor (the near
   side).
Hopefully Bally'll be visible lower screen when WKU is on offense in the second half.
If I can get my tie 60 min of CBS in the Davidson-Kansas game, I can get Bally on ESPN2.
   I'm a good agent, but he might trade me for Boras.
Do you want MEAC scores? YOU GOT EM: (7) Hampton 51, (10) Delaware State 32; (8)
   Florida A&M; 71, (9) Howard 58
What a finish in Indy!!! Butler got three chances to win with a 3, Cleveland State is
   dancing! Two-bid Horizon!!! Gary Waters: waterworks!
WE DID IT!!!
Meanwhile, USA has come out of the break with a little basktball juice in their bellies.
   WKU lead cut to 4!
South Alabama on a 13-2 run, leads 38-37! Is there a Bally Hex over the Hilltoppers?
WKU 1-for-8 from floor since Bally appeared on screen. CONSIDER: Last March, Sweet 16
   plane malfunctioned when Bally & I got to BG airport.
CONSIDER: I had a pic of Big Red and Bally lined up before the game, but my camera
   malfunctioned and didn't focus correctly.
WKU jumps back up 51-46. Was just kidding, there's no Bally curse. At least I hope not... I
   want to avoid any/all kidnappings in the future.
Elsewhere: Montana State takes down top seed Weber State in the Big Sky semis, 70-61...
   final tomorrow is Portland State vs. MSU...
Estimated attendance in Ogden tomorrow: 12
Just announced that the Sun Belt men's tourney attendance is the highest since 2003. Look

at this 2/3 empty building. Whuuu?!

OMV with the daggahhhh. 60-53 Western Kentucky, under three left in the Sun Belt title game.

WKU looks ready to win. Jacket's off, I'm getting ready to, um, "document" this.

:22 left; 62-56 WKU. Signing off for now.

#FAIL WKU fans didn't even attempt a floor storm. One glare from a security guard, and the entire student section backed off. #FAIL #FAIL

Very subdued celebration, considering. Congratulations to Ken McDonald, the happiest man in the building by about 3 jigowatts.

Sorry you couldn't make it to wherever this is, Most of Bowling Green. Hope you're celebrating.

Asshole cop chased WKU fans who were trying to get on the floor. He's off duty now, and the kids are partying on the court. DAMN THE MAN

Some are still under the impression that this is just an.. http://tinyurl.com/dx39h8

I lovelovelove that Bally got face time on SportsCenter, and the closest I ever came was a phoner :)

HOT SPRINGS, Ark. — With our third-to-last GMHN of Season 5, we .. http://tinyurl.com/bxeozf

GAME NO. 96 — (2) Nicholls State at (7) Texas State, Southland quarters. After an act of Congress, finally got a WEP password.

Lot more charming and well-organized than the SBC — folks put out color-appropriate pompoms for the fans of the 4 schools in the session.

Texas State leading 49-45 at 13:09 2H. Been to T-Dough before, but didn't know the Nicholls St. student paper was the Nicholls Worth. Cute!

The wireless here only loads two out of every three pages/images/anything. Sorry again about the chat postponement.

Nicholls back in lead 54-53. OK, reason chat was ppd. = the Katy school dept's WebSense blocks TMM for "unsuitable content." Lollycopter!

I'm assuming that my site's being blocked here because Bally gets naked sometimes in the cartoons.

Nicholls on a 12-4 run with four left, up by six, looks like Texas State only had 35 minutes' worth of basktball juice again.

Nicholls State through to the semis of the SLC over Tex St, 80-75. Texas-S.A. has a cool bird/bug mascot that's supposed to be a Roadrunner.

GAME NO. 97 — (3) Sam Houston State vs. (6) Texas-San Antonio... Southland quarters... Katy, Texas. Bearkats. Roadrunners. Who you got!?

UTSA jumped out to a big 18-9 lead, but Sam Houston is storming back with a bunch of transition junk. 23-22 at 6:12 1H.

DeLuis Ramirez (SAMH) with a buzzer-beating 3 at the half! UTSA is up 34-30.

It's turning into a 3-fest, but a very well-executed one. Both teams running plays and getting open looks. UTSA is up 48-41 at 15:05 2H.

5:12 to go here in Katy, UTSA holding on with a 61-54 lead. Four Runners in double-figures, and they're sharing the luv.

#6 UTSA extending the lead out to doubles, it's 69-58 with three to go over #3 Sam Houston. Looks like Bob Marlin's stuck in Huntsville.

Bigg Sexii at the line for UTSA putting delicious icing on this game. UTSA advances 83-74, will play NIcholls tomorrow in the semis.

GAME NO. 98 — (1) Stephen F. Austin vs. (8) Southeastern Louisiana. Southland quarters. Oh yeah.

Eric Bell is every inch of 5-3. Man among boys out there. SFA out to a 9-2 lead early.

SFA band was playing contempo-jazz nuggets like "Vehicle" and "Slammin'," but then busted out "Hot & Cold." Good job. SFA 29-24, 3:26 1H.

37-28 Stephen F. at halftime. Getting awesome Bally pix.

Not to be outdone by the currentness of SFA's band, SE La. drops "Party Like a Rockstar." An attempt at it, anyway. 46-39 SFA, 14:56.

Elsewise: A-14: Xavier and Temple advance. NMSU and Utah St. into the WAC semis.

Game No. 100 will be Ball State-Buffalo MAC semi tomorrow.

On press row discussing Shawn Atupem's Cameo/Ewing/Gerald Levert hairstyle from last night's NEC game. WORD UP http://twitpic.com/21lju

We're getting a superstar 3 exhibition from Josh Alexander (SFA) tonight. 25 points. This is pretty much over, 61-52 Lumberjacks at 1:26.

Shock in from the A-14... Rhode Island goes down to Duquesne. One plausible three-bid scenario left: Temple beats Xavier and Dayton.

We're singing Cameo songs on the row, but we can't get the proper lyrics to "Candy" because of the restrictive Chinese Olympic filter.

That's it... game three of four finished. SFA advances by a 67-56 score, will play A&M-Corpus; Christi/Texas Arlington winner tomorrow.

Getting the impression that we should be referring to them as "A&M; Corpus Christi." That's the way it was at the mock selection too.

GAME NO. 99 — (4) [Texas] A&M; Corpus Christi vs. (5) Texas-Arlington. The last Southland quarterfinal.

OK, everyone who wants some Bally Southland style, here you go! http://twitpic.com/21nkh

Marquez Haynes massssive oooooop for Arlington... up 20-18 with 6:28 remaining in the first half.

Marquez Haynes just personally erased a five-point Corpus Christi halftime lead with a couple of 3's. TAMCC 36, Arlington 36 at 16:21.

Texas fans do the "Hook 'Em Horns" hand sign. Texas A&M; Corpus Christi has picked up the "hang loose." They're Islanders.

Conspiracy theory: Izzy the Islander is actually a Scooby-Doo villain. Ruh-roh, it's Old Man Wickles underneath! http://tinyurl.com/ddu7jw

UTA HC Scott Cross suspended Ro'ger Quignard (12.6 ppg) for a TRV. The right way to do it, though it risks a loss. TAMCC 60-50, 7:48 2H.

But Southland TMM POY Anthony Vereen engineering a comeback! Corpus lead down to six.

Vereen has scored the last seven points for UTA, the Corpus lead is now three with 3:37 left. T! M! M! ... P! O! Y!

Elsewhat: Dayton survives Richmond 69-64 in the Atlantic 4... and gets Duquesne in the semis. An NCAA bid is the Flyers' to lose, basically.

MEAC was getting too chalky, anyway. Coppin State takes out No. 4 North Carolina A&T; to move into a 2008 CG rematch with Morgan in semis.

This here might be outside Arlington's reach, but it's Foul Time and that's where the magic is real. TAMC 74, UTA 69 with one minute to go.

Corpus' Horace Bond has a big tat on his shoulder that says "Game Ova." Just missed a FT that would have iced this... oops!

Corpus misses 2 more FT's, 18.7 seconds left, Haynes (35 pts.) going to the line! TAMC up by four!

GAME OVA. Corpus Christi 79, Arlington 72. Your SLC semis: SFA/Corpus; Nicholls/San Antonio. One's going to the Dance!

I go, and it is done; the bell invites me. Flying to Columbus tomorrow, in Cleveland for the MAC tourney this weekend.

GAME NO. 100 — Buffalo vs. Ball State, MAC semis. Did it again.

SHOKK OMG: Temple over Xavier in the Atlantic 3.

Winnarz: American repeats PL! Morgan > Coppin, MEAC semis (SC State/Norfolk u/w); Jackson > PVAM in SWAC; SLC: 6 UTSA (upset) > 2 Nicholls

One thing: the Q dropped "The Diff" from the scoreboard since 2 years ago ($hscore-$vscore), hopefully to promote math skills for kids

Buffalo up by 11 with 20 secs left, fans chanting "Just like foop-ball." What does that mean? I don't get it.

Trying to convince Mark Adams to come to our PIG Party. Wish me luck!

GAME NO. 101 — (1) Bowling Green vs. (5) Akron, MAC semifinals at Cleveland. Unfalconbelieveable.

Xavier turned it over on one of every five possessions today vs. TU. Told you that bad ballhandling would hurt X in one-and-done situations.

Here, it's 10-6 Akron. Bowling Green not quite in the building yet.

Why is BG playing so frustrated? Down 12-9, body language is the down-20 kind.

Please join CSCBFPV: the Committee to Stop College Bands From Playing "Vehicle."

Reminder: in the eyes of the NCAA, it's not when in the conf tourney you lose, it's to whom it's to. Utah State and Dayton in bad positions.

BG is playing the kind of basketball you'd expect from a team that's mutinying against its coach. Horrible attitudes. 21-13 Akron, 3:09 1H.

Pop break: The Game saved "Mercy" from itself as well as its fake-ass Amy Winehouse arrangement. Disagreements not accepted.

Aggressiveness. Bowling Green. Tonight. All in the same sentence. BGSU five quick points out of the break, only down by six now.

SWAC final is set: Jackson State vs. Alabama State. Please do me a personal favor and watch this game. It's going to be really good.

More Bally WAC fun: http://twitpic.com/21p26 http://twitpic.com/21kcr http://twitpic.com/21id5 http://twitpic.com/22bwa

With Morehead State, a Southland low seed, Chattanooga, the Big West and the SWAC out there, the 16-line is looking mighty crowded...

Atlantic 2 final: Temple-Duquesne. Yup, I had that title game matchup picked back in November, didn't you?

Nate Miller has 15 of BG's 32, the rest of the team is mentally somewhere else. I'm guessing the Goasis down in Ashland. Love that place.

Yup, BG's back from the fudge shoppe. Tied at 40, big 3-point possessions by Brian Moten and Scott Thomas. 8:52 left.

It's a 13-2 Bowling Green run, if you're counting. Get this "Duke" off my teevee, I want to see some hottttttttt WAC action!!!

The guy in the stands who won the Fathead NCAA bracket looks like he wants to trade it in for a two napkins and a straw.

Looks like a 3/5 final in the MAC. If the leagues without strong teams keep sending low seeds, that is GREAT NEWS for the double-champions.

We're final here, 63-55 Akron wins. Bulls-Zips tomorrow night. It'll be a NCAA bid for a long-suffering program, that's guaranteed.

Bally had an exciting first week of playoff action, visiting .. http://tinyurl.com/bupyhm

GAME NO. 102 — Buffalo and Akron for the championship of the MAC. A box of Kraft M&C still gets you in!

Slingboxing the A-2 game, waiting for the MAC to start.

Still looking for an A-East title game blogger recap that doesn't mention Tony Kornheiser. #fail

Buffalo and Akron both long-suffering teams. This could be the happiest court storm I've ever been in.

Rumor at the Q is they're going to squelch the storming with overwhelming security. Happened last year, apparently, when I was at the A-14.

Waiting room in hell: "If you like it, you shouldn't put a ring on it" on a 24/7/365/1000000000000/infinity loop.

Temple 65, Duquesne 59 at 2:00 2H... who will be the ATLANTIC ONE?

I've written a special song for the winner of the Atlantic 14 that I want to share with you.

For the 2nd straight year, TEMPLE IS THE ATLANTIC ONE! Now here's some metal that will melt your balls off!

OMG SHOKK: horrible crowd at the MEAC title game and a upper-level curtain. The CIAA OUTGREW Winston-Salem. What an embarrassment.

The timeout trivia answer was Romeo Travis, and the AK-Rowdies all spontaneously did the chant they used to do when he played. Neat moment.

This is a hard slog... 17-12 Akron with 7:30 1H. Honestly, the MEAC game is more interesting.

MEAC: The more they show endline shots, the worse the attendance looks. They need to put this in Baltimore NOW, no more excuses.

29-20 Akron here. Buffalo's offense is suffering from self-defense.

Excuse me while I take about 200 pictures of the Kraft vs. MAC halftime mascot game. Kool-Aid Man and Zippy are the fives.

Under a minute to go in the MEAC, Morgan by 16, malfunction put three minutes on clock. Norfolk was all, like, shit. More of this?

Congratulations Morgan State, MEAC champs. Now, about the declining info situation there... who the F won the band/cheerleaders/Miss MEAC?

Akron is putting the HURT on now. 10-2 run out of the break. Looks like I'm going to storm the floor with Zippy!

I don't care how much security they put up, that Akron student section looks like it will not be denied.

I need Twitassistance with my MAC All-Tournament Team ballot. Anyone out there want to help influence college basketball history?

I'll say it again: please watch the SWAC game if you have ESPNU. Tough, active match so far. Alabama St up 9-8 on Jackson St at 10:00 1H.

Swacvillain.

You might be a loser if: you own a Fathead NCAA bracket. You ARE a loser if: you paid $30 + shipping for a Fathead NCAA bracket.

The last time Akron and Cleveland State were in the NCAA's was 1986. Huggy Bear. Kevin Mackey. Bread was a nickel.

Buffalo band playing "Paint it Black." Fans turning their heads until the darkness goes. 53-41 Akron with 3:51 left.

57-45 2H, Akron up by 12. Coat and tie off, have three letters in Sharpie on my left hand for another team's storm luck. End transmission.

No stormin' in the MAC. Not even an attempt.

I got to hug Zippy, so that sorta made up for the no storming. I feel bad for the kids though. Watching the end of the SWAC game.

Congratulations to Alabama State, YOUR SWAC champions. On to the Wickity.

I know you're listening in Reno: STORM HARD, and hold Bally aloft!

Don't know how anyone who saw USU play and looked at its stats doubted its ability. Oh that's RIGHT everyone just judged it based on SOS

Awaiting approval of first weekend credential app.

Bally's going to Minneapolis!

GAME NO. 103 — Ala State vs. Morehead State. PIG Party!

This place is almost full. I'm guessing there'll be a PIG attendance reord set tonight.

Morehead up 15-10, but the band scoreboard shows an Alabama State blowout.

sob sob LEAVE CHIEF KICKINGSTALLIONSIMS ALOOOOOONE sob

In past, Dasani tanks behind benches just had color scheme and logo — NCAA no-ad policy . No doubt who's responsible for hydration now, huh?

Remember the Daria episode where the school was covered with Ultra Cola ads? That's what media backstage is like, except with Vitamin Water.

OK, we heart the SWAC, but its teams have to start scoring points at the Tournament. ALST at 24 in 26 minutes.

Pph of post by nearby blogger: "Calling it the opening round confuses it with real basketball." With coverage like that, who needs coverage?

Instead of east-west or other somesuch directionals, press row is unofficially divided into The Side Erin Andrews Is On and The Other Side.

Morehead State is your PIG Champion for 2009. Print up the t-shirts!

Morehead State HC Donnie Tyndall told me I look like Rick Barnes. What a sweet guy!

Quick stayover in Indianapolis at the best hotel in the entire world.

GAME NO. 104 — (14) North Dakota State vs. (3) Kansas. BISON FEVER

There are a lot of NDSU fans here 45 minutes before game time. I'd guess 5000.

Green/gold NDSU sections: 16, Red/blue KU sections: 2

Things are changing: they didn't make us sign a two-page blogging policy this year

Gus Johnson/Len Elmore at our pod. If there's an upset, guaranteed you'll get a great catchphrase for it.

OK, two pregame things: 1.) I'm first row in the lower left corner near the photo pit, so look for Bally.

2) I've attached something to the court (under the curtain) that relates to 2008, for NDSU luck. I'll tell you what it is if all goes right.

Nervous enough to throw up, which could be grounds for revocation of my media credential.

12-12 at 14:42 1H. Lord, the floorburns. Pure go-after-it, take-it desire.

27-25 KU at 6:47 1H. Bison playing as if the season comes down to each possession, which is a pretty good approach yes it is.

Can't allow runs. Can't allow runs.

I've learned something today. Never underestimate the run-killing power of BISON FEVER

Woodside 16 points, Collins 15 points. It's a star-off! KU 40-34 at 1:03 1H.

Woodside's stuttersteps are drawing quite a few fouls. Is that showing up on TV? 'Cause it sure doesn't seem like Kansas scouted for that.

KU up 43-34 at the half. It's better when you don't have to play from behind.

Time for a halftime beverage. What's this! "Vitamin Water?" ::sip:: Egad! The only vitamin in this water is Vitamin SUCK! #adbusters

That's for you, Coke representative who just spammed The FormTM.

I was hoping for this. I'm in the same corner as the Flyer Pep Band! Go crazy or go home!

NDSU and Utah State... simultaneous runs! Let's do this!

I want all of you to get up out of your chairs. I want you to go to the window. Open it, stick your head out, and yell... BISON FEVER!

Woodside just broke YOUR ankles too. 56-52 11:48 2H.

Reminder of how things work: NDSU will not get borderline call for the rest of the game.

That's what makes these upsets Real.

For all you art history majors, that last Woodside layup was a tribute to "The Creation of Adam." KU 60-55, 8:38 2H.

Reminder: There's a little reminder of 2008 (illegally) attached to the court near my station, and it's working. Can you guess what it is?

C'mon, focus... both USU and NDSU...

Woodside and Collins talking to each other and laughing. Priceless.

Clarification: I burned the basketball tie after the Davidson-Kansas game. But that's the right track...

Woodside 32 points... KU by seven with 4:17 2H.

Aldrich. Need less of it.

C'mon, Aggies, finish this.

Here comes that goddamn chant. 80-70 44 sec.

NDSU gets a standing ovation that's about 10 times louder than "Rock Chalk Jayhawk." Bison Fever forever.

NDSU out, USU out. Perhaps now you can see why we prefer conference tourneys to this.

Winning a game like this is a lot like walking through a three-alarm burning building, staying calm, and coming out alive.

GAME NO. 105 — (6) West Virginia vs. (11) Dayton. And then there's Dr. Willie Morris and the UD Flyers Pep Band to cheer us up.

NCAA basketball makes me thirsty. Look, some "Vitamin Water!" ::sip:: Ugh! Hworf! You didn't feed this piss to NDSU, did you? #adbusters

Nice start by Dayton, 7-3 after two and a half minutes.

London Warren with the Larry Bird bounce-off-the-back out-of-bounds play! You like that, Gus?

Scene:NDSU players in sweats shuffling out into a holding area full of crying people. Trust me, to be in front of a TV is preferable to this

Dayton players all trying to do too much, it's as if they're attempting to blow West Virginia out early. DUDE. CHILL.

Screw tempo-free stats. I want to know point, rebound, turnover differential when the Flyer Pep Band is wearing the wacky airplane hats.

NCAA is getting better about in-arena out-of-town scoreboards. I think they're live. Two years ago, they'd update every 15 minutes.

5-min. MTO thought: YOU need to create a ridiculous obsesso-blog about the CBI... 2000-word previews, breakdowns, press conf. streaming. cbimadness.com is available.

West Virginia is exhibiting power-conference swagger without the appropriate talent or confidence.

Quickie score update: MIZZ 22, CORN 19 — 5:14 1H; PITT 24, ETSU 22 — 3:53 1H; ASU 35, TU 26 — H.

The West Virginia band should rename itself "The Sound Of Anal Retentiveness." It's totally getting pwned by Dayton's. 28-22 3:15 1H.

If Dayton is going to win this, it's going to have to be over with five minutes to go. NO free throw contest.

We're at the half here in the Homerdome, Dayton is up 33-28. A 20-minute break is long enough for a nap with a REM cycle.

Four upset possibilities going right now. We're looking for six, have one (WKU) in pocket.

Did You Know? Any sports-talk radio host who wants to can get a credential to the NCAA Tournament, and they talk all the way through games.

Relatedly, sports bloggers are now credentialed to share observations similar in substance to those of sports talkers. Which belongs less?

Answer: sports bloggers and talk-show hosts are the only ones who should be allowed on press row. This should be a fun vacation, not work.

Second half, and Dr. Willie's got the spangle-suit going! It's time for the A-14 to pull out a win! (Or two! Here comes Temple!)

Keep hangin' in, ETSU! Does Jamie Dixon actually, physically get eaten alive by Pitt boosters if he loses this game?

Flyers have plenty of basktball juice right now. Up by eight at 13:24.

Never mind... here comes that West Virginia run we knew was coming. Fire-retardant suits, Flyers.

Just found myself in awkward small talk with a BC official. Forgot who they were playing, intimated they were still in the Big East. OOPSIE

Reminder... 1989: (1) OU 72, (16) ETSU 71, tied as closest 1/16 game with GU-PRIN. How many times have they referenced that on TV, I wonder?

Dayton's now whizzed away the lead. Nervous time in the fan section behind me.

We have so little bandwidth here at the Metrodome that the out-of-town scoreboard is ahead of the MMOD feed.

57-54 Dayton at 4:02 2H. This is the free throw contest I was afraid of.

Mickey Perry.... BLOCK MONSTER! And the Wright two-point dunk shot! Dayton by five!

ETSU comes down the floor on MMOD, I can cheat by looking up at the OOT scoreboard to see if they scored or not. Fun way to watch a game.

UD's Charles Little with the layup, and one! He's really playing BIG today! #fakerickreilly

1:12 to go... Dayton up by five with the ball! Do it for our capital city, Flyers!

Little with the HUGE bucket, 65-58 UD! We love your band, selfless play, and your Title R compliance but you've got to pull this out!

Warren with the steal! :26.8, Dayton by six! WVU intensity coming out of the huddle: zero! Finish this!

:14.2, WVU 3-miss, at the line to try to make this double digits.

NO.. but Wright rebounds.... the Johnson dribbles the clock out!!!!!! DAYTON WINS

Security's trying to clear the Dayton fans, but they don't want to leave!

Dr. Willie's standing on a chair in front of the student section, getting them Flyered up!

Band girl yelling into cellphone: "Omigod! Omigod!" UD fan: "We don't want to leave! We want to stay here forever!"

Dayton's first NCAA win since 1990 (Illinois). Chris Wright with 27, Charles Little with 18, Marcus Johnson with 10. WVU shot 36.7%.

Place is cleared out. Sitting on an empty press row talking floor percentage with Brian Gregory.

UD: 46% FG, 14/23 (61%) FT, but scored at least 1 pt on 57% of possessions. That matches UNC's national-best avg. Floor percentage, baby.

I've felt for a while that TMM Season 5 is destined to end in Indianapolis at Sports Bubble Stadium. It would make sense.

Burning question about NCAAT photographers answered: "Does that tape you have to put around your ankle leave a stain on your pants?" "Yes."

GAME NO. 106 — (7) BC vs. (10) USC. BC: great comeback after going 4-12 in the ACC a year ago, and USC has solid inside de... Ah, screw it.

There are more NDSU fans making the most of their ticket strips than BC and USC fans combined.

Watching a game like this reminds me why a lot of people don't read TMM. It's hard to maintain attention towards teams you don't care about.

I'm seriously nodding off here. The combination of two teams that combined for 16 conference losses, and zero arena buzz is making it tough.

A dude just blew a layup, then another guy made a dunk... look, Song Girls!... I don't know anything about basketball. I'm a fraud. Crap.

I think when I ran some numbers, USC has the biggest average height of any D-I team. That's all I have that's interesting about them.

That was an AWESOME blown dunk by number 0 on the Trojans! USC up 29-27 at 2:21 1H.

UL 35, MORE 33 HT... Reminds me of the time on MST3K when Joel and the bots rapped about the classic movies they wished they were watching.

"You know this game is supposed to really excite me, But all I can say is, 'No! Bite me!'"

Len Elmore just walked by. He's dragging ass too, but it's more impressive because he's seven inches taller than me.

OK, CONTEST! The prize is a NCAA Final Four record book, which is good to have but hard to find in non- PDF form. Includes shippin'. Ready?

Trivia! First to tweet in the answer: who was the last NCAA Tournament rep from the American South Conference (hint: 1991)?

A couple more trivias this half. Of course, you know you can cheat and use BBState's Tournament Wiz. That's how I'm getting the questions.

MORE Trivia! You know how many times a 16 has beaten a 1 (0) and how many times a 15 has beaten a 2 (4). How many times has a 14 beaten a 3?

Some dork in a sweatsuit is practicing PBP into a Blackberry two seats down. The game atmosphere is now complete.

Pictures, accounts and descriptions of this game are expressly sucky.

For the next 7:08 the OVC is still one of five undefeated conferences in the Tournament (Big 12, C-USA, Sun Belt, WCC). Just remember that.

USC is such a great story. They lose O.J. Mayo, then make it back to the NCAAT and quite possibly win a game... okay, who's laughing?

OK, final trivia. Sortatoughie: the SWAC is now the conf. with the longest wait for a NCAA win (93). Ivy is 2nd (98). Which league is third?

This IS a tough one... nobody's got it yet. Remember, this is for an official NCAA Final Four record book, chock full of geeky stuffs

Sorry for the unnecessary suspense, but the internet connection just slowed down to 1400 baud.

Well, THAT'S over. RMU-Michigan State in about 25 minutes.

Xavier wins to put 3 Red Liners in the 2nd round. There were 6 last year, so even if Cle State and Siena win tonight, 2009 is a step back.

Big ups to the NDSU fans, who've kept this place packed all day. Contrast that to many groups of fans who leave when their team is done.

9 hours of hoops leaves me parched. I'll try this "Vitamin Water." ::sip:: Eyargblah! Tastes a lot more like ASS than potassium! #adbusters

GAME NO. 107 — (2) Michigan State vs. (15) Robert Morris. I need a miracle... every day.

OK, all you HD watchers... look for Bally in the lower left near the photo pit!

C'mon Siena, c'mon Cleveland State! Trying to get some Bally luck out there to Dayton and Miami!

Good start for RMU. Shooters getting points. 8-7 MSU three minutes in.

Cleveland State POUNDING Wake Forest early. With a pounding instrument.

Robert Morris is not afraid to take it to the hoop against this team, and that fearlessness will get them far. 15-11 MSU, 14:55 1H.

All games of TMM relevance in the late session pointed towards Indianapolis.

Low seeds can either try to put in 40 minutes of full-on Soldier Shit, or try to fake their way to a win. RMU has signed up for the former.

The long TV timeouts definitely hurt NDSU's focus earlier. There's a lot of emotion and activity in RMU's huddle.

MSU 19 RMU 18 10:54 1H — OHST 17 SIE 15 6:00 1H — CLST 20 WAKE 10 11:22 1H

Three for three. Let's get six. We can still get six.

I haven't seen RMU live since last season. Mike Rice was popping veins yelling at his team.

Doing it now. RMU goes as far as the amount of intensity it has in the tank. 26-23 MSU at 8:29 1H.

CLST 29 WAKE 12 7:48 1H — OHST 26 SIE 23 2:19

All the NDSU fans — and there are thousands — are slowly getting behind RMU. It's like they're deciding en masse if it's worth it.

If the Bison fans put their Bison Fever behind RMU and it's close down the stretch, it's going to be loud and it's going to be a factor.

It all comes down to this session. We have three through, six last year. This is the gap between "irrelevance" and "mid-major pride."

Robert Morris up, 28-26... but Draymond Green tied it for MSU. 5:44 1H. Ohio State and Siena are at the half, Buckeyes up 28-23.

Rob Robinson just blew a dunk and people laughed.

No, not 37 minutes of sustained effort. You blink, and the other team has a run. 41-30 now,

MSU extending.

Halftime in Mpls., 41-30 MSU. Apropos of nothing NCAA, but isn't it kinda cool that Davidson and SMC are playing in the NIT on Monday?

Siena fading: 36-27 Buckeyes at 16:34 2H. We're still at the half, so is CLST-WAKE.

BALLLLL controlllllllllll, Siena....

Just made an awesome play after the ball went out. I passed the HELL out of the rock back to the ref.

Three stages of an upset falling away: 1.) the initial run the other way, 2.) the stupid chucked shots, 3.) acceptance. RMU is in Stage 2.

Siena back within four. Cleveland State up by nine. Wish Greg Gumbel's magic voice would come in right about now. MSU 51-32.

RMU down 64-42. Your name is Bob and there's nothing you can do, the ladies won't go out with you... because your name is Bob.

Siena down six at the 5 minute mark, Cleveland State up by nine in the seven-minute zone.

No, Cleveland State up by 15!!! Thank you, magic scoreboard that does everything I want!

There's no line on the Horizon, Mr. Bono, but there's ASS-KICKING BASKETBALL!

Siena ties it! Feeeeeel the surgggggggge!

NDSU fans packing up and going home. It's a shame, because RMU coulda had them on their side right about now. 68-49 7:29.

The :35 second buzzer in the Metrodome sounds more like a smoke alarm. Shrill, dude.

Personal attendance upset streak: 2005 (Pacific), 2006 (Mason x 3), 2007 (SIU), 2008 (Davidson), 2009 (Dayton). Intact.

Hasbrouck!!!! C"mon Siena! 56-55 Ohio State at :47.6!

Siena's tied it up!

Injury to insult as well as insinuated indignity, MSU's band is playing a half-tempo version of "What is Love?" Like like the the the death.

Siena-Ohio State... overtime! Cleveland State is up by 17! PROTO-BEAST!

Siena first bucket of OT.

Hey, we've got enough bandwidth to run MMOD now! Everybody left! YES! Siena up by four, 3:24 OT!

Ubiles at the line... both FT's! Siena 62-61 at 1:47 OT!

77-62 is the final here in Minneapolis, Michigan State over Robert Morris.

63-62 OHST, within 30 seconds... foul. 9.1 seconds left. Nervewracking.

DOUBLE OT

can't take it

WE'VE GOT FIVE!!!!!!!!!!!!!!!!!!!!!!!

#onions #onions #onions #onions #onions #onions #onions #onions #onions #onions #onions #onions #onions #onions #onions #onions #onions

Pure basketball joy. Western Kentucky, Dayton, Xavier, Cleveland State, Siena. We are NOT going home.

Heading to the office. Theme song of the day in Minneapolis is the Ben Folds version of "In Between Days."

OMG OMV! I bet that one's been used before.

Wave those red towels, Hoops Nation! C'mon WKU!

Ugh-MPFN.

Having to watch TV darlings Gonzaga and Duke celebrating within 10 minutes deserves its
own special Vitamin Water flavor: "Groin Punch."

Ladies and gentlemen, the Memphis bracket is now closed.

I blame McDonald for signaling timeout 8 times. Didn't he know that the rule is 20
iterations of "T", with giant foam clown hands? IDIOT.

DUDE, what does this team have to do to get proper respect... http://twitpic.com/2c9sn

GAME NO. 108 — (11) Dayton vs. (3) Kansas. Will ditch the second game to watch SIE-UL
if we're not safe in three hours time.

I will pay any college band $100 to learn "Dirty Boots."

Walking into the Metrodome, double-breasted, silver Nikes, shades on, pet basketball, SY
"Goo" in the iPod, ready to FUCK UP SOME BRACKETS

An hour before tip; the Dayton fans are here and very loud.

I don't know if I mentioned this, but there hasn't been any journostar power here in Minn
this weekend. But Luke Winn just showed up!

In lower left corner near the photo pit and UD pep band again. Resisting urge to yell with
Dr. Willie or chant the Statement of Theme.

Chris Wright fist-bumping the officials before the tip. Dayton as a whole looks pretty loose.
Kansas a little tight and businesslike.

Kurt Huelsman is trying his dear heart out, but he's proving little more than a speed bump
against Alrdich. 6-2 KU at 16:32 1H.

XU 8 WISC 5 11:33 1H... keep it slow, X.

Dayton is turning the ball over almost every time down.

MINNEAPOLIS — You work in an office. It's a big office with hundreds of.. http://tinyurl.
com/d7ue8u

11-4 KU, and here comes the Dayton pressure.

13-7 KU with a Fabrizius 3, against a smaller KU lineup. ARIZ 5 CLST 0 18:33 1H — XU 16
WISC 11 7:53 1H

Collins 10, Aldrich 6 of Kansas' 21 points. Need to stop at least one!

Dayton pressure working, but still too many coughs. Holding own on the boards. 23-16 KU
5:46 1H.

Fabreeeeeeezius for threeee! And a sweet Wright tip-in! 23-21 KU, and Bill Self takes a TO!

Nervous time elsewhere: WISC 23 XU 20 1:39 1H — ARIZ 19 CLST 10 11:45 1H

Michigan State band is setting up, and they're rooting for UD-they have their reasons.
Remember that the whole pod is pointed towards Indy.

Sales of Cole Aldrich's "Secrets of Free-throw Shooting" DVD just went through the roof.

Kansas up 29-23 at the half. WISC 27 XU 25 HT, ARIZ 24 CLST 14 6:59 1H.

The only reason Dayton is in this game is because Kansas is missing FT's. Need 20 perfect
minutes...

I can only imagine how ugly that Xavier game is. XU 35 WISC 33 12:10, both teams
shooting 33%. ARIZ 35 CLST 25, still at the half.

Dr. Willie's mugging for the camera in his sparkle suit.

Kansas: "Please beat us." Dayton: "You sure? Really? You mean that?"

If the Flyers have a run in them (and they rarely do), now's a good time for it.

KU 40 UD 30 10:15 1H — ARIZ 39 CLST 27 17:45 2H — XU 40 WISC 37 7:00 2H

Chucking dumb shots and counting on the usual good offensive rebounding to be there isn't the way to get this done. 44-30 8:10 2H.

Xavier has nobody in double figures, up 42-39 at 6:32 2H. Wisc has six turnovers and is shooting 30%. Freeeeeky

XU 49 WISC 41 3:54 — ARIZ 46 CLST 40 12:34 2H

KU 49-36 5:38 2H. And the passionless, eternally entitled KU fans get up and clap in unison. Vomitous.

UD is not getting calls anywhere near the borderline. I'm so close that I can hear the skin slaps, and KU is not being called for anything.

Then again, Flyers aren't helping themselves any with crappy shots. Frustrating for everyone. Band's frustrated. Fans stunned and quiet.

But Xavier appears to have this. We're safe, and the site will live another week.

But where will we go? Looks like Cleveland State's bringing the heat!!! Apologies to Katy Perry, but you're hot and you're COLE!!!!!

ARIZ 52 CLST 46 8:37 2H — XU 57 WISC 47 1:07 2H

If there was a half a point given for bounding it off the back iron, Dayton would be in this. Rock chalk... Jay-hawk... screw you.

Great season, Dayton.

But the A-14 marches on. Xavier beats Wisconsin 60-49!

Wanted to go back to the media area and watch the end of CLST-ARIZ, but guess what? Everyone's watching freaking Pitt.

Sitting on press row watching the end of the game on MMOD, ducking USC's shootaround clangs. My lawd.

Geez. Why is keeping focus for 40 minutes so hard? Don't say "big time players making big time plays" or "good coaching."

This is why I swear off drinking during the season. I could use a 150-proof Vitamin Water right about now.

Congratulations Xavier! As is Sweet 16 tradition, we change the header: http://www.midmajority.com/

FYI Watching CBS producers convince cheerleaders to make the "steering wheel" motion for the cutaways is really sad and pathetic in person.

The word of the day is: ARRGGHHHHHHHHHH

Siena is fighting so hard... Win or lose, this is how you carry yourself in the Tournament...

FWIW I'm not watching that corporate crapfest out on the court. I don't care if it ends up being the greatest NCAA game ever.

Siena ties it at 59!

Holy FUCK did you see that Jackson layup!!!

Siena has 5 turnovers. Ball control, baby!

8 perfect minutes. Let's do this.

7 perfect minutes needed...

Focus, composure, blah blah blah

Exciting and Fun are totally mutually exclusive.

sigh

My mission, and I choose to accept it: help make Xavier loveable. It's going to be an interesting week.

I hear you, I hear you all. BUT... Xavier's done just as much as Gonzaga has, but has received a fraction of the credit. Why is that?

There's also an ugly reality about how the CBB media-gang operates, and Gonzaga fits in with why Duke/Carolina are easy national sells.

I'm going to leave that one to Stephen A. Smith though.

Final Official Hotel stopover in Indy, I can see Sports Bubble Stadium from my window. Thanks for following this season and God bless. -30-

BONUS

GAME NO. 109 — (4) Xavier vs. (1) Pitt. Whatever I did to deserve this seat, karma will put me in hell.

I am practically sitting between the announcers. Once more into the breech, my friends.

Good 2006 memories, not just b/c the guy in the X section with a Mason jersey: I came here to see the women's CG after Indy. Better game.

Reading X's postseason guide just now. Assuming they included every article, guess how many national features there were on X this season?

3 — 800-word jobs by DeCourcy (TSN) and Goodman (Fox), and the Dana O'Neil story from Nov. The rest in the pack (about 40) were local.

Scoreboards here are broken or something. No way X is 2-for-9. It's 9-5 X at 15:14 1H. Verne just scratched his ass. By George!

Remember when CJ Anderson and Bobby Gonzalez were together at Manhattan, and the future was full of possibility? Yeah, this is better.

X's band has a very good cowbell player. Pitt is up 14-12 and is trying too hard to deliver a 1st round KO.

Derrick Brown is good at two-point dunk shots!

This may be obvious at home, but the Musketeers are playing their asses off.

Pitt players jawing at each other. THAT can't be good!

Pitt spent all that money, and they couldn't buy a team with chemistry or heart. Second time I've seen them, and they're plenty unlikeable.

Halftime, X up 37-29. Writers scrambling for Xavier media guides.

NCAA FUN FACT: Xavier fans in real life are much nicer than the Xavier fans on message boards.

Dude... Verne and Bill have mad male groupies. They're trying to crawl over me to get to them.

And now, America, watch me enjoy a delicious piece of chocolate.

OK, Xavier has more margin for error b/c of its talent, but 20 perfect minutes would be good here.

I've had 15 e-mails in the last few minutes congratulating me on my CBS face time. I wish I'd shaved. Or slept last night.

@julia_flyer Put it this way: This is the closest to Verne Lundquist's lap as I ever want to be.

Pitt is good at making basketball dreams die. X lead cut from eight to two in three minutes.

Contrast this to Mason-WSU 2006, when I was in media overflow between George Michael and Tony Reali. I'm movin' on up now! (c) Primal Scream

Just want to point out again: Pitt fans outnumber X fans 3-to-1, and X hasn't won over the unaffiliateds (yet).

I know there's that whole "we're big time" thing, but look how hard Xavier fights. They want to rip this away from these entitled bot-men.

When Xavier is as lazy and entitled as this Pitt team, then they can be "big time." Agreed?

Happy to report the tide is turning. Unafflilated fans on the endlines are coming over to X, because Pitt is playing like ass.

CONTEST! Regionals program plus shippin' to the first person who can give me Verne Lundquist's famous call when Mason beat UConn in 06.

OK, X has to buckle down here. Pitt is doing that talent thing.

You can be as lazy as you want for 35 minutes if you're capable of bursts of 185 mph speed. Urgh.

UConn wins. The Boston crowd boos. I like living here sometimes.

Pitt not only deserves to lose this game, the ETSU victory should be vacated as well.

Ass.

Double ass.

This is just insulting to good taste.

The final kick in the balls of the 2008-09 season.

All gone.

Quick update before I go. In 36 hours, we've raised as much for Season 6 as we did during the week-long bailout. Overwhelmed and thankful.

And do we forsake a 2nd-row courtside seat for Nova-Duke?

Of course we do! Because BOTH TEAMS CAN SUCK IT. Good night, and remember — Vienna waits for you.

[Test pattern]

INDEX